AMERICAN OZ

AN ASTONISHING YEAR INSIDE
TRAVELING CARNIVALS
AT STATE FAIRS & FESTIVALS

MICHAEL SEAN COMERFORD

Comerford Publishing

PRAISE FOR AMERICAN OZ

Wonderful, eclectic, rich, collection of characters … Excellent. Well done!

— JOANNA LANG, INTERNATIONAL JOURNALIST

By turns emotional, erudite, enlightening and ever engaging.

— RICK KOGAN, AUTHOR/COLUMNIST/BROADCASTER, AT THE *CHICAGO TRIBUNE* AND WGN RADIO

"Reminiscent of The Big Fish and the gritty writings of Studs Terkel and John Steinbeck, with a dash of Jack Kerouac, Tony Horwitz, and even Hunter S. Thompson thrown in, American OZ will take you on the adventure of a lifetime. It will kick your COVID blues."

— STEPHEN REDDICK, HISTORIAN, EDUCATOR

"Unlike any book I've ever read! Buckle up and get ready for this book to bring you on the ride of a lifetime!"

— SUZY MARTIN, WRITER/JOURNALIST

"Having been born and raised in the carnival business, I found it to be an extremely authentic."

— DAVE GALYON. HIS BROTHERS DONNIE AND RONNIE GALYON WERE CONJOINED TWINS WITH THEIR OWN CARNIVAL EXHIBITION.

Published in the United States by Comerford Publishing LLC., at MichaelSeanComerford.com

Library of Congress Cataloguing-in-publication data

ISBN 978-1-952693-007

The R-keys at scene breaks are linchpins used extensively in traveling carnivals holding rides and equipment together.

The photos on the back cover from left to right: the Mexican reefer bunkhouse for Butler Amusements in San Mateo, CA.; a jointee at the State Fair of Texas; view from the Grand Carrousel in Chicago; a Giant Wheel setting up in Waycross, GA.

Reader reviews are easy and free, free, free! Help the people and stories of American OZ find the voice they deserve. Please review at Goodreads or your favorite book buying site.

This book is dedicated to my daughter, Grace Comerford; to my parents, Gordon and Alice (Flatley) Comerford; and to my sisters, Colleen, Maureen, and Katie. To the extraordinary people in traveling carnivals. To every driver who picked me up. And to luck.

You just grow more when you get others people's perspectives.

— MARK ZUCKERBERG, FACEBOOK FOUNDER
& CARNIVAL CUSTOMER

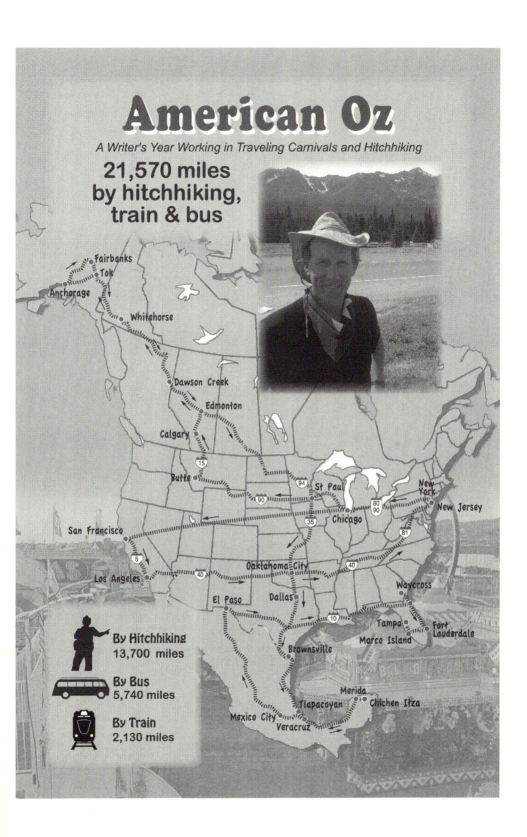

American Oz

A Writer's Year Working in Traveling Carnivals and Hitchhiking

21,570 miles by hitchhiking, train & bus

By Hitchhiking
13,700 miles

By Bus
5,740 miles

By Train
2,130 miles

Fairbanks
Tok
Anchorage
Whitehorse
Dawson Creek
Edmonton
Calgary
Butte
St Paul
New York
New Jersey
Chicago
San Francisco
Los Angeles
Oklahoma City
Waycross
El Paso
Dallas
Tampa
Fort Lauderdale
Marco Island
Brownsville
Merida
Chichen Itza
Tlapacoyan
Mexico City
Veracruz

CARNY LINGO

TERMS USED IN AMERICAN OZ

Bally – A routine drawing a sideshow crowd
Carny – A carnival worker, usually on rides
Carny Code – Unwritten worker rules
Cutting Up Jackpots – Telling carnival stories
Gaff – Tricks, illusions or way of fixing a game
Hole – Job slot or a joint space
Joint – A booth for games
Jointee – A person working in a game joint
Plush – Stuffed animals and toys for prizes
Possum Belly – A storage area under a ride
Red Light Job – Wage theft
Ride Jockey – A person running rides
Showman – An entertainer. Sometimes a jointee
Slough – Carnival teardown; rhymes with cow
With it – Worker traveling with the carnival
Website for more: Carny Lingo

CONTENTS

ACKNOWLEDGMENTS

All the stars of American OZ were not drivers and carnival people. There are too many to thank by name, but here are a few.

Mary-Margaret Green is a renowned journalist/editor who worked for the *Washington Star, Washington Post, and Washington Times.* Her keen eye and generous spirit were inspirations.

Freelance editor Kevin Kohler was a fan of American OZ and asked to edit the book. His editing and advice were invaluable.

All-star writer Caren Chesler housed me for a time in Harlem and provided contacts. She is a true believer in the power of the stories.

Chicago author/broadcaster/journalist Rick Kogan was a major backer. Rick has a genius for seeing the best in people.

INTRODUCTION

Sometimes out on the road, life is gorgeous.

I was a ride jockey, jointee, and a hitchhiker for a year. I was slinging iron and pushing plush across the USA. Thousands of miles of sleeping, eating, and working with carnies, showmen, and sideshow freaks. The year ended in a way that made sense of the journey. The world runs on untold stories.

The year began with an omen, a Chicago blizzard that said, "Get back fool." I was nearly flat broke when I jumped on a westbound train named the California Zephyr. I didn't have money to get back. I was living on a thread, and had to make the year work.

The Zephyr blew across the Mississippi, Colorado, Humboldt, Wasatch, and Truckee rivers. We passed through the Glenwood and Ruby canyons and across the Rocky, Pequop, and Sierra Nevada mountains. We beat a path across the Bonneville Salt Flats and the Forty Mile Desert on the way to the San Francisco Bay.

My plans to spend the season with one carnival fell apart early. I thought my year was finished until I began hitchhiking between carnivals. I saw the drivers as part of the greater story.

Drivers were the Americans carnivals served. And carnies in

Alaska are different from carnies in Mexico. People are products of their place in this world. Geography became context.

I could empathize with carnival people making their home on the road. I'm the oldest of four kids in a family that moved ten times before settling in the Chicago area. In my young mind, I linked moving to a new home with a life of discovery. Sights unseen. Amazing people. Wonder.

I bicycled three times cross-country. I rode freight trains and herded cattle out West. And I hitchhiked around the U.S., Europe, the Middle East, and North Africa. As a journalist, I worked in Chicago, New York, and in the so-called "Wild East" after the fall of communism in Hungary and Russia. I toured almost a hundred countries, stopping to study at a Tibetan Buddhist monastery in the Himalayas. I've interviewed homeless people, immigrants, CEOs, and billionaires.

Millions of people every year go to state fairs, street festivals, and church parking-lot fundraisers. Even more have childhood memories of the smell of cotton candy and running amok with friends on and off rides. People remember the rides, games, and the overpoweringly unhealthy food. They want that again this year and next.

Yet the questions remain. Questions about safety, fixed games, and the person putting us on rides. Are these people evil or dangerous?

I wrote hundreds of thousands of words in background notes in bunkhouses and all-night diners. I posted videos and blogs from the road. The blogs and videos drew a real-time following because the life-or-death cliffhangers were potentially deadly.

I drew inspiration from other writers who lit up the realities of lives undetected by history's radar. Writer and journalist Charles Dickens walked ten to twenty miles daily, often at night, to capture the metaphysical feel for the streets. Pulitzer Prize-winning writer Studs Terkel wrote *Working*, giving voice to the thoughts of working people about the work they do. Years ago, I wrote nearly one hundred stories for a jobs edition at a daily newspaper and named it after Terkel's book. He called the newsroom to say he approved.

American Oz owns the same kind of zeitgeist-capturing power in the compelling, funny, and outrageous stories of carnival people. They deal with migration, poverty, and a host of social challenges. Home and family are on their minds when far away from both.

I worked at getting carnival workers to relate the true inner geography of their lives. Yet they talked about their lives in their own ways. They spoke of seeking love and meaning in their lives on the road.

This book is factual. All the quotes are real, although no attempt is made at portraying regional or racial accents. There's a daydream vignette, but it is made obvious to the "reasonable person" standard.

American Oz is unmatched in the miles traveled, people interviewed, and issues explored. No carny ever worked for ten carnival companies in ten states in a single year. None ever worked and hitchhiked coast to coast, north to south, and down to Mexico. The journey was unique, and so are the heartfelt stories.

Moments of insight and inspiration changed me and will change the way readers see the next street fest or state fair. Expect humans at their best and worst. Reversals of fortune and fun-loving people.

Buckle up for a behind-the-scenes ride around the world of traveling carnivals in America. It's a magic rollercoaster never ridden before.

PART I
CALIFORNIA

FEBRUARY, MARCH

WRESTLING IN A SILICON CHASM

OAKLAND

From Alaska to Mexico, New York to Cali
From Dallas to Chi-town hear my bally,
Change your life, it's meant to be,
Win big money, free, free, free,
Be shocked, be amazed on every page.
Be younger, be smarter in a tech age,
Say no to the square life, say no to the blahs,
Say yes to the wonders of American Oz.
— The Bally of American OZ

ose Dog's eyes fixed on me as he danced around the trailer in agony. He wanted to transfer all the pain in him onto me.

It was well past midnight and difficult to tell a person from a shadow inside the eighteen-wheeler truck trailer. I was helping the carousel foreman, Rose Dog, tear down the carousel before moving the carnival to the next town.

Carousel beams were placed on the trailer floor before we lifted them onto a side rack. We were not in sync picking up opposite ends of the first carousel sweep, and his fingers crushed between the beams.

"You smash my fingers again, and I will fuck you up," he said. "I make my living with my hands."

A violent ex-con and former Grambling State defensive back, he was twenty pounds heavier, twenty years younger, and in a psychotic rage.

The carnies outside the trailer stood staring in at us. With the klieg lights behind them, I couldn't tell if their half-lit faces were scared or excited. If they were anything like me, they loved a good fight. Mother of God, I didn't want this.

We picked up the next carousel beam. Rose Dog dropped the beam again.

Clang. . . ang. . . ang. . . ang.

"Goddammit!"

Rose Dog launched himself around the trailer holding his hands in fits of pain. The crew expected him to retaliate.

"You smash my fingers again, and I will fuck you up. I will fuck you uuuup!"

I wasn't responsible for pinching his fingers. He was placing his fingers at pinch points. He did not see it that way.

"I swear to God if you smash my fingers again . . ."

Nobody, least of all me, expected what happened next. We bent down to pick up another beam.

Clang. . .ang. . .ang . . .ang.

"Ooh my fucking God!"

My mind raced, but no thought of running away crossed my mind. I traveled two thousand miles from Chicago to Oakland to work in carnivals. This was where I ran away to.

I'd worked the entire show for Butler Amusements from setup to the slough. Nobody is part of a carnival crew until they've worked a slough. The teardown was an initiation.

Rose Dog's fury jumped into my body. From the start, I wanted to feel what carnival people feel. I forgot who I was and felt anger. I might attack him before he attacks me.

A SPY IS BORN

HAYWARD

My first day in carnivals began a couple of weeks earlier at a different show, in a carnival oasis in Hayward.

It was pitch black when I arrived at the packed carnival lot in the Hayward industrial park. Classic Amusement crew boss Tim drove us onto the lot in a raggedy carnival van. Rides and food wagons were parked close together with narrow pathways.

The lot was like a folktale forest with enchanted beings with ride names Mind Winder, Pirate's Revenge, and Super Sizzler.

Tim walked me around the rides to the long white bunkhouse trailer near the back fence. He warned me about the demons living in the eucalyptus trees behind the trailers. Skunks, raccoons, a fox, and one wild turkey lurked in the backlot underbrush.

"Watch your step around here," he said. "You don't want to step on a skunk."

Skunks are nothing. I worried about wild turkeys. If they get the wrong vibe, they will go wild turkey on your ass. If they like you, a wild turkey is a good omen.

When I told him I intended to write about the carnival, he told me not to use his real name. He said it as if his life depended on it, and it may have, which could be one reason why carnival workers are so misunderstood. Many are actively hiding in plain sight.

Wood pallets paved the way between bunkhouse trailer rooms. A plastic container box was my front doorstep. In my five-by-seven-foot bunkhouse room, I put my sleeping bag on the wood bed. Music by Led Zeppelin and the Doors played from another bunkhouse room. A black pit bull named Max patrolled nightly between the rides.

Going to the bathroom at night called for walking through a dark maze of carnival rides to the warehouse. And at any moment, a rabid wild turkey could fly off the Super Sizzler to peck my eyes out. On my first night in my bunkhouse room, I whispered what would become a nightly mantra, "What have I done?"

I woke early to the sounds of birds and the small animals near my door. The carnival lifestyle feels so much like camping because, both awake and asleep, it is an outdoor life.

During the peak summer months, about forty people worked the rides, games, and food joints. That first morning was a casting call. Walking out from behind trailers and rides came Murphy, Damien, Tim, Country Love, and Monster. They sported do-rags, ponytails, beer bellies, tattoos, and keyhole smiles.

Murphy was the first to come out of the pack talking. He was a forty-ish white man dressed in an old black t-shirt and jeans. With a nod of the head to follow him, Murphy walked ahead of me and showed me around.

"All I ask our guys to do is always pay attention. If you get distracted or someone is talking to you, tell them to shut up. Or I'll tell them to shut up. Or you can lose a foot."

He wasn't kidding. He could tell you foot stories. Somewhere there must be a graveyard for carny feet.

When Murphy walked by a ride, he'd rattle off how much Classic's owner George D'Olivo paid for the ride at the national convention for traveling carnivals in Gibtown, south of Tampa, Florida.

Gibtown's not on any conventional map, and yet it is the focal point of an elusive, mobile nation whose population, GDP, and borders are unknown. Murphy described the capital of a phantom carny country existing within the borders of the United States. If true, I had to see Gibtown.

Back in Chicago, I'd searched the internet for carnivals in the San Francisco Bay Area serving Silicon Valley. I wanted to see the Silicon Chasm from a traveling carnival's perspective.

San Francisco has the most billionaires per capita in America, 1 per 11,000 people. The Bay Area is third in the world, behind New York and Hong Kong. It also has among the highest number of homeless per capita. The gap between the richest in history and the poorest is called the Silicon Chasm.

When I reached D'Olivo by cell phone from Chicago, he laughed when I told him I wanted to blog all season.

"Come, come," he said, "everyone in California blogs."

The conversation was so off the cuff that he forgot all about it until I arrived.

While I was waiting to meet D'Olivo that morning, Murphy provided the build-up. D'Olivo was once a professional wrestler. In my mind, Murphy became a pro-wrestling ring announcer building up the arrival of the main event.

In this corner is George D'Olivo. The preening. The bulked up. The Beautiful Bo Paradise! He fought the greats of the wrestling circuit. He fought on the same bill with Hulk Hogan at the Cow Palace in San Francisco. Yes, don't let his beauty fool you. Beautiful Bo Paradise was an unholy terror in the ring.

Professional wrestling in America started in traveling carnivals called "at shows," or athlete shows. Fixed fights and storylines later worked their way into mainstream professional wrestling. Beautiful Bo Paradise was what is known as a jobber, whose scripted fights called for him to lose to the headliners.

Summoned into D'Olivo's headquarters offices at the front of the lot, I sat across from him on an old brown couch low to the ground. D'Olivo was in his forties and one of the sharpest people in the carnival business.

I reminded him that I intended to write about his carnival while working. At first, he said he remembered agreeing to the deal. But he soon began talking around the topic. Leaning back in his seat, he spoke about his carnival playing mostly to middle-class and upper-class venues. The show returned to the industrial park before traveling to the next show.

Classic Amusement was not a traditional traveling carnival, but it operated in the right region, during the right time in history. The tech giants were growing in power at a blazing speed. Apple, Facebook, Google, and the City of San Francisco became Classic Amusement customers. Classic's route was the Silicon Chasm.

D'Olivo was a big personality. If I stayed there all season, he would not be boring. From his point of view, his carnival was already a reality TV show. All it needed was a writer and a venue.

"We have so many characters around here," he said. "I see those reality TV shows, and they're boring compared to us."

The more he talked about it out loud, the more he worried out loud about storylines. Billionaire wrestling promoter Vince McMahon was his mentor. McMahon kept tight control over his writers and profits. He used writers to boost business. If I wasn't that kind of writer, then I was a threat. When D'Olivo was a wrestler, the writers told him to lose even to guys he could beat. He learned writers could hurt you.

On second thought, he said, he wanted time to reconsider the alien in the midst.

ONE EVENING, I was passing the time at Monster's bunkhouse door. He was drinking beer on his trailer step, talking about the prisons where he served time for firearms, drugs, and assaults.

Monster was in his mid-thirties with a salt-and-pepper beard and only a few stubs for front teeth. At six-foot-four and 300-plus pounds he enjoyed walking around the compound shirtless, his belly hanging over his belt like a white mudslide.

Just when I thought all his stories were lewd and violent, he lowered his voice to tell me how he'd won his new $400 NASCAR jacket. A young girl on the midway was caught in a rainstorm, so he took off his coat, and left his game to put the coat around her shoulders. A carnival owner's wife was moved by his act of kindness and gave him a new jacket with racing patches.

"Monster has a heart of gold," I said.

He didn't like my comment.

"Not always," he said.

I realized he didn't tell the story to show his kindness to children. He was bragging about his jacket. When I began the year, I wondered if I'd find carnival people were more in touch with their childhoods because carnivals focus on kids. The answer seemed to be the same. Not always.

Monster's stepfather and uncle were early members of the Hell's Angels, and he grew up to become an enforcer. His longest prison term was for shooting a man in the shoulder after a carnival game dispute. The customer stole money off the game counter.

"I was aiming for his head," Monster said.

Monster's stories about violence and prison soon turned to stories of love. After work each day, he went seeking drinks and women at the Dark Horse and the Hollow Leg. He was a lady's man. His smart phone was loaded with pictures of sexy women. Women went crazy for him. Who am I to doubt a Monster?

"Don't let them meet me," I said. "Women find themselves strangely attracted to me."

He laughed because we both knew Monster was the real king of strange attractions. Yet if D'Olivo read Monster's stories on my blog, my year in carnivals was finished. I was cornered with no way out.

MY FIRST CELL phone call in California was to my seven-year-old daughter, Grace. She lost another tooth earlier in the week. Grace was a little creature with baby teeth falling out, skinned knees, and fear of "the bad people" she saw on the news.

She loved holidays like Father's Day and her birthday. She bragged to her friends that her dad "is never boring," which hid the fact he was never home. She told her school counselor, "I really miss my dad."

I told her how to feel about missing people we love.

"Love cuts both ways, sweetheart. Sometimes it's the greatest feeling in the world, and sometimes it hurts more than anything ever. We love each other. That makes us lucky. It's the best way to be."

Most carnival families are separated during the season, and so too my own broken family. Grace was still dealing with the divorce. Parenting books said kids her age are particularly susceptible to separation anxiety.

On my end of the line, I hung up and felt like I'd said the right things. On the other end of the line, Grace hung up the phone with tears in her eyes.

MY TRAVELING GEAR INCLUDED A BICYCLE, a sleeping bag, a suit bag, a laptop, a camera, a cell phone, clothes, and two books. One book was a guide to writing and publishing books. The other was self-help book by Tim Ferriss, *The 4-Hour Work Week – Escape 9-5, Live Anywhere and Join the New Rich*. The title is almost a perfect carnival bally. The sales pitch promises success and the easy life if you buy the book.

I also brought a suit and tie. If this saga became a shipwreck, I didn't want to look like a castaway. The mother of all doubts sat screaming on my shoulder. Carnival work is tough for a young man. It was 2013 and still winter. The next week I was turning fifty-four. My God, what have I done?

AFTER A WEEK-AND-A-HALF OF PAINTING RIDES, I was a model hardworking employee. Yet D'Olivo cringed everytime he saw me taking notes.

He called me into his office for a sit-down. Yes, I was fired. Yes, the concept was impossible. Honestly, give up now.

"No carnival owner will hire a writer," he said. "I worked under Vince McMahon, and he owned the writers. They wrote what he wanted. There's no upside for me to have you here. I don't think anybody else will hire you either."

Traveling carnivals are a horrible allocation of fixed assets. Rides lose their value fast. Every carnival undercuts the next. The margins are slim. Family-owned carnivals are liquidating. Labor problems are getting worse.

"The new face of carnivals is Mexican. They work. They drink their beer. They send their money home. They're good family men. They're like our fathers were in the 1950s."

In some big carnivals, Mexicans are more than half the crew.

"You don't speak Spanish. You won't get to know them if you can't speak to them."

As he spoke, I could see the solution unfolding. Instead of one carnival, I'd join many carnivals. I'd learn basic Spanish and get close to Mexican carnies. I'd go to Mexico to see the roots of the Mexican carnival experience.

The next morning, D'Olivo subtracted the bunkhouse rent money and paid me sixty dollars for almost two weeks of painting and assembling. Then he shook my hand and chuckled.

"More than you had when you came."

He wasn't playing the villain. He was curious about my next move.

"Butler," he said, "is setting up in Oakland."

Putting on my safari hat, I rode my bicycle to the Bay Area Rapid Transit (BART). Getting off in the Coliseum Industrial district, I rode around the giant, rusting, candy-colored cargo-container Jenga-block jungle. I could see a carnival rising on the edge of San Francisco Bay.

Gone were plans to spend the year with Classic. Gone too were open, honest interviews. From that morning forward, people wouldn't know I was writing about them. Against my will, I became a spy.

FIRED TO HIRED

OAKLAND

*R*iding tall in the saddle, one hand on the handlebars, I rode my bicycle on the grass past dozens of carnies setting up dozens of rides.

A carny shouted out to me before I dismounted.

"Looking for a job?"

He directed me to the crew boss. Lee stopped work to look me up and down. He was a big man in his forties, tall, with a booming voice and baseball mitt hands. If I didn't make a good first impression, if Lee told me to keep riding, I was flat out of ideas.

"Do you have a place to sleep tonight?" he asked. "Do you have black pants? Can you pass a piss test?"

Lee never said the words, but I knew what he was saying.

Hot damn! I was hired. Just a couple of hours earlier, I was fired from my first carnival. By noon, I was a working carny at one of America's legendary carnivals and in one of the greatest American cities, Oakland.

Lee pointed the way to the carnival backyard, crowded with bunkhouse trailers, trucks, and RVs.

"It's not much," Lee said. "We're fixing up the bunkrooms. But it's better than sleeping on the streets tonight."

I asked to stay in the reefers, the allegedly air-conditioned trailers for Mexicans. About fifteen men fit into a reefer trailer. The bunks were stacked three beds high, with a small kitchen and two showers. By staying in the reefers, I'd live rent free and get to know the Mexicans. The suggestion surprised Lee.

"We've never integrated the reefers before," he said, looking around to see if that was even possible.

I waved off the idea, in part, because I feared there was no safe place to store my laptop. I also was too tall for the reefer bunks. My stinking carny feet would have stretched into the next fella's face.

Lee was a good judge of men and correctly judged me. I was a homeless man desperate for a carnival job. February is still cold in Northern California. I was grateful for the work and the shelter, no matter the ungodly hours, no matter the bunkhouse bed. I was a newly minted Butler man.

THE OAKLAND BUNKHOUSE room was smaller than the Hayward room. Classic promised $10 an hour and charged $100 a week for a bunk. Butler paid $325 per week and charged $50 for a bunk.

The contract came with an unspoken fine print clause that you work until the work is done right. No overtime pay. You're always on call. Home is the carnival. Work is the carnival. The only place you can escape is at night in your dreams, and carnivals roll through those, too.

The sticker on my bunkhouse door read, "Don't Steal! The Government Hates Competition." My neighbor's door read, "This Definitely Was Not One Of My Three Wishes."

Three doors down from my room lived a jarocho named Salvador. Every jarocho I met was proud of the moniker, which meant he came from the eastern Mexican state of Veracruz, along the Gulf of Mexico.

Salvador was Butler's translator and Mexican crew boss. The Mexican carnies said Salvador had a young way about him. He laughed every other sentence, rarely losing his temper. A human ball of energy, he wore a hard hat saying "Atomic Man."

Employee trailers had twelve single bunkrooms, six on each side. The trailer was put up on blocks, and people stored their belongings underneath. A three-step ladder was needed to climb into a room.

Outside the trailers were card tables loaded with hotplates and crockpots. Beside them were grills and five-gallon water jugs. Folding chairs and overturned plastic buckets were for sitting. At night, grills lit up like tribal campfires. Out came the tequila, beer, and pot. Mexican music from the reefers mixed with the hip-hop from the American trailers.

I went to my room that first night and climbed up about five feet into the bunk. I pulled my notebook from my back pocket, rested the laptop on my stomach, and typed the day's notes. The breeze off San Leandro Bay blew in a foggy, deep chill. Warm in my sleeping bag, I took inventory of my progress.

Butler is a storied carnival. The late owner, Butch Butler, and his father, Bud, set up their top people in their own carnivals. Other carnivals owe their start to the Butler family. Butch Butler died the year before I arrived. Flags honoring Butch's memory waived around the carnival. The best way to understand traveling carnivals was to travel with the best carnival people.

Then doubts started creeping in. What if D'Olivo was right and Butler people heard about me? Stories of savage beatings are legend on the circuit. Sometimes coworkers give the beating. Sometimes the owners do it themselves. Midway machismo is a fact of life, and turning the other cheek isn't in the carny bible. When tempers flash, you have to face what's coming.

That first morning in Oakland, I rose early and watched tired men file out of their bunkrooms. Two-thirds of the men were from Mexico, and I gravitated toward them. They knew their rides and worked fast. The Mexican work ethic was group oriented. A dozen or more men joined together to move heavy yellow electrical lines across a lot.

In the afternoon, I switched over to working on rides with the Americans. Lee started calling me "Employee of the Month."

One day Lee and a group of supervisors were standing around talking when I decided to join their conversation with a joke.

"Lee, what does a guy like me have to do to end up running a place like this?"

Lee and the others laughed at the audacity.

"You gotta marry a girl in the office," said Lee, who'd married a girl in the office.

Dean was another boss, also married to a girl in the office. With a phone to his ear, Dean chain-smoked and squinted while he paced the carnival lot.

Jesse was a game owner and the top boss of my unit. The son of a prominent carnival family in the Southwest, he was mild-mannered when I saw him. His family had ties with carnivals across the country. Jesse owned his own carnival joints and games, which he subcontracted to Butler. Known to be a great manager and "lot man," he surveyed every lot, holding a poll with a wheel at the end.

Where to place rides is a science because a good crowd-flow strategy is a difference-maker. The Ferris wheel should be in the back to draw customers to the back of the lot. Loud rides shouldn't be too close to games. The Midway is the main walkway. The best money-maker games start on the right side of the Midway because people tend to head there immediately after the gate. A good lot man can boost profits for everybody. A great lot man sets the mousetrap.

~⌐

BUTLER'S African American crew was small, but I worked closest with them. When I first said hello to Rose Dog, he took pains to ignore me. The next time we met, I said hello again.

"I didn't tell you my name the first time, did I?"

Rose Dog, thirty-nine, was a six-foot-two carousel boss with a volatile temper. He may have still been on parole from a six year sentence for beating his wife. He loved talking about where he served time.

Huey was a tall, thin, muscular black man in his forties. The most senior member of our unit, he ran a giant circular rollercoaster called the Ring of Fire. He lived in a beat-up RV with a white woman in her twenties named Sabrina. They shared the RV with a snake and a varying number of dogs. The first time I saw Huey, he was riding his bicycle along a dirt path, yelling in jest at the Mexican carnies.

"Punk-ass bitches," he yelled.

They yelled back profanities in Spanish, and everybody laughed. Huey's taunt was only partly in jest.

The Lolly ride foreman was of mixed African American and Hispanic heritage. The Lolly is a swing ride, a smaller version of the much taller Yoyo.

"My name is Harvey, like the rabbit," he said, referring to the 1950 film *Harvey*, about a delusional man talking to an invisible rabbit.

Harvey was an ex-con who spent thirteen years in prison for attempted murder and drug trafficking. He was innocent, but he did time in supermax prisons in Illinois and California before agreeing to a plea deal.

A man of average height, in his forties, Harvey spoke fluent Spanish thanks to his Mexican mother. Being half Mexican didn't help him much with the jarochos.

"Harvey is crazy," the Mexicans said.

Harvey and his wife, Rhonda, lived in a single, small bunkhouse room a couple of doors from mine. Rhonda was a big, friendly white woman who worked in the ticket booth.

Harvey talked to himself in pop culture clichés that flowed together in long Joycean stream-of-consciousness sentences.

Hell hath no wrath like a woman scorned. Lucy someone has some s-plaining to do. I've been bamboozled. I'm a cowboy, on a steel horse I ride . . . wanted dead or alive. Oh, I wish I was an Oscar Mayer wiener, that is what I'd really like to be. I'm a Hungry Man. It's good to be full.

If he was working on a ride and holding out his hand, his whole monologue might really just have meant, "hand me that hammer."

THE MENTALLY ILL are another category of carny. Nobody can afford a primary care doctor. Most people in need are undiagnosed, untreated, and unmedicated.

On my first day at Butler, Eagle wanted to initiate me with classic carny prank jokes. A thin, nervous white man in his twenties, Eagle told me to ask a crew boss for lightbulb grease. No? Go find the carnival key on the midway. No?

I was forewarned about the tricks for greenhorns. I never went hunting for left-handed monkey wrenches, board stretchers, or red light bulb paint either. Eagle told the crew I fell for every trick, and he laughed until there was an awkward silence. Will there be a flock of Eagles in this carnival?

Picky Picky talked to himself in rambling and aggressive monologues. He was a short, strong Mexican man. Salvador said Picky Picky was schizophrenic, but he was just guessing. Picky Picky's main jobs were collecting garbage and odd jobs like driving the carnival van. A possible schizophrenic driving you around in a van as he screamed at personal demons was terrifying even to carnies accustomed to running rollercoasters. Yet every week we stepped on board the schizophrenic express to the grocery store or kingdom come.

Picky Picky's condition created a memorable scene one evening when top carnival hands took the evening off to attend an awards banquet. Because the carnival was shorthanded, Picky Picky was drafted to help the rest of us on rides during the show. Just before the front gates opened, Picky Picky walked out onto the platform of the Giant Wheel, a ninety-foot Ferris wheel made by Wichita, Kansas-based Chance Rides.

Picky Picky cussed out the empty midway in English and Spanish. His voice echoed from one end to the other.

"You assholes. You think I'm going to just take this shit? You think I will do this all by myself? You going to a party? You assholes."

One man shouting at an empty midway is like a man in an empty church shouting at God. Moments later, the crowds rushed in, and he ushered people onto the Giant Wheel. The usual wheelman ran the Giant Wheel.

The carnies at Butler used classic carnival lingo. Mexicans who knew little English still knew donnikers were toilets, and church calls were general crew meetings. Jointees ran games, and ride jockeys ran rides. Some wanted to be called carnies. Others were insulted by the term and insisted on being called showmen. The basics of carnival life were on the price board of the commissary truck.

Deodorant $3.00

Breakfast Sandwich $2.00

Condoms 50 cents

That night in my bunkroom, I bundled up against the February cold and began to plot my year. Earlier in the day, a wild-eyed carny told me he'd hitchhiked to the carnival from Yakima, Washington. After being fired by Classic and widening my ambition to work at more carnivals, I realized I could hitchhike to many carnivals. For the first time, a bicoastal carnival year came to mind.

I laid awake waiting for sleep and listening to the bay muffling Oakland's din. It wasn't quiet. It was city quiet. The only clear sound across the valley was the whistle blow of a midnight train.

SALVADOR CAME out of his bunkhouse in the morning, kneeled down on one knee, touched the ground, and made a sign of the cross. Salvador prayed at every new jump location. Jumps usually last from a weekend to a week, longer if the carnival works at a state fair. I asked him about the prayers. They were for our protection. Were we in danger?

When the show opened on Wednesday, I was assigned to the Super

Slide. It's a wavy multi-runway slide with gunny sacks for sliders. Placed at the front of the midway by the gate, the Super Slide gave me the perfect overview of the carnival. The top of the Super Slide was my photo stand for Oakland and the San Francisco Bay.

Three local hires, Rosemary, Jeremy, and Reese, made me responsible for setting up the schedule for the Super Slide. We worked in rotations of two hours on and two hours off. The rules for the ride were clear. Three tickets. One gunny sack. No handholding. No lap rides. No face-first sliding. No jumping. No kids under thirty-six inches. Look for wrist bands and stamps on the right hand. Beware of counterfeit tickets. No drunks.

I developed my routine at the ground-level gate.

"I have only one real rule, kids. You must have fun!"

Repeated hundreds of times a day, it became a claim to fame.

"Mister, we know your one rule," the kids said. "We had fun. We really did. We're going again."

From the top of the slide I watched kids race their friends up the stairs. They ran around below me, from games to rides to food wagons. Parents watched their children and were happy too. Fried food and perfumed candied air rolled in on the fog. Every type of person walked through the gates. Dozens of game joints blasted music.

Huey ran the Ring of Fire for maximum screams. Crowds jammed in for Rose Dog's carousel. Harvey's Lolly Swing rose and swung riders around in high, wide circles.

The whole carnival lifted off the dizzy ground. Food stands sold snow cones, candy apples, deep-fried Twinkies, funnel cakes, and elephant ears. Flirting, eating, screaming people in a chaotic blaze of lights and music. All to a trumpet playing at high register more, more, more, again, again, again.

Beyond the carnival and on the bay, rowing crews crossed neon waves glowing from the carnival lights. On the other side along the interstate, rush-hour lights merged into the show. Standing at the top of the Super Slide, I was above the illusions of the carnival.

One evening, I watched a charter bus pull up to the back gate and a couple of dozen men filed out. They were Mexicans at the end of their 2,500-mile bus ride from the foothills of Veracruz. They carried six months of belongings in their arms on their way to the reefers. I expected to see weary migrants, but from that height and distance, all I saw were the laughing men.

The fog came across from San Francisco Bay like stagecraft. Bright colored pennants on carnival tent tops snapped in the wind like wishes.

SPRINGTIME IN CARNIVALS is a time for dreamers. Jeremy, Reese, and Rosemary opened up about their dreams one rainy night standing under the Super Slide.

Jeremy acted out all his stories. His nightly walk home past gang-bangers was terrifying and comic.

"I wear this ugly-ass cap, these dusty old pants, dusty old coat. This puffy backpack looks like I don't got nothing in it or like I was out robbing cars. If they stop me, I say I got nothing. Check me out. I don't got no wallet, nothing. I don't wear my earphones. I just keep walking."

To show us how he avoided the gangs, he walked fast under the Super Slide with his hands in his pockets and head down. It was Jeremy's one-man show.

"If they stop me, I say you got the wrong guy, go get someone at the Coliseum."

His last apartment was a $650-a-month, government-subsidized studio. His kitchen and bathroom were in the same room. Living there exposed him to more violence than the streets.

"The stairwell was like the OK Corral. The elevator was always broken. There was always some kind of drama going on in there. People were always partying. Every time I went down the stairs, I'd look down and see if I'd get mugged."

Then he cupped his hands on both sides of his mouth and acted as if he were yelling down a stairwell.

"Hey, I'm coming down. I ain't got nothing. Don't kill meee!"

Jeremy's backpack was usually full of pirated DVDs. Carnies joked that if you watched Jeremy's movies, you could hear people yelling at the screen.

Rosemary was a middle-aged, heavy-set black woman with an infectious laugh. She laughed at everything Jeremy said. All she wanted from the carnival that season was money enough for a comfortable night's sleep in a new bed.

Reese wore thick black-rimmed eyeglasses and spent his extra cash on rap music recording studios. He backed up and rapped for us, waving his arms to profane, chopper beats. I didn't know anything about rap music, but I knew enough to ask why he was rapping under a Super Slide. He was no carny. He was an artist.

When the time came, the Giant Wheel lights went out and people yelled, "Down!"

Ride jockeys scrambled to close their rides. Jointees turned down their game-joint awnings. Grab wagon concessionaires put away food.

Ferris wheels are commonly compared to eyes: the London Eye, Tianjin Eye, Dubai Eye, Eye of the Emirates, Budapest Eye, and Orlando Eye. Ferris wheels are the focal points of the Santa Monica Pier in California, Galveston Historic Pleasure Pier in Texas, and Navy Pier in Chicago. When the Eye is open, the carnival is awake. When the Eye closes, another life behind the rides and games lights up.

PEOPLE SUGGESTED I switch to a newer bunkhouse trailer. The trailers were newer but still old. A ballad drifted across from the radio in another bunkroom. A young woman sang along. She meant every tender word. I fell asleep happy.

The next morning, I found bites on my arm. Carnies later took one look at the bite patterns and confirmed I had bedbugs, the carny plague. The bites spread to my inner thigh and head. My forehead swelled so much that my hard hat no longer fit.

I decided that same day to wash all I owned and move back to my original bunkhouse. I had to do my laundry during my two-hour work break. Loading my laundry onto my bicycle, I rode two miles to the laundromat near the corner of High Street and International Avenue.

High Street was a dangerous area, so I was on my guard. Sitting inside the shop, I kept looking back and forth from my laundry in the machine to my bicycle leaning on the laundromat store window.

When I rose from my chair to empty the drier, a bike thief jumped on the bike and rode away. I'd owned the bike since the 1980s and nicknamed it Pan. It meant something to me. It had a name. I ran in my socks into the parking lot, stopping strangers. "Did you see anyone riding away on a black bicycle?"

Was I really going to run down a bicycle thief in my socks? I ran into the local Hispanic market and then around the corner. Turning the corner, I saw young black males standing in a group talking in the windows of passing cars. I heard an exotic bird call. Wait a second. There aren't any exotic birds in Oakland. Frozen in my socks, I realized it was a warning call.

To hell with the bike. I turned on my heels and began speed-walking away in my socks, in short, fast steps like a clownish mime.

A skinny teenager on a BMX bike came riding out of the crowd toward me.

"You better get out of here, mister. Those guys over there think you're a cop."

A wizened old black prostitute waved me down from across the street.

"I know you," she said. "We partied last week. How are you?"

I didn't know if I was sorrier for myself or my doppelganger.

Back at the laundromat, I realized my work shift began in thirty minutes. Grabbing my two bags of laundry and sleeping bag, I began running back two miles to the carnival. I ran with my laundry and sleeping bags flopping in opposite directions. I ran next to commuters driving home from work and past a shipwrecked fishing boat where homeless people slept and smoked crack. My running made me that special kind of silly person that occasionally appears in cities to comments like, "you don't see that every day, do you mom."

Arriving in time for my shift, I later retold the story to the great amusement of other carnies. I wanted to make them laugh, but I became a target of good-natured taunts.

"Hey, High Street, going back tonight for a date? Can you pick me up some weed?"

I was afraid my carny nickname would forever be "High Street."

I moved back to my original trailer with my laundered clothes, but the laundromat did not rid me of those satanic bugs. I used industrial pesticides, but they gave me headaches. I worried the bugs might live, and I might die. The whole embarrassing affair resulted in me no longer lugging a bicycle across the country. I mailed my uninfected bicycle packs, suit, and ties back to Chicago.

The day after the theft, I walked up to Dean, Jesse, and Lee. I acted out the whole story. Jeremy couldn't have done it better. They laughed at first until Lee stopped laughing.

"You're lucky. One year, one of our guys wandered off around there and was hung."

﹏

KITTY CALLED herself the Goldfish Lady and seemed to love everyone at first sight. She was in her fifties with bright white hair and clear, shining brown eyes. She took long puffs on her cigarette when she was making a point worth remembering.

Her goldfish game was in a circular joint, with small bowls floating in a plastic pool. The prize for throwing a ping pong into the bowl was plush or a fish. Spend ten dollars, and you were guaranteed a tiny fish in a plastic bag of water.

Kitty rigged the game in favor of kids and the disabled.

"I don't care. I'll pay for it out of my pocket if I have to. But I want to see them happy."

A registered nurse by trade, Kitty was shanghaied by her love of carnivals.

"I don't do it for the money. I have a bunkhouse, a trailer, and a three-bedroom house in Chico. I do it for the kids. These are my babies. I never had babies."

The money was terrible that early in the season. She was making just enough gas money to get to the next jump.

I mentioned that I thought of my daughter Grace when I saw laughing kids in the carnival.

"I see my unborn children," she said.

She took another puff and thought about it.

"If I can make a child cry because they got a fish. If I can make a memory. If a kid says, 'Remember that year I went to the carnival and won that fish?' It's worth it."

Like all people running goldfish games, she told stories of fish living well into inexplicable old age. She owned a four-year-old goldfish that was getting fatter every day.

She said the sweetest words ever spoken to her were, 'I remember you. You're the Goldfish Lady from last year.'

"That feels good," she said. "I do it for my babies."

After a long, slow puff, she looked me in the eyes and snuffed her cigarette out on the ground for emphasis. She was never more serious in her life.

FOR CARNIVAL WORKERS, the slough is the show finale. The whole carnival jump leads up to the teardown-night ordeal. Doing my best to avoid Rose Dog, I began slough night working with a Mexican crew on the Shrek funhouse. The Shrek is a kids' gym and features the green ogre Shrek on the façade. Inside are rope ladders, body bags, a swinging bridge, and a slide.

Jesus and Faustino worked fast. They told me where to go and what to do. At one point, a spring backfired directly into my face. It left a scratch and a bruise, but no scar. Then Jesus dropped a two-pound steel pin from the top of the Shrek, hitting me on the crown of my head. If slough was a cartoon, the bump on my head would have risen to the sound of a slide whistle "awe-whoop." I should have worn my hardhat.

Rose Dog later called me over to work the carousel. He was angry because I chose to work with the Mexicans. Taunts and profanity came raining down. The insults made me smirk. Rose Dog wanted to slap the grin off my face.

Three times his fingers smashed. Three times he blamed me. Three times he threatened to "fuck me up." The crew heard his threats. Rose Dog and I faced each other in silence. I widened my stance and readied for him to come at me.

I am six foot five with my own history of violence. Yet my age and weight made me the odds-on underdog. Before I went to work in carnivals, I made a solemn vow to never be involved in a violent encounter.

Here it comes. Fight dirty. Trick him. I once overheard him say he broke his neck in a car accident. A violent scenario flashed in my mind. Grab his head. Twist it off. Stick it on a carousel spike. Turn on the engine and give the old girl a spin.

I have since realized my get-away plan from the blood-soaked crime scene of my imagination would have involved a bicycle . . . which was stolen at the laundromat . . . where I also was nearly killed.

Rose Dog stared at me. It was an American stand-off. He opened his eyes wide. He puffed up. Walking toward me, he bent down and picked up his side of the pig iron carousel beam. We lifted it together and slid it along the side of the truck trailer. We worked until dawn, and we shared the heaviest lifting. The abuse didn't stop until we walked away in silence to our bunkhouses.

Before going into my bunkroom, I stood staring up at the stars looking for something I recognized. I saw nothing. I'd lost my bearings. This wasn't over. I'd crossed a dangerous man.

THE MORNING AFTER SLOUGH, the carnival site was an electric field devoid of energy. After a week of crowds, bright lights, and noise, the carnival lot was the aftermath of an epic party. Trucks drove around the lot all night, hauling away rides and joints. A few rides remained. Hundreds of seagulls squawked on the gravel parking lot, fighting over trashed plates, cartons, and plastic bottles.

Walking around the lot, I saw a Mexican sitting alone on a midway bench. No rides or tents nearby. From behind, I watched him staring at the hazy sunrise. A huge, red Oracle arena sign was in his line of sight.

What would a high-tech oracle say about the future of sloughs? How long before we have self-sloughing rides folding up and driving themselves to the next spot? Fewer, higher-skilled carnies might become the norm. All-night sloughs would become history.

The injuries to my face and head were still thumping. Sloughing the carousel came close to a bloody ending. Robots can take the sloughs.

The day after slough was payday, but a few rides still needed to be torn down. I was the only American to go out to help the Mexicans finish the last of the work. When we finished, there were a few more hours left before pay time. The Americans were preparing for the jump and resting. The Mexicans looked at the empty carnival field and saw an empty soccer field.

Hardhats went flying to the grass. Out came the soccer ball. They brushed back their jet-black hair and ran out onto the vacant lot where once a major urban American carnival stood. They all missed church on Sunday, but soccer was their Monday morning religion.

One player wore pink Bermuda shorts and a designer shirt, dashing around the field like a painted bird. He may not have been the best player, but he was the flashiest. They played in front of a crowd brought up from Mexico on a carnival conveyor belt. Every shoulder-high kick drew whistles and cheers. Across the field, men ran through drifting clouds of dust. They owned the field of play.

THE POWER of a carnival payday puts all else to shame. The web said God is dead. Climate change is gone. Death is cured. Payday's today.

Out of the shadows and into the light, she walked. The office lady held a long list of names and envelopes filled with one-dollar, five-dollar, ten-dollar, and twenty-dollar bills. The all-male crew completely surrounded her.

She shouted out the names on her list. Men pushed their way into the middle of the crowd as if they'd won the lottery. I wasn't sure where I stood. After the confrontation with Rose Dog, maybe they thought I was trouble. I'd get paid but told not to go to the next jump.

Then she called my name, smiled, and handed me the fat envelope. At that moment, I crossed another hurdle. I went from a local hire to a traveling carnival man on my way to the next jump.

Dean took half the crew north, and Lee took the rest of us south. Our next jump was in Hayward, where Classic Amusement was based. At the last minute, I hitched a ride with a truck driver hauling a Tilt-a-Whirl. We were driving off the lot when the driver saw Rose Dog on foot.

"Come on in here," the driver said.

"No, I'm walking," Rose Dog said.

Rose Dog planned to walk the fifteen miles from Oakland to Hayward. He was angry at the Mexicans for securing rides before the Americans. He'd show them. He'd walk it. Then everyone would know how angry he was. They'd be sorry.

We drove next to him for a while on the lot. The driver finally talked him down. Rose Dog climbed up into the cab and sat next to me. Last night was still unfinished business for him, and he wasn't a forgiving man.

Dozens of trucks, cars, and RVs pulled out of the lot scattering dust clouds up against the orange-red twilight. Plastic-bag tumble-weeds blew across our path. Flying hordes of seagulls returned triumphantly to their parking-lot kingdom. They stood legion, in a menacing vigil. The industrial biome returned.

In the truck, Rose Dog talked about his six-year prison sentence for beating his wife.

"Now I beat up people who hit women," he said. "I had a talk with Jesus about it. I'm forgiven."

I drifted off, squinting out the window, searching for a wild turkey flying ahead, leading the way back to Hayward.

UP, UP, AND AWAAAY!

HAYWARD

*R*ose Dog wanted me to run the carousel the way he ran it, in a constant state of sexual arousal. When Rose Dog ran the merry-go-round, I called it horny Jenny.

A carousel, aka a Jenny, may run on electricity, but that's not what made her go up and down, round and round. That was Rose Dog.

In the Southland Mall parking lot, carousel training started with a lesson in etiquette around the old girl. Rose Dog acted out the proper way to approach female customers.

"First, you open the gate," he said in his Louisiana accent.

Rose Dog swung the gate open and bowed like a Southern gentleman.

"Then you greet all the ladies. You tell them they are looking fine. Then you make sure all the ladies are strapped in. Then you tell the ladies they are looking fine. Again."

A young woman drove her car around the mall parking lot, stopping in front of the carousel. She leaned her head out the window.

"When do you guys open up?"

Rose Dog stopped everything and perked up.

"We open Wednesday. Come by. I'll set you up, baby. Maybe you can bring me a hot cooked meal."

On more than a few occasions, I watched Rose Dog whispering in a woman's ear while she mounted a carousel horse. Some women giggled. Others seemed to taste a bad California lemon. He boasted real successes. Women went back to his bunkroom. On his fantasy carousel, he was a merry-go-round Romeo.

Rose Dog's training was abusive. I asked too many questions. Nobody cares if Chance Rides makes Americana Ferris wheels. Strap in the kids, stupid. We are both going to jail if you screw this up.

"There are eighteen rides. You can go to jail for twenty years for each ride. You do the math. If you fuck up, I'm the boss, so I go to prison too. And if I go to prison with you, you won't like me very much."

What were we sweethearts? And is there really a prison for carousel carnies? Is it anywhere near Murphy's carnival foot grave-yard? If Rose Dog's math was correct, we'd be going to prison between 20 and 360 years. Maybe we'd be friends by then, but I doubt it.

The carousel is the heart of the traveling carnival. Carousels have a fanatical fan base. The horses are standalone art in galleries and public spaces. They're in movies, books, plays, photos, paintings, sculptures, and songs. They are make-believe out for a spin.

The Americana carousel features eighteen fantasy rides, including a Puss-in-Boots cat, a deer, a sea monster, a zebra, and an Easter bunny. Sphinxes adorn the sides of the carousel benches.

One horse on the Butler carousel wore a ribbon with the name "Sydney," the name of Butch Butler's daughter. Sydney is the carnival's logo, a smiling Easter Bunny in a tuxedo waving atop a carousel horse. It was another reminder that behind this show was a carnival family.

Dismantling and setting up the ride usually took four or more of us. Rose Dog and I took turns inside the semi-truck trailer, picking up 170-pound horses and putting them into slots. Rose Dog was sure I would drop a horse.

If I broke a horse, Rose Dog warned, the carnival would charge me fifty thousand dollars per horse. Would they take an IOU? Putting up the carousel's pie-topped tarp roof required climbing inside the tent, bending backward, and pinning the tarp to hooks. The steel diamond plated floor planks took two workers to lift.

Customers rode the fiberglass horses up and down, moving five miles per hour counterclockwise for two-and-a-half minutes. It's not fast, scary, or high tech. Add the calliope organ music, and the carousel becomes a time machine.

Carousels may seem sleepy, but the lines are among the carnival's longest. When we opened the gate, kids ran like Greyhounds for the carousel. When kids dismounted, they fed the horses imaginary carrots and lovingly said goodbye.

One evening, a waifish Hispanic preschool girl rode Sydney while pretending to be a beauty queen. She waved and blew kisses to the crowd.

"I love you too, California. Ooh, I love you too."

The crowd played along and cheered at every pass. On those nights, it was easy to see humanity under the influence of carnivals.

Parents took pictures of their smiling children to keep forever. Lovers and rowdy teens acted out their own games in slow circles. Carousels have real power in carnivals. Carnival people and carousel fans still get married on carousels.

Rose Dog kept harping on me to watch the riders. I couldn't keep my eyes off them. People came to the carousel depressed. When they left, there wasn't a sad rider among them. Doctor Carousel.

The carousel was Rose Dog's theater, and it mirrored another Broadway play that year. In the revival of the Rodgers and Hammerstein musical *Carousel* on Broadway, Tony-nominated actor Joshua Henry played the first black Billy Bigelow.

The Bigelow character is a carousel boss and a criminal who hits his wife. Rose Dog was a black carousel boss and a criminal who hit his wife. Jesus forgave him.

Other guys might have a hot car, but Rose Dog's chick magnet was a merry-go-round. I once complimented Rose Dog on taking pride in cleaning the carousel tarp, poles, and horses. Rose Dog lowered his voice in reverence.

"You noticed that? I like my carousels like I like my Cadillacs. Shiny."

Before prison, he was a warehouse manager, golfing at the best golf courses. He bought Cadillacs. Since his divorce, all his alimony checks went to pay his gardener. His success in life was due to being raised right.

Rose Dog went to an all-boys Catholic high school in Louisiana before going to Grambling State. A scholarship player for the historically black college, he either dropped out or was kicked out.

Love of the carnival life seemed to be in Rose Dog. He thought everyone noticed if his ride was set up and torn down fast. He swaggered around the lot.

His eldest son was a source of pride, too. His son made the McDonald's 100 basketball list that year and signed a letter of intent to play basketball at Marquette University in Milwaukee, Wisconsin. His son won't drop out either. His son won't make the mistakes he made. His son also refused to speak to him.

"I understand that, after what I did to his mother," he said. "I'll save my money and go see him play someday. I'll dress up and go to the stadium."

He consistently mispronounced the university's name. I didn't mention it, nor that I attended Marquette.

Anger was Rose Dog's most available trait. One morning Rose Dog told us about a dream he had the night before, of being in an argument with "this dude." In the dream, he shoved a carousel pole through the dude's chest.

"That is fucked-up, isn't it? Ha. Ha."

He left it up to me to guess if I was that dude.

The Southland Mall was a short distance from Classic Amusement's headquarters. I was worried a carny from Classic would somehow blow my cover, either at the carnival or later over drinks at the Hollow Leg.

During setup the jointees turned up the music while they washed tarps on the parking-lot concrete. Pink, white, and powder blue tarps were doused with liquid soap. Long-handled brooms became imaginary dance partners. Barriers of race and nationality were forgotten. Mexicans and Americans brushed side-by-side on top of the tarp to the disco beat of *Car Wash*.

Working at the car wash
Working at the car wash, yeah
Come on and sing it with me, car wash
Sing it to me, car wash, yeah.

Lee told Harvey to train me on the Lolly Swing. Once I could run both the Americana and the Lolly, I could give work breaks to Harvey and Rose Dog.

Much like Rose Dog, Harvey wanted me to run the ride his way. Harvey put people in their seats with hair-raising jokes. He was an unstable ex-con who'd spent years in a supermax prison. If his jokes were a guide, he believed life was scary, crazy, and funny if you survived.

"I hope you're not sitting in seat number five," he'd say, "because that one falls off."

When the rider in seat five panicked, Harvey feigned surprise.

"Just kidding," he'd say. "I must be thinking of seat six."

Just as the worried person in seat number six began to ask about safety, Harvey turned on the Lolly.

It was at the Lollys where I first developed full routines. I felt the call of show business. Pressing the "on" button, I walked out from behind the control stand during the time delay. Palms up, I was ham-actor Moses raising my arms up like I was parting the Red Sea.

"Up, I say. Up, I say. And awaaay, I say."

All the seats rose up, seemingly at my magical command. When riders returned to earth, I ran from seat to seat and asked everyone if they loved the ride. None of the other ride jockeys made up skits to go with their rides. They watched my routines change all night.

"I never saw someone with so much energy," Huey said.

I ran between seats. Half mad and half possessed, I sold it all night long. Kids came running up to me later, asking how I made the ride go up. Parents brought friends to watch the act. The Lolly lines grew with repeat customers.

Each night, we brought our ticket bags back to the main-office trailer to be counted. The next day, the ticket totals were posted at the main walk-up window. Before I began using my Lolly routines, the carousel was the top earner. When the Lollys became the top earner, Harvey began ribbing Rose Dog. The status quo was upset. Rose Dog knew the dude to blame.

HARVEY COULDN'T PASS a dumpster without leaping inside, searching for cans and plastic. Both inside and outside his room, there were plastic bags filled to the point of exploding. He didn't see trash. He saw beer money.

Another source of street cred was his skill as a master street chef. He'd worked in Mexican restaurants and watched his mother cook. Like all great chefs, he was renowned for his specialties. The meal that made him famous in the railroad yards across California was "homeless chicken."

"If you can make a great chicken when you're living at the side of the railroad tracks," he said, "then you are good."

It sounded like a version of hobo stew or Mulligan stew, made from whatever was handy.

The spending habits of Harvey and Rhonda were bizarre. After Oakland, they paid $130 for a night in a hotel. The next day they bought a cell phone and shopped for a new TV. Harvey purchased a stool to sit on while running the Lolly. They ate at restaurants and ordered ribs delivered to the trailer.

Rhonda was a big, lovely woman with a good sense of humor and a baffling tolerance for Harvey's abuse. She talked out of one side of her mouth. When she wanted to be funny, talking out of the side of the mouth added to the funny.

On a van ride with Mexicans to the laundromat, Rhonda told us how she and Harvey were once slapped with a $120 ticket in Hayward for jaywalking.

"We got a big fat ticket in the mail," she said.

A Mexican in the back of the van decided to have some fun.

"Oh, wow, man. I would love to get a big fat chicken in the mail."

"Not a big fat chicken in the mail," she said. "A big fat ticket in the mail."

"Now you've done it," I said, "I'm hungry."

"You can't get blood from a peach," she said. "With our luck, we'd get a judge who didn't get laid the night before."

Then I steered the running joke in a stranger direction.

"Ask him, 'Judge, did you get laid last night? Because if you didn't, I want another judge.'"

I still wasn't sure if Rhonda was playing along or giving real advice.

"It's true, try to figure out if the judge has been laid," she said. "See if he's smiling or something. Because if he isn't smiling, you might go to jail or back to Mexico."

The more I thought about the jaywalking rap, the angrier I felt. A cop gave a poor, itinerate carnival couple a ticket, knowing they'd have to quit the carnival to make the court date. Fines accumulate with every missed court date. The ticket amounted to more than their life savings.

What would a Silicon Valley billionaire have to do to be fined more than their net worth? Even walking across a street, poverty humiliates.

~⌣⌢

FROM OUR TRAILER doors in the Hayward Mall parking lot, we saw the back fences of local homes. More than one carny wondered what it would be like to get off the road. Maybe own a home like those so close to our bunkhouses. What does "home" mean to people living in rented, mobile, seasonal bunkhouse rooms?

Metal Head was a carny who'd lived the square life and returned to the carnival life. He was a Hell's Angel millionaire. He worked with Smiley in a souvenir joint in Hayward.

At forty-seven years old, Metal Head was a mountain of tattoos, cigarettes, leather jackets, jeans, and boots. By his estimation, his net worth was between two million and sixteen million dollars. I asked him, which was it, two million or sixteen million? He just nodded yes.

He worked first in rides and then in games for seventeen years. His carnival nickname was Metal Head because when a Gravitron accident sliced off the top of his skull, a metal plate was surgically implanted.

During those long seasons on the road, Metal Head wondered what it would be like to have a home and a sucker job.

A fight changed his life. Rowdy local teens one night were harassing a pretty jointee he knew. He went up to the biggest loudmouth drunk and broke his jaw. Then he looked at the group of kids and asked, "Who's next?"

"She was so surprised, her mouth was down to there," he said, pointing to his feet.

It was love at first punch. They married and found a life outside of carnivals. He became a Home Depot warehouse manager, reinvesting and doubling down every time the stock split. He made money, but his home life fell apart in a messy, bitter divorce.

When I met him, he was wealthy and semi-retired. He spent his days working on cars, fishing, and going on parental visits to see his six-year-old son. Money wasn't the object when he worked the souvenir joint. He wanted to get out of the house. The carnival was his first home, and he missed being with it.

HAPPY EASTER, KISS MY KEISTER

MARTINEZ

On the Martinez setup, I turned fifty-four years old. I put red leis around my neck and gave extra leis away to the crew. I tooted a birthday-party horn while setting up rides.

"This ride is ready. Toot! I have a leveling board. Toot!"

Jointees offered me whiskey. Rose Dog yelled at me. Harvey gave me chocolate-chip cookies. Far from family and friends, I cherished those cookies.

"I love you, man," he said, repeating another old TV commercial, "but you still can't have my Bud Light."

Grace sang happy birthday to me on the cell phone. I told her I scored cookies for my birthday. Her present was waiting for me to come home.

My family tradition on birthdays is to ask, "In all your years, what have you learned about life?"

That birthday night, in a cramped bunkhouse in Martinez reeking of sweaty socks, I thought of how little I owned. How little I felt. How little I'd learned about life.

The Japanese haiku poet Basho was around my age when he wrote *The Narrow Road to the Interior*. Inspired by itinerate poets, Basho left everything behind to walk a 1,500-mile journey into the wilds of fifteenth-century Japan. He said clouds inspired wanderlust in him. Living on the road would be a fresh well of insights.

Before leaving his home behind, he wrote a letter to a friend noting that the previous owner of his hut was a monk who put a sign outside that read, "Hut of the Phantom Dwelling."

"We all in the end, do we not," he wrote, "live in a phantom dwelling."

I was in a bunkhouse hut, living an itinerant life. My old life was annihilated. I owned almost nothing, not even Basho's hut. I didn't feel lonely so much as an unmistakable aloneness.

I took the last bite of my birthday cookie and closed my eyes. A consoling thought crossed my mind, a carnival Zen. Off to sleep I flew, drifting on Basho's clouds.

THE MEXICAN WOMAN who cut hair for the Mexican side of the crew couldn't speak much English. She laughed when she finally understood I wanted my hair to look like Salvador's hairstyle.

She sat me outside on a fold-up chair. Her barber's apron was a black Hefty trash bag. She was less than five feet tall and was forced to reach high to cut my hair. The wind blew the sheared hair from my shoulders. The trash bag haircut cost five dollars.

Before she finished, someone tapped me on the shoulder. Jeremy had taken a train and a bus from Oakland to Martinez to join us. I made a joke about him following me.

"Where are you going next?" he asked. "Doesn't matter because next time I see you, I'll be driving a car. I'll get your number and call you. Or I'll just use my GPS."

Jeremy clowned like he was driving a big car with his pockets full of money. A natural storyteller, he walked with an up-and-down swagger that changed tempo with his moods.

Coworkers complained that Jeremy was always on the make and bumming too many cigarettes.

"He needs to get his hustle together," Harvey said.

Hustling cigarettes and videos was small time, but hustling up a car raised questions.

Later in the day, Lee shouted to the crew to gather for a talk about the upcoming weekend.

Jeremy was standing in the back when he noticed two men crossing the lot toward him. He acted as if he didn't see them and walked away.

Rose Dog noticed too.

"He's being followed," he whispered.

The two men were undercover cops. They caught up to him, and after a couple of questions, they slapped the jewelry on him. They led him away in handcuffs, his head down, his gait still unmistakable.

Lee denied knowing anything about the arrest. Carnies told me it was best not to ask. Rosemary, who also made it from Oakland to Martinez, said she talked to Jeremy. She told me what he said. It was a serious charge but second-hand information. All I knew for sure was I'd never see Jeremy on the midway again.

A FREAK-SHOW PERFORMER showed up one night at my Lolly Swing. She wanted to see a manager. She worked for Butch Butler and suggested she should get a few free rides for old time's sake.

Tall and thin, she was dressed in high black boots and a black leather jacket. She had long black hair and deep blue mascara. I could envision her as the sideshow beauty in years past.

She'd worked the blade box, walked on glass, and handled a twelve-foot python named Julius Squeezer. She'd paid her sideshow dues.

When she showed up at my Lolly Swing, she was a local hairdresser with a colorful past. Nobody in our unit remembered her. She gave up quickly. We were ride jockeys and jointees, not her sideshow tribe.

Seeing her fade into the night was unsettling. She was with it back then, but we were with it now. Did she put sideshow pictures next to her salon chair and tell stories to her clients? Did she reminisce about her tight carnival family?

WEARING his dark sunglasses and his Oakland Raiders jacket, Lee called us out of our bunkrooms for the Sunday update and a raffle.

"Church call. Church call. If you hear this, you're already late."

About fifty of us came shuffling out past the 1001 Nachts, a swinging seated "magic carpet" ride. The Butler managers surprised the crew with an Easter Sunday buffet laid out on the balloon-dart game counter.

It was a carnival Easter feast with free food and a raffle for pickled pig's feet. Ham, salami, turkey, cheeses, potatoes, pasta salads, cookies, and colored eggs lined the throwing counter. Tickets were drawn from a bucket on the midway.

If any of the Mexicans won, a roar went up from their groups. If a boss or a Butler family member won a prize, jointees hooted, "It's a fix." One jointee won three prizes in a row and rubbed it in. He bowed to the losers in the crowd.

"Thank you," he said. "Thank you."

A woman in the back of the crowd shouted, "Happy Easter, kiss my keister."

Dark rain clouds followed the Easter brunch. The Sam & Dave version of *Gimme Some Lovin'* rolled down the midway. A hammering rain turned the dirt lot to mud and sent people for cover under game awnings.

One grandfather embraced the storm by running around in the rain and jumping into puddles with his grade school granddaughter.

Spring storms give carnival people time to air their hopes for the coming year. A Classic Amusement carny once said he was saving to buy a dollar store. Harvey wanted to start a computer repair store connected to an internet cafe and a strip bar. Both men were veterans of past carnival seasons. Both were homeless a month prior.

"They'll all be broke by the end of the season," Lee said. "If they saved just fifty dollars a week, they'd have a couple of thousand dollars at the end of the season to do something with."

Lee was referring to the Americans. The Mexicans have a different experience. They do all they can to save for their families south of the border. The Mexican organizer for US carnivals, according to Salvador, told his recruits to thank God for all the money they would make up north.

"He told us all to get on our knees," Salvador said, "and thank God that we have this chance to work up here."

Ten hours of rain left everyone soaked to the bone. Our sneakers were caked with muck up to our ankles. I helped Rose Dog slough the carousel and later moved to help Harvey tear down the Lolly. Harvey's thoughts and methods were disorganized. He cursed the ride and his life.

Late in the morning, I hung back and told Harvey to "go bother Rhonda." He didn't laugh. Round-shouldered and muddy head to toe, he walked behind the rides to his room.

All those sleeping carnies. Klieg lights flickered off the blue and gold Oriental dragon head on the rollercoaster. Iron monsters folded in on themselves while colorful ticket joints stood selling tickets to nowhere.

Soft sounds crept back, hanging on the leaves. A low, breezy, updraft whistled around the rides. The empty, dark carnival was a childlike out-of-tune concert of pig iron flutes.

SHOOT THOSE BASTARDS ONE, TWO, THREE

BAY POINT

*B*efore the show opened, Rose Dog walked out in front of the carousel and onto the empty midway in Bay Point. He wore his baggy black pants, black sunglasses, new shoes, and a powder blue Butler shirt and hat. He turned and shook his head at the carnival.

"Drama, drama, drama," he yelled. "That's all we get round here."

A young Hispanic guy in his twenties came aboard in Martinez. With a boxer's flat nose, Juan was short and walked with a wide gait. He shadow-boxed once in a while around the lot.

The five-foot bags at the Shrek gym resembled boxing body bags. Juan took to hitting them like the movie character Rocky Balboa hit slabs of meat. Sticking, jabbing, circling, Juan saved his best stuff for an upper right hook. The hook was designed to take down taller men.

Lee liked him. Rose Dog ridiculed him at every turn. As for Juan, he liked getting drunk after work and passing out inside the rides. The money he saved on a bunkroom he spent on his habits. He told stories in an un-embarrassed way.

"Any of you guys have a fat girlfriend? Oh my God, it takes a lot of work to get around her. A lot of work. Phew!"

Rose Dog was berating Juan one day for every kind of imagined wrong when Juan snapped mid-sentence. The upper right hook hammered Rose Dog's left eye, and he fell backward like a pro-wrestler into the tin fences around the carousel. Juan jumped on top of Rose Dog in the high uncut grass. Rose Dog cried out.

"Ow wee . . . Ow wee."

The sounds Rose Dog made didn't quite match his tough-guy persona. The smaller and lighter Juan couldn't win a wrestling match. Neither drug abuser could last long. When carnies jumped in to pull them apart, Rose Dog was whooped.

Rose Dog stood there stunned with an eye swelling to the size of a black-and-blue Easter egg. He turned to look at me.

"There's puss coming in my eye. I hope nobody sees it. What did I say wrong?"

At church call the next Sunday, Rose Dog stood in the back wearing black sunglasses. Lee praised Rose Dog for not retaliating.

"He was the bigger man," Lee said. "That's the kind of man we want at Butler these days."

Lee really was saying an old-time carny would never have let such a beating go. Lee guessed that Juan broke his hand on Rose Dog's face. He joked that "black people's heads are harder." There are no politically correct police on carnival lots.

Rose Dog didn't retaliate because his broken neck was worse than he let people know. He'd lose a second fight too.

Juan won the fight, but finding work was going to be tough with a busted hand. Juan was broke again. A steady diet of Camels, pot, and whiskey catches up with most people.

From another perspective, Juan kicked some ass. He decked the boss, collected his pay, and rode away on his bicycle. Free from the mad carnival.

SALVADOR DISLIKED Bay Point because of the gangs. Gangbangers one year threw rocks at the carnies from local apartments. Yet the carnival was a wildly popular annual event in the neighborhood.

We squeezed eleven rides onto a tiny lot. At night we were a loud, technicolor, alien space ship just a street away from ranch homes the size of three-car garages.

Bay Point seemed young, with black and Hispanic kids bicycling past and playing in parks. On set-up the first day, Rose Dog ran after a local kid riding his BMX at top speed around the rides.

As the week progressed, Salvador's concerns about Bay Point mounted. Several times we chased away ticket counterfeiters and a purse snatcher. A teenager climbed to the top of the nearby billboard and sat waving to a rowdy, cheering crowd.

Our final day was Hispanic Sunday, which was my name for the day because we drew mixed crowds all week, but Hispanics dominated on Sunday.

"It's family day for us," Salvador said.

Clouds gathered around noon, darkening and moving closer. Carnies at their rides tipped their hats back and stared at the sky. The danger of lightning strikes is great around crowds of people and tall electric structures, making carnivals risky places during storms.

Five Mexican food carts were parked close together on the side street across from us. Long lines formed for the two-wheeled wooden carts. Corn cobs with mayonnaise, cheese, and chili powder were hot sellers.

Watermelon and mango slices sold next to deep-fried chips. Shaved-ice snow cones were scooped from grubby coolers. Vendors used their stained juice bottles to squeeze sugary flavoring on the shaved ice.

Most of their items were two dollars or less. Our food and drink were four dollars and up. The side street competed with the carnival, and all the transactions were in Spanish.

Parents sat in lawn chairs and the flatbeds of pickup trucks. Their kids ran around the carnival with all-day passes while the parents visited. The twenty-five-dollar wristbands were popular. Kids grew dizzy riding again and again. They were in kid heaven until they reported back at the end of the night, googly-eyed and zonked.

There was no room for a Giant Wheel in Bay Point. When the

lights went down on the Super Shot tower ride, shouts rang out from one corner to the next, "Down!" Jointees and ride jockeys turned in their tickets. Because it was Sunday, the crew's next-day payroll was probably in the office trailer's safe box.

When the main-office trailer door opened for more money to come in, three gunmen burst in behind. They pointed guns point blank in Jesse's face. He handed over the money, and they ran out of the trailer. The men disappeared into the unlit neighborhood. Nobody pursued them.

Lee hobbled with his bum knee up and down the midway shouting the news.

"Three guys with nines (9mm semi-automatic handguns) just robbed Jesse. It just happened five minutes ago. Go slough your ride."

The office women locked the office trailer door. Carnies ran around to see if anything else was being robbed. People leaving their bunkhouses for the slough were told the breaking news. When I returned to my ride, the storm was whipping up. I spotted police in the front parking lot, responding to a report of a dented fender.

"Because it happened on private property, ma'am," the cop said, "there is little we can do."

Lee told me to stay out of it, so I did the opposite and re-entered the fray. I approached the sheriff's police.

"You guys know there was an armed robbery just five minutes ago, right?"

"No, where?"

I led the officers down the midway to the main-office trailer and knocked on the door.

"Who is it?" asked a woman inside.

"It's Mike. I'm with the cops."

Crying women in the office trailer opened the door enough for the police to squeeze in.

When Lee arrived, he shouted at me, "Get back to your ride."

Making my way back to the Lolly in the pouring rain, I wondered why the cops weren't called sooner. Then I realized Jesse did not call the cops. Carnivals don't call cops. If the police investigated, there were visas and outstanding warrants to consider. We couldn't afford to lose workers.

Back at the Lolly, I saw Harvey working alone in the rain. I told him about the robbery. On a whim, I kidded the con.

"Come to think of it," I said, "where were you during the robbery?"

"I was in my bunkhouse. I didn't even know about it until you told me."

"Did anyone see you in your bunkhouse? Nobody? Is that your alibi?"

Harvey hated the joke. He thought people might want to blame it on him, given his criminal history.

All around the lot, a trash bag army tore down the rides. The Mexicans wore yellow hard hats and black plastic trash bags for rain gear. They cut holes in the bags for their heads and arms.

I was rain-soaked through my jacket and pants down to my skin. The cold numbed my fingers. It was tough to hold a wrench, much less squeeze a pair of pliers.

Driving wind and rain in the dark made climbing a ladder tricky. We held onto our hats and yelled for hammers, pins, and R-keys.

Harvey bent over a bucket of tools. At that moment, my yellow hard hat blew off my head and flew twenty feet like a canary-colored cannonball, inches from Harvey's face.

Bemused, Harvey stood up with the rain beating against his face.

"Wow, your hat went that far?"

If my hard hat had hit him, it would have knocked him silly.

Harvey and I finished early in the evening. He was ecstatic. For him, the armed robbery didn't compare in excitement.

The morning after the robbery, every carny knew how it should have gone down.

"I would have gotten some men together," said one jointee, "and gone after those assholes."

"I would have pulled out my Glock," another jointee said, "and shot those bastards, one, two, three."

CARNIVAL IMPROV

DALY CITY

*W*e set up our trailers and RVs on the San Mateo Fairgrounds at the halfway point between the fabulous wealth of San Francisco and the ludicrous opulence of the Silicon Valley.

We lived a life stripped close to the bone. My bunkroom was recently deloused with a bug bomb. People were broke every few days. Donnikers and kitchens were outside. Drinking and shower water came from the same garden hoses. Too hot. Too cold. Bad food. Bad teeth. No doctors. No voice. No easy way out.

The Silicon Chasm is the divide between the young royals of a high-tech Versailles and peasants living in a Bruegel painting. If a new social order is being born, there'd be no more fertile place for a French-style revolution than along this peninsula. Yet class warfare wasn't brewing in the carnival quarters. Life was battle enough.

Carnies suffer envy, but like anyone else, they most envy their neighbors. The Silicon Valley lifestyle is a lucky lottery number away for them. Or they don't think of it at all. Mexican carnies seemed even more oblivious to the local inequities and talked in terms of US-Mexico comparisons.

Carnival workers in most states are exempt from the Fair Labor

Standards Act, which means common overtime and other rules don't apply. The "contracts" with workers assume forty hours of work. Yet we always worked more than sixty hours a week, not including travel time and the time needed to set up living quarters at each jump.

My $325 a week amounted to $8.13 an hour if we worked forty hours, but we always worked more. With my $50 a week for rent, my take-home pay was $275. If we were working sixty hours or more, that amounted to $4.58 cents an hour, which meant we had to work more than an hour to buy a Big Mac.

We were paid in cash, so it was up to us to take out our federal, state, Social Security, and Medicare taxes. Nobody filled out quarterly tax forms. Ride jockeys like me wouldn't have to worry because we wouldn't make enough to be taxed at the end of the year. Carnies can be more invisible to the IRS than they are to riders.

An American ride jockey's budget-breakers were cigarettes, beer, pot, coffee, snacks, fast food, cell-phone bills, rent, and "entertainment" costs. A pack of cigarettes could cost twelve dollars at the local gas station. Cell-phone charges were at the top of a carny's monthly bills. International calls were an extra burden for Mexican carnies.

Taxes, child support payments, and health insurance were monumental hurdles. Dropped phones, new sneakers, and cold medicines were budget busters.

My major expenses were childcare payments, a new phone, and cellular service. Finding a quarter on the sidewalk could make my day. My focus on my pay was not universal. I saw people quit before payday and not come back for whatever they were owed. Some blew a week's pay at a strip joint.

From the carnival owner's perspective, government labor restrictions are the biggest headache. The survival of traveling carnivals depends on the flow of H-2B visa workers, most of them Mexicans and South Africans.

On the San Francisco Peninsula, the hottest labor issue is H-1B visas, primarily for high-tech foreign workers. H-2B visas are for the working poor.

Studies show the H-1B visa holders take high-paid jobs Americans want. Many H-2B visas go to farm worker and carnival jobs, which are not prime employment targets for Americans. Mexicans do not take a significant number of American jobs, but they keep carnivals alive. The best carnival jobs, from jointees to managers, usually go to Americans.

The wealthiest zip codes in America include Atherton, Los Altos, Portola Valley, and Woodside. About seventy billionaires live in the San Francisco Bay Area. I daydreamed about a tech celebrity sighting. Facebook founder Mark Zuckerberg, Oracle founder Larry Ellison, and Google co-founders Larry Page and Sergey Brin had homes in the Bay Area.

They might want a whirl on my carousel. I'd read Brin loved swinging on trapezes. Anyone who loves the trapeze has an affinity for carnivals. His children were the right age for carousels. Imagine what those billionaire techies could do for carnivals.

In 2020, Atherton topped Bloomberg's Richest Places list, with an average household income in excess of $525,000 a year. Our proximity to the wealth belt was as real to us as Mars.

SMALL TEARS MESSED up her deep blue mascara as she sat with her morning cigarette and carnival coffee. It was a couple of mornings after the Bay Point robbery. The woman was about my age, sitting on a folding chair on the San Mateo lot.

"I'm sorry. I'm crying at nothing ever since it happened. I know it happened for a reason. Everything happens for a reason. I believe that."

Belief was a big deal for Tammy. "Believe" was tattooed boldly on her right ankle, along with a dragonfly signifying freedom. She wore a white tank top, with her cigarettes tucked into one bra strap and her cell phone tucked into the other.

Tammy lived out of her red Dodge Durango. She slept on a mattress in the back and showered in one of the trailers. Each night she took the night's cash from her portable ticket booth to the main office trailer. With ten thousand dollars or more in the bags, she walked shaking from the ticket booth to the trailer office.

On the previous Sunday, she delivered the money to the front office. She and another woman were still nearby when the gunmen leaped out of Jesse's trailer. One man pointed an automatic pistol within inches of her face.

"Don't move," he yelled.

Her eyes focused on the gun.

"One minute everything was fine," she said, "and the next, I really thought I would die."

She grabbed the other woman, and they both fell back into the grass. That was two days earlier, and she still couldn't talk about it without tears.

It was impossible to tell if the territory of her inner life was merely being examined or forever altered.

"I know I'm here for a reason," she said.

Her existential crisis unearthed regrets she wanted to tell me.

"I live for my grandchildren. I work all season so I can buy them anything they want when I get back. I was seventeen years old when I had my first child. I was just a kid myself."

Her ex-husband was abusive for years before she left him. She thinks "most families are dysfunctional" but says that's no excuse for her family.

"I was both mom and dad for my kids, so I did all the disciplining. As a grandparent, I know so much more. I wish I knew then what I know now. I live for one thing, those grandkids."

I was witnessing a quiet breakdown. Tammy should have sought crisis counseling. Yet this trained nurse, mother, and lifelong caregiver wouldn't seek help for herself.

As she collected herself, she mentioned she'd suffered three heart attacks the previous spring. She was shaken to her soul, a soul she had to believe was in God's hands.

"I know God has a purpose for me."

From across the fairgrounds, I later saw her alone in her outdoor fold-up chair, wiping away tears again. She looked abandoned. What tattooed belief. What dragonfly freedom.

～

SECRETS in the bunkhouses have short lives. Family, friends, coworkers, and rival carnies move in live webs of gossip. Every cell-phone call, every fight, every loud fart was audible through the thin trailer walls.

God help you if someone was having sex. Everyone noticed the rocking and could hear. A favorite prank was for a carny to bang on the door of a couple having sex, then run away laughing.

People saw you go to the shower. They ate with you, worked with you, and wasted time with you. Secrets were kept for a while, but eventually, everyone knew who was sleeping with whom.

As in most neighborhoods, people watched what their neighbors owned. Keeping up with the Joneses on the San Mateo lot meant the Joneses in the next bunkhouse, not the Atherton Joneses.

The castle in our kingdom was Jesse's new fifty-seven foot, custom-made Residential Suites trailer. Managers lived in RVs and campers hooked up to satellite TV dishes. Bunkhouse carnies watched videos on their mobile phones.

One of the game supervisors, Todd, personalized his bunkroom with his own carpentry, a refrigerator, a TV, a stereo, and a custom-made bed.

Bunkhouse rooms reflected their surroundings. One day, carnies working on the Gravitron pulled the foam from its stand-up boards. They brought back the foam to their bunkhouse rooms for bed cushions and floors.

We were pulling foam from the Gravitron one afternoon and stapling new foam on the stand-up boards when Rose Dog asked to work the staple gun. He'd never used one before.

As he tested it, it went off, "Snap-snap-snap-snap." He stapled his bald head. The staples pierced the skin but didn't stay in like stitches.

Blood dripped down his head and around his left ear. The Mexican crew laughed.

He angrily held out the gun and turned it around so it pointed at his eyes. A slip of his finger would have stapled his eyeballs.

"This fucking gun," he said.

I was standing next to him. He put the gun down before another, worse accident. Wiping the blood off his head, he turned and looked at me.

"Shut the fuck up," he said.

JOINTEES AND RIDE jockeys gathered in the shadow of my bunkhouse trailer for a day of dominos, smokes, and dancing juice. Vodka, Mickey's, Red Stripes, Coronas, Budweisers, and sodas sat on the asphalt.

Kools and Marlboro Reds lay on the playing boards. The playing table was two Coleman coolers with ride-leveling boards on top.

Sitting around in folding chairs was Huey, Sabrina, Rose Dog, and a jointee named Steve. More people joined later. Every point drew a reaction. Every domino was a statement.

"Bam," Steve yelled. "Bam again."

Steve rubbed it in when he won. Rose Dog accused people of being liars and cheats. Huey was losing, too, and it shook him. Worst of all, Sabrina was beating the men. They steamed as she raked in the money.

"She's lying or stupid," Huey said. "I'm a genius at this game. I always know what you got in your hand. But she's winning. She's lying or stupid."

Sabrina was an experienced jointee working rides that season, maybe to be closer to Huey. When the men tried to win their money back, Sabrina smiled triumphantly at the marks.

I heard the night deteriorated after I left to spend the night writing. Alcohol and arguments. The next morning was a cats-be-sad workday.

SAN MATEO WAS our jumping-off point for two spots, Daly City and Saint Timothy's Catholic Church, near the fairgrounds. The jointees were licking their chops going into Daly City with its Asian population. They viewed Asians as gamblers.

The first day of setup, we drove in a rickety carnival van along I-280 to Daly City, named after a farmer who donated land to the homeless after the 1906 San Francisco earthquake. I liked that the city was named after a rich man helping the homeless.

The carnival was set up at the closed and abandoned Sierra Bowl. We worked the leveling boards hard to balance the rides on the sloped and cracked parking lot. Tempers flared when people argued over stolen leveling boards.

Harvey loved Daly City for its dumpsters. He never passed a dumpster without diving inside filling bags with plastic bottles and cans. Apparently, the dumpsters near the carnival lot were undiscovered by local dumpster divers. Harvey started talking like one of the nouveau riche.

"I'm not too proud," he said once, while still inside a dumpster. "I remember where I came from. I'll buy us all beer with this."

I loved the setup in Daly City, as I did all setups. It must have been visible. Jesus saw me joking and working on rides. He worked with me on my first slough, dropping a heavy pin on my head.

"You are the only happy one around here," he said. "Everybody wants to work with you."

At breaks, I roamed the neighborhood with its Chinese restaurants, salons, barbershops, and appliance stores. Town & Country Billiards was in a triangular building with high windows and ceilings. Fourteen tables and no booze allowed.

Hanging on the wall were movie posters of *The Hustler* and *The Color of Money*. Both movies were favorites of the fast-talking wise guy jointees. The all-time favorite ride jockey movie was *Joe Dirt*, starring David Spade as a ride jockey who gets the girl and seeks his real parents. Freak show showmen often cited the 1932 classic *Freaks*.

The House of Catfish N' Ribs featured a logo of a catfish and a pink pig disco dancing. Wood chips fueled the stove. Pictures of singer Bessie Smith and heavyweight boxing champions Jack Johnson and Joe Louis hung on the walls. The place was known for barbecue sauce, fish, cornbread muffins, and pies.

During a break from running the carousel, I splurged on the lunch special. BBQ chicken, white bread in a plastic bag, homemade potato salad, and a soft drink for five dollars. The place was so authentic looking, I had to taste the food myself.

When the tall black cook sidled up to the counter, next to the worn Bible, I told him the carnies raved about his barbecue. He was stone-faced.

"You must know Huey," a woman shouted from the back of the kitchen. "He comes here every year. Tell him we say hi."

When you've been on the carnival road as long as Huey, places like The House of Catfish N' Ribs are your kitchen. On sunny days, Huey disappeared somewhere with his fishing rod. He knew every secret fishing hole along the circuit. Huey loved riding an old bicycle backward around the lot for fun.

In Huey's zoo of a van, the number of dogs increased in Oakland with a new litter of puppies. Sometimes I heard the van comically disturbing the quiet of the night. Huey and Sabrina engaged in a call-and-response routine with the dogs.

Callout – "Shut up! Shut up!" Crowd response – "Bark. Bark?" Call out – "Shut up! Shut up!" Crowd response – "Bark. Bark?"

Huey knew he wanted to be a carny the moment he first walked onto a carnival midway at eleven years old.

"I stood on the midway, and I just said, 'Wow.'"

When people ask why anyone works in carnivals, I tell his story because it is like so many others. Carnivals speak to kids, and kids talk back. Huey was an inner-city kid who grew up learning to run every ride in carnivals.

Everyone respected Huey. He stood silently next to Lee on the stage in front of the crew at every church call. Huey wasn't a manager, but his presence was symbolic. Huey was the real deal. He was a lifer.

Huey's informal status didn't mean he was paid more. His pay was an ongoing insult to his ego. After nearly three decades of work and all his expertise, he earned $375 a week. I was paid fifty dollars less a week. His van ate up the difference in parking, electricity, and water bills. He wasn't always happy about it, but he knew where he belonged.

I'd been working in the Bay Area for two months. It was time to commit to Butler or leave. I was communicating online with Old Carny Boy, the moniker of a veteran owner who loved my blog. He said he would guide me. He had contacts in L.A. carnivals. If I went to L.A., he'd line up a hole. I was skeptical because he only knew owners, and they didn't knowingly hire writers.

I'd committed to working at many carnivals, but I didn't know how to do it or where to go next. It wasn't a plan. It was improvisation.

NO COMING BACK THE SAME

SAN MATEO

I rode the inaugural ride of the Orient Express rollercoaster around the grade-school parking lot of Saint Timothy Catholic Church in San Mateo.

"Hee-haw," I roared at every turn. "Heee-haaaw."

In a mood for mayhem, I was the only test rider on Orient Express. It's a kiddy rollercoaster with a giant Chinese dragon head.

With my Butler hat held high above my head, I whooped like a cowboy village idiot. The Mexicans setting up rides stopped to watch and laugh. The good Lord only knows what our Catholic school overseers thought.

A homeless man stood by the fence, furious about a carnival operating on holy ground. He knew how to quote the Bible.

"Jesus went into the temple of God and cast out all them that sold and bought at the temple," he said. "My house shall be called the house of prayer, but ye have made it a den of thieves. A den of thieves."

In the Bible story, Jesus of Nazareth was outraged at goods being sold at a local temple, so he made a makeshift whip. The Prince of Peace began whipping people and overturning the tables. I hoped the homeless man wouldn't come back with a righteous whip. Besides, I was a ride jockey. Leave us alone. The jointees are the thieves.

Lee told me to help Huey and Sabrina set up the Ring of Fire. It's a rollercoaster that travels along a forty-five foot vertical loop, like an upright hula hoop. Held together by outriggers and steel cables, the Ring of Fire required Sabrina and me to be on the ground, pulling cables.

Sabrina wanted everyone to know she was as tough as any man. She owned a pit bull back home in Oklahoma, along with a large knife and gun collection. On setup, she wore dark sunglasses and jeans rolled up to her knees. Her ponytail hung below her shoulder blades. With her lit cigarette in the side of her mouth, she'd squint through the smoke as she talked.

She ran away from home at fifteen years old, a teenage desperado. Her freedom came at a price, though, and she rattled off the injuries and accidents along the way. One day, a group of carnies were cutting up jackpots, trying to top one another's injury stories.

Out came their stories about gunshot wounds, stabbings, accidents, and other bloody misfortunes. Sabrina was right there telling stories with the best of them. Most of the stories ended with the phrase, "Didn't hurt that much."

Huey and Sabrina were madly in lust, joking about it as if they were rich and we were poor. The two disappeared one mid-afternoon under the Ring of Fire's possum belly, under the ride and behind a tarp skirt.

One of the Mexicans saw them slip away. Soon a group of young men were whistling and jeering. Sex under the Ring of Fire? On a church lot? Huey and Sabrina laughed and yelled back that they were trying to nap. When Huey and Sabrina crawled out from underneath the possum belly, they smiled slyly and left the rest to our imaginations.

The Saint Timothy carnival was ethnic, musical, and delicious. Hula dancers swayed to traditional drums. Rock bands played with all their might. Dancing young people jammed the parking lot.

Church food joints dished out homemade foods from Hawaii, Mexico, Samoa, and the Philippines. On Filipino day, tents served adobe chicken, pancit noodles, arroz calde porridge, lumpia veggies, and cake tops.

That day, Huey ran the Eagle 16 Ferris wheel, a sixty-foot-tall wheel with three thousand lights. He gave free rides to people he liked. He felt like a favorite son returned.

"Samoans like me," he said. "I remember some of them from last year."

The Samoans reminded Sabrina of her rocky childhood. A Samoan girl from Hawaii lived in her group home as a teenager. She invited Sabrina to spend Christmas with her family.

"Always be kind to kids," she said, "They'll never forget. I never did."

The weather was perfect. Catholic school kids in their uniforms ran around with their friends. Parents tagged along with one eye on their children and another on the party.

THE SAINT TIMOTHY'S Catholic School principal was playing winky face with Rose Dog. That breaking news came from the source himself, Rose Dog. He let us all know on the van ride back to the bunkhouses.

Harvey knew it was a lie because the principal was flirting with him. Each thought the other was ready for a fully padded funhouse room. What followed was a profanity party free-for-all.

Harvey blamed drugs for making Rose Dog delusional. Rose Dog's eyes opened wide. He looked at Harvey like it was time to call 911. Only a madman would question his hold on the hot school principal.

The argument was so heated, I wondered what bombshell of the midway looked like. The woman I saw the next day was an innocent-looking Catholic school principal, oblivious to the sexual upheaval she was causing in her wake.

Rose Dog wasn't limiting himself to the principal. I saw him help a young mother and child onto a carousel horse. When the mother kissed her daughter, Rose Dog leaned in asking, "Where's my kiss?"

The husband was a few feet away behind the fence. He kept smiling, unaware of the carousel Casanova.

Carnival workers are in show business. I've seen attractive young women giddy to talk to a real carnival showman. Free rides, free plush, and free flirting were enough for young women to quit their sucker jobs for a new adventurous life. I'd never heard of a Catholic school principal running away to carnivals, but we'd take her.

ON MY FRIDAY BREAK, I told Lee I was leaving after Sunday's slough. L.A. had some open holes. He didn't seem to believe I was leaving for another carnival job.

"This job isn't for everybody," he said. "I wish you wouldn't leave."

When I told Harvey about leaving, I assumed he'd be happy. Somewhere along the line, Harvey had joined Rose Dog in telling people I was an undercover cop. He told the Mexicans I was an undercover immigration cop.

"You gotta be crazy to leave," Harvey said.

The entire carnival knew within minutes. Salvador's brother Rodolfo was among the well-wishers.

"You are a good man," Rodolfo said. "I know you will be successful at anything in life you want to do."

I took pictures of Rodolfo, Salvador, and other carnies from their hometown. I wrote down their names and phone numbers. I told Salvador I might visit him. He rolled his eyes and laughed me off.

Salvador was right to be skeptical. I didn't know if I would have the money to make it to Mexico. I put their contact information in my pocket, instantly losing it.

Huey suggested I should admit my mistake and ask Lee for my job back.

"It hurts me you're leaving," he said. "Stay. I want you to."

Tammy didn't like the news either.

"You're the only person I cried with after the robbery," she said. "Don't go."

Another ticket lady named Grandma pulled me aside to say I couldn't go because she liked me. Her ex-husband, like Tammy's, was an abusive drinker. Despite the odds, she'd raised two of her own children, four stepchildren, and four foster children. She was a great-grandmother seven times over.

Grandma wasn't the only foster or adoptive parent I met in carnivals, but she was typical in feeling she had a special mission. She was in carnivals because of the children.

"Kids are the soul of life," Grandma said, "before life and poor parenting corrupts them."

In that Catholic church parking lot, she turned the concept of original sin upside down. She believed children were born as pure "souls of life." Grandma thought if we did this carnival thing right, we'd add happiness to the lives of children.

"Happy children," she said, "will change the world."

The tech royals of Silicon Valley love talking about changing the world. So do people in carnivals.

As the weekend progressed, old carnies called me a fool for leaving. They pointed out that Butler worked every week and paid on time. I was surprised I hadn't thought of that earlier. How would it feel working for a less ethical carnival?

When Sunday church call came, Lee and Salvador stood at the front of the Oriental rollercoaster. Redwood City was our next jump, they said, and the people there love carnivals.

Lee looked down from the deck into the crowd and at me.

"You might have heard Mike is leaving us. He's headed to L.A., to another family. We're all going to miss him."

The crew went quiet. Then came a rolling blast of cheers.

"*Póg mo thóin*," Mexicans yelled, the Gaelic phrase for, "Kiss my ass." I taught them the line on Saint Patrick's Day. "*El Grande*," others yelled.

I bowed and doffed my hat to the crowd, knowing everything had changed. I was all wrong about the year. Objective reporting wouldn't cut it. I was part of this thing and so was my point of view. I'd have to examine how I was feeling and changing. I wasn't coming back from this one the same.

That night's slough was cold and long. I alerted the crew working with me that the Lyrid meteor shower might be visible just before dawn. At about 4 a.m., the few of us left were frustrated and yelling at each other.

Harvey talked to himself out loud as usual until he put down his hammer.

"I saw a meteor, Mike, like you said."

Without food or breaks all night, nobody was in a good mood. The Tornado was the last ride to be torn down. Lee paid the Mexicans, and they drove in the van back to the bunkhouses.

The American workers were left to finish the job. Huey couldn't take it anymore. Rose Dog tried to calm him down. At that point, only Huey, Rose Dog, Harvey, and I were left standing at the Tornado.

"You just don't get it, you dumb motherfuckers," Huey yelled. "The Americans are still working. A white guy and us. It isn't fair. It isn't fair. The Mexicans run this place. Not us."

At least two Mexicans filed pending lawsuits in U.S. courts alleging uncompensated marathon work hours. Butler managers were careful to keep Mexican hours down. The Mexican labor force was highly valued, and rightly so.

We all should have it better, not one group at the expense of the other. On the peninsula that personifies growing economic inequality, we fought over scraps.

Huey hitched a ride back to the carnival quarters. The rest of us finished as the grade school day began. We rode back in the van to the fairgrounds in a half-awake dream state.

We walked on to the lot as the white trailers lit up with the sunrise. I crawled up into my bunk and laid my head on a bundle of shirts I used for a pillow.

No jobs were waiting for me in Los Angeles or New York. I didn't know where I was going or what to expect when I arrived. I was hitchhiking across the county to carnivals unknown.

PART II
SAN FRANCISCO
TO NEW JERSEY

HITCHHIKING

COAST-TO-COAST NAKED

Somewhere along the line I knew there'd be girls, visions, everything;
somewhere along the line the pearl would be handed to me.

— JACK KEROUAC, ON THE ROAD

*A*n abandoned TV set sat on the Route 92 on-ramp at my hitchhiking spot. After hours of waiting, my imagination picked me up for a ride, and the TV lit up.

"Hi, this is Jack Kerouac. Am I blowing your mind right now?"

Kerouac's *On the Road* launched generations of young people in search of adventure, inspiration, and self-discovery on the road. His book was an anthem for beatniks, then for hippies, and eventually a younger version of me.

"Where are you?" I said.

"I think I'm in Viking heaven because I'm allowed to drink and get high all day, but there's no hangover. But now I have a new addiction. It's awful."

"What?"

"Game apps on my iPhone. I'm playing games and not talking to my friends. Did I mention I hang with Jack London, Harry Kemp, and Jim Tully?"

Those are some of the greatest American writers on carnivals, hitchhiking, hoboing, and adventure travel.

"It's great being dead," he said. "You should join us."

TV Kerouac had a real black sense of humor.

"What's it all about, Jack? Any insights from the other side?"

"The only truth," he said, "is music."

A car passed by, and TV Kerouac vanished.

Music distinguished me from other hitchhikers. I sing softly all day. If there are no cars in sight, I'll sing with all my might. That day it was Woody Guthrie.

As I went walking that ribbon of a highway
I saw above me that endless skyway
I saw below me that golden valley
This land was made for you and me

After a short ride to the Foster City on-ramp, I stood beside the road for another hour before the po-po visited me. The Forest City police officer who got out of the squad car was a big man, a weightlifter in his twenties. Ready for trouble, he walked up asking for my ID.

"Move slowly," he said.

I put my palms out and reached down into my fanny pack for my wallet.

"Do you have any weapons or anything sharp? Anything I should worry about?"

I was hitchhiking naked, which is hitchhiking without a weapon for self-protection. I assured him my fanny pack contained nothing bad inside.

"I know you have nothing in there," he said. "If I thought you had something in there, I'd have run you down."

I laughed. He didn't crack a smile. If he arrested me, the charge probably would be vagrancy. Returning to his squad car, he called in my Illinois license. He walked back toward me saying he stopped because he wanted to check out if I was a "wanted man" or "high."

"I am neither high nor wanted," I said. "In fact, I am feeling quite low and unwanted."

I told him I was headed to Los Angeles or New York. I wasn't sure which. Saying it out loud made me feel insane, again.

"You know," I said, "some people in the carnival thought I was a cop."

"Why? Because you have all your teeth?"

He suggested I take the scenic Route 101. He was sure I'd have a tougher time getting someone to take me across the San Mateo Bridge.

As he drove away, I knew I'd crossed a significant hurdle. California cops would not haul me off to jail for hitchhiking.

A carload of teens outside Hayward threw a full McDonald's Coke cup at my head. I was standing in the same spot for hours, smiling at each passing car. Suddenly a cup whizzed by my face. A direct hit might have knocked some sense into me and turned me around. Instead, I reached down and took a look at the cup. Ronald McDonald was holding an umbrella and dancing. It read, "Smile. Even when it rains."

I slept that night in a farmer's field. Twice the next day, state highway patrolmen along I-580 drove me to on-ramps. They didn't want me to cause an accident. They didn't want to waste time hauling me in, either. After miles of walking along the I-5 shoulder under a California sun, I felt like a walking mirage.

Then a white eighteen-wheel Freightliner swerved across lanes onto the shoulder. The driver opened the passenger door and shouted at me to hurry because a cop was coming up from behind. I ran fifty yards with a full backpack up to the truck. I threw my oversized bags up into the cab, grabbed the door handle and swung up into the high cab.

Juan called himself the Crazy Mexican and said he was hauling toilet seats from the Canadian border. He was sleep-deprived, and I guessed a bit buzzed. We drove six hours and 350 miles from the junction of I-580 and I-5 to suburban Los Angeles.

He was in his early forties and wore a dirty t-shirt and jeans. His black hair was thinning, and his belly hung over his belt. Born in the Mexican border town of Tecate, he came to the United States when he was ten years old. He'd been driving his whole adult life. The North American Free Trade Agreement, NAFTA, made it tough, with too many cutthroat load bids from Mexico.

Crazy Mexican told me about his prison stints for drug possession. He also went in for grievous bodily harm to a fellow driver in a bar fight. He mentioned an outstanding warrant in North Dakota.

Driving up on a weigh station, he pulled over, and I watched him forge his log sheets. When we went through the weigh station, I kept looking forward as he talked to the officer at the window. If asked any questions by the officer, I was to say I was a trainee.

His stories veered from the violent to the disturbing. One time, he said he picked up a hippy couple hitchhiking and bought them food along the way.

"I asked the guy, 'Can I fuck your wife?' I mean, I gave you a ride, and I bought you food. How about some payback?"

"Hell no," the boyfriend said.

So, Crazy Mexican stopped the truck and left them off in the middle of nowhere.

Bruce Springsteen, the Bee Gees, and Prince played as we hauled ass. From the western edge of the Central Valley, we saw the San Joaquin Valley, Tehachapi Mountains, Tejon Pass, Pyramid Lake, Santa Clarita Valley, Santa Susana Mountains, Newell Pass, and the San Fernando Valley.

I saw more nuts, fruits, and vegetables than I could name. The Central Valley produces half of the nation's fruits and vegetables, ninety percent of seventeen crops. The valley was gorgeous to someone who only saw green fields. My perspective changed when I thought of climate change in the valley. Then the valley looked as beautiful and vulnerable as a carnival before a hurricane.

The Interstate Highway System gets criticism for not being as colorful as the old Route 66 or so-called Blue Highways. Interstate 5 proves interstates don't reroute travelers away from real America. Interstates are America.

Crazy Mexican dropped me off late that night near a Catholic church in Corona, in suburban Los Angeles near I-15. He suggested I sleep next to a Catholic church in a bush. It was too cold outside to sleep in a bush, unless it was a burning bush.

That night I typed notes at an all-night Denny's, eating the all-you-can-eat pancake special. Old Carny Boy, my online connection to L.A. jobs, was not responding to emails. Should I stay in L.A. and find my own carnival holes? After giving it a thought, I decided I wanted to head east anyway. I took out my roadmap and plotted a route toward the Atlantic Ocean.

I planned to stay on I-40 across Arizona, New Mexico, Texas, Oklahoma, Arkansas, and Tennessee before heading north on I-81. When I reached the coast, I'd look for work in the New York area. Sitting in the L.A. Denny's with an empty syrupy plate, I felt a bit unhinged and wildly free.

IDA HIT the brakes when she saw me hitching in the Chihuahuan Desert outside Albuquerque. Her pickup truck swerved across lanes to pick me up. She had a humanitarian policy about hitchhikers along desert roads.

"If they're hitchhiking in the middle of nowhere," she said, "they need help."

In her seventies, Ida was thin, white-haired, desert tan, and full of her own strong opinions. She was returning home after cleaning houses. Social Security wasn't enough for retirement. She dropped me off in Moriarty near the TA Truck Stop. In the field behind the building was a single tree and a cardboard mat, an indicator that other travelers camped there before. I pitched my tent in high grass for the night.

In Moriarty, I-40 intersected with the most famous of all-American roads, Route 66. The Los Angeles-Chicago route was once called "America's Main Street" and "The Mother Road." It was also the main street in Moriarty. Shops along the road didn't let you forget it either, with lots of red, white, and blue Route 66 road signs.

The next day, I met a hitchhiking Marine in front of the TA Truck Stop. He called himself the Lone Wolf. He wore a Vietnam Veteran hat and held a sign saying, "Old Homeless Veteran." The sun and cigarettes aged the sixty-two-year-old. His grey beard hung down from his chin like an old mop. Lone Wolf's apparel was vintage needy.

In private, he was a proud Marine. Whenever he needed cigarettes, food or beer, all Lone Wolf needed to do was fly the sign. His veteran sign worked like magic. He wanted for nothing.

That Saturday night, he panhandled forty dollars and paid thirty dollars for a hotel room. On Sunday, he raked in seventy dollars in two hours. After buying cigarettes, beer, food, and the room, he was broke by morning.

Lone Wolf made it clear this was his dream life. He wasn't saving for a better future or worried about being broke tomorrow. His today was eternal.

"It's the freedom," he said. "Feeling free and no landlords breathing down your neck and turning off the heat or the lights. I've had that."

A native of Lincoln, Nebraska, he'd married three times and had three children. He was not sure where they were. He had one grandchild and "may have another by now." Why did he leave his homes and families? Evading the question, he said, "I'm sure it was something."

Hotel rooms were okay in extreme weather, but he loved sleeping outdoors and waking up to the sunrise.

"Mornings are my favorite part. You see the sun come up. The air is cleaner. You get in touch with nature."

A drifter for most of the previous thirty years, Lone Wolf didn't care where he was going. He went where the driver was going. His best ride was from Tipton, Georgia to Albert Lea, Minnesota. He climbed into the eighteen-wheeler with no idea where he was going and no idea what to do when he arrived. The driver bought food and clothes for him. When they reached Albert Lea, the driver reached into his pocket and gave him $140 in cash. Lone Wolf stepped down from the ride, looked around, and hitchhiked back southwest.

He said happiness is a state of mind.

"You can change your mind. I'm happy. Of course, there are good days and bad days. But it's all what you make it."

The last I saw of Lone Wolf, he was carrying a six-pack of Budweiser and looking for a quiet spot to drink. I told him about the cardboard patch behind the TA Truck Stop. Off the drifter went to drink alone, sitting under a single tree in the middle of the field.

Off I walked, riffing on the Irish song, *The Beggarman*.

> *I got the sky,*
> *I've got the road,*
> *Don't ask why,*
> *the world is my home.*

STANDING inside a pressure system kicking up tumbleweeds and dust devils, I'd have been miserable if I weren't so in awe of the action. Twisty, sandy funnels skipped and played across the desert.

So many tumbleweeds blew into the nearby Motel 6 parking lot that they blocked the front door. It was my third day on that same Moriarty on-ramp, and I was feeling like my luck was changing.

In a cloud of desert gravel, Navajo Mike appeared in a dusty, 2001 Silverado. He was fresh from the annual Gathering of the Nations, the largest Native American powwow in the country. More than 1,500 Native Americans gathered for the weekend at the University of New Mexico. Navajo Mike was on the long road home to Amarillo. It's a four-hour drive into the Texas Panhandle.

"We're going to get to know each other," I said.

Navajo Mike was born in a small town in the Navajo Nation, which straddles Arizona, New Mexico, and Utah. It's the biggest Native American semi-autonomous region in the country.

A power company employed him, and he worked on substations

and power lines in small West Texas towns. His beard was light. He was strong, but no weightlifter. Soft-spoken, he talked about heart-breaks and mistakes.

The lack of sleep on previous nights was getting to me. In my half-asleep state, I noticed five dust devils around us. Four satellites surrounded a single strong dust-devil tower. In the hands of someone more supernaturally minded, the dust devils would have appeared to be visiting someone they knew.

Mike began telling me a birth-omen story about himself. I remembered the birth-omen stories. Genghis Khan was born with a blood clot clenched in his fist. An ancient temple burned to the ground the night Alexander the Great was born. Jesus was born under a star.

"This is the story my grandma and my mom told me," he said. "When I was one year old, a dust devil picked me up and pulled me over their heads and carried me off. They tried running after me, trying to grab me. After six hundred feet, the dust devil dropped me down into their arms."

He looked over from the steering wheel at me.

"It's a true story and a good story."

He was the child of the dust devil air. There is a Navajo proverb, "Sit still, the earth will talk to you." He wondered what the earth was telling him.

I later found the obscure Navajo myth online. The story was no myth to Navajo Mike. He felt he should live up to the dust-devil promise of great deeds ahead.

WHEN I WOKE, my bag with all my clothes was gone. It was stolen. I'd taken a short nap in an Amarillo roadside park. My laptop was safe next to me but I left my bag several feet from where I slept.

The local Target didn't carry backpacks, so I bought a red luggage bag on rollers. From that point on, I hitchhiked with a new, bright red suitcase. It made me look like I was waiting for an airplane beside the interstate.

That night I found another outside spot to put down my sleeping bag. When the rain started, I tucked my head inside the sleeping bag and didn't move for a while. Then it occurred to me that the rain was rhythmic. It wasn't raining. Sprinklers were spitting rapid-fire water at me.

I struggled out of the sleeping bag as if under fire in combat. Water jets bounced off me. I picked up my sleeping bag and dropped it. I picked up my new luggage and dropped it. By the time I was out of range, I looked like I swam to Amarillo.

Changing into dry clothes in the bushes, I wasn't sleepy anymore so I walked around that night in wet shoes. A woman saw me at about 2 a.m. at a gas station and waved me down to give me three dollars. She looked so broke, I felt like giving it back.

I stood in the Texas sun for three days, running out of songs to sing to myself. At twilight, I began eyeing a bank of trees to sleep under when out of a distant vantage point, a dusty white 1998 Mercedes-Benz Sprinter ambled closer at a gas-saving pace.

When the Sprinter stopped for me, I stepped aboard a rolling felony driven by nomadic, drug-dealing, idealistic grifters through the Texas-Oklahoma night.

A ROUND-FRAMED Sancho hopped out of the passenger door wearing black jeans, a black shirt, and a black porkpie hat. The driver, Don, waved me in to sit next to him and his dog, Buddha.

They were driving 700 miles to Memphis. In the back of the van was a mattress along with shelves of rock-polishing equipment.

On the dashboard lay heaps of pot, tobacco, and a couple of books from *The Indian in the Cupboard* series about a little boy who puts a toy Indian in the cupboard, and it comes to life as an eighteenth-century Iroquois Indian.

Don was all beard and bones. He appeared to be living on cigarettes, pot, alcohol, hallucinogens, and Argentine mate. His hairstyle was a dreadlock free-for-all that suggested his chaotic worldview. With a marionette frame, Don reminded me of Don Quixote.

His Sancho was shorter and stockier. He loved to scratch his belly, which his shirt only partially covered. He was the sidekick but no comic foil.

In Don's mind, they were sallying forward into a more enlightened world fueled by bumming, theft, and chemical-induced fantasies of world peace.

Buddha was Don's two-year-old rescued mastiff/golden retriever. He sat between my legs all night. Buddha's position gave me cramps and caused me to shift in my seat during knee-slapping philosophical discussions.

Smoking a pot pipe shaped like a deer antler, Sancho told me that he once ran a carousel for a Texas carnival. The carnies gave him pot laced with crack because they suspected he was a cop. The crack made him go crazy.

"Don't take no dope from no carnies," he said.

With that advice, his eyes rolled back into his head, and he passed out backward onto the van mattress. His porkpie hat stayed on his head as if nailed there.

Don told me how he broke up with the love of his life that very morning. His object of worship, his Dulcinea, was a whiskey-guzzling bitch.

"You know what the difference between a bitch and a whore is? A whore is a woman who'll sleep with anybody. A bitch is someone who sleeps with anybody but you."

She'd headed west with his best friend, so Don headed east toward his family home in New Jersey. Don was a polisher and seller of semi-precious stones. He'd stolen the stone polisher in the back of the van. They'd been in Amarillo at the same time as me. I knew in my guts, they stole my clothes. What a prize, too. The clothes stank of carnival sweat.

Don drank Mickey's malt liquor and smoked from the deer antler as he told stories of spending years in prison for "stupidly" flooding his small New Jersey hometown with acid tablets. He alluded to other "stupid" arrests, including bongo drumming while high as a satellite in a Boulder mall.

An amateur pharmacist of illegal drugs, Don could list a long line of ingredients in each hallucinogen. He referred to serotonin levels in the brain and studies that backed him up on the benefits of psychedelics.

The Grateful Dead and Wu-Tang Clan played from 8 p.m. in Amarillo to 5 a.m. on the Arkansas-Tennessee border. Don only stopped talking to sing along and point out great lyrics.

Don and Sancho traveled to festivals selling and bartering pot, acid, and stones. On the road, they lived by bumming money at gas stations. Sancho was cocky about his skills. At one gas station, he bummed twenty dollars off a cop. He bummed from a guy at the next bathroom urinal.

At one gas station, I angered Sancho when I bought a one-dollar bag of chocolate-chip cookies.

"Stay away from me while I do my thing."

Yet another bumming rule I learned on the road. It's not good to eat cookies while bumming.

Within minutes of his blunt advice, he began puking beside the van in a loud "awwing" sound. He sounded like an actor overacting. Puke shot out his nose.

Sancho nonchalantly wiped the vomit away with his forearm. He then complained about "shittin' like a Mexikin" in the bathroom. Sancho wiped his mouth and spat so close to me that I jumped out of the way.

Don looked at me and suggested it must have been the water in one of the hotels that made Sancho so sick. As if it couldn't have been the boatloads of booze.

Don drove for a while until we heard pounding on the vehicle from the back. I turned around, and Sancho's chipmunk cheeks were filled with vomit.

Round two. Don swerved to the shoulder of the road. Sancho jumped out for a series of unreal, gut-twisting firehose vomits. Again, his spew almost hit me.

He noticed I was still holding a bag of cookies from the gas station. "What? Do you live on cookies or something? Goddamn."

Right on, puking man. Too many cookies are unhealthy.

After Sancho passed out again in the back of the van, Don and I spent the wee hours of the morning talking. Senora and Flagstaff, he said, are great towns for hitchhikers. "Hippy Hill" outside Murfreesboro, Tennessee, is great for hanging out and playing pool in a teepee built in a tree.

Don gave me tips on how to volunteer before festivals. Once you're an official volunteer, you can ignore your assignments and sell rocks and drugs inside the festival.

By the time we made it to a McDonald's in Van Buren, Arkansas, I was sick of Grateful Dead songs. In a thoughtless comment, due to a lack of sleep, I mentioned I was older than band member Jerry Garcia when he died. Buzzkill for Don.

I stepped out of the van and rubbed the Buddha-cramps out of my legs. Don and Sancho went back to sleep. It was 5 a.m.

The long night of pot, puking, and drug-fueled talk faded away like a puff of smoke from a low-burning deer antler.

BEAR, Ru, and their dog were sitting at a picnic bench in the nearby park in Van Buren. The young couple spent the previous night in a hotel, so they were clean and ready for whatever the day might bring.

Bear was forty-one years old with a big grizzly beard. Ru was in her twenties, with a folk dress and a bright outlook, at least that morning.

When they woke, Don and Buddha walked over from the van. They started talking about their mutual interest in polished stones and festivals. Sancho tried to bum pot off the couple, but it's tough bumming from other people who live off bumming.

Bear and Ru were hitchhiking across the country. They'd made $170 the day before by sitting in the Walmart parking lot flying their cardboard sign. They'd bought new clothes, a portable stove, and checked into a hotel. They'd spent their Walmart money. All they had left in the world was eight dollars.

It didn't seem worth it to save for a better life. The way they saw it, they were living a better life. Enough money always seemed to come along. It was a magical, sweet life.

Bear was a veteran of twenty years on the road. An endless cycle of bumming money, selling rocks, and smoking pot kept him forever young. Bear felt he was getting away with too much fun. He had a way of talking that suggested, "Can you believe I'm getting away with this?"

They knew hobo lingo and definitions of a bum.

A hobo travels to work,
A tramp travels but doesn't work,
A bum neither travels nor works.

Ru chided Bear for being a home bum, sticking to a place too long. She took it back quickly for fear of offending. Ru was in a giggly mood. She told me she was the "only traveler" from Punxsutawney, Pennsylvania.

She gave me a cell phone number of a friend to call if I ever got stranded there. It seemed absurd. I wasn't headed anywhere near her hometown. But it made perfect sense in her drifter world.

Part of the adventure is waking up broke and not knowing where you'll be that night. Starting out for one place and ending up in another is a minute-to-minute option.

Bear said he knew a hidden creek to hunt for stones, meet traveling kids, and score more weed. Ouachita National Forest was down Route 71. Don and Sancho were headed to the Memphis Music Festival, but plans change. I was out, and Bear and Ru were in.

They were on a caravan ride to an underground meeting spot. They left me behind because I wasn't like them. Real drifters drift.

As I walked to I-40, I could see Don and Sancho out there one step in front of the law, grifter drifters on the road of excess. Even if disaster awaits them, I won't judge their journeys by their ending.

I'll think of them the way they were that morning, young and dizzy with excitement about an improvised turn toward a crystal-clear mountain creek filled with unpolished jewels and a new high. I'll try not to think of them wearing my stolen clothes while they do it.

MY FIRST RIDE OUT of Van Buren was with an Arkansas preacher. He appeared healthy compared to the people I'd been hanging out with the previous few days.

Once again, sleep deprivation was to blame for my ridiculous lack of judgment when I told a Southern preacher a religious carny joke.

"A carny and the pope die at the same time. They meet Saint Peter at the pearly gates.

'I see you both have been good men,' Saint Peter says. 'Come right in.'

Peter shows the carny his mansion with a Ferris wheel in the front yard. Bottles of beer grow from every tree.

'Thanks Pete,' the carny says.

Saint Peter brings the pope to a tiny room with a cot and an over-flowing donniker.

'Saint Peter, you've got us mixed up,' the pope says. 'He's the carny. I'm the pope.'

'Oh, I didn't get you guys mixed up,' Saint Peter says. 'We get lots of popes up here, but we get darn few carnies.'"

I even put in the "darn" where a "damn" should be. But the preacher didn't buy it.

"I think that's a Catholic joke," he said.

Of course, because popes don't go to heaven. The joke stopped being funny to an Arkansas preacher the second I mentioned the pope. There aren't a lot of popes in heaven. The carny joke was preposterous.

He asked me about hitchhiking. I told him about weather and hitchhiking. When it's good weather, it brings out the good Samaritan in people. When it rains, you're on your own.

It's like life. When you're doing well, everybody is your friend. When you're down, people find reasons that it's your own fault. As if God's displeased. But people need each other more when it rains.

"You're going to steal my story for Sunday, aren't you?" I said.

"I like it," he said, smiling.

Bear and Ru warned me about Memphis. Do not get dropped off downtown. There's no place to sleep. Memphis is unforgiving.

When I reached a hitchhiking spot just outside of Memphis, I told the next driver, "I don't want to be left downtown."

MALCOLM DROVE straight to downtown Memphis.

"Trust me," he said.

He drove his beat-up economy car on an insider's tour of Beale Street, the nightlife strip in Memphis sometimes called "The Home of the Blues."

Malcolm was once an up-and-coming drummer before the drugs and alcohol bit him back. He'd spent many a wild night along Beale Street. He showed me who played which joint. Louis Armstrong, Albert King, B.B. King, and Muddy Waters rang out along the strip of his memories. They were the greats. The Beale Street he knew was a wonder of the world and his personal ruin.

Malcolm took job-training classes and volunteered with the Memphis Union Mission. When he brought me to the mission, a line of men waited outside to secure a place to sleep for the night. "He's with me," he told security, skipping to the front of the line.

Before going on his way, Malcolm said the mission band was chock-full of all-star ex-Beale Street cats.

The big guy at the front desk, Mike, was a guitar player in the mission's band. Waiting for my paperwork, I asked him about his story. He described himself as a disgraced Seventh Day Adventist preacher. He also was a sex offender who did six years in a prison psych ward.

Ushered over to the Great Chapel, I looked around at the crowd of predominantly African American men. I talked to several men who worked in past carnivals. None of them was eager to leave Memphis again for a traveling carnival paycheck. They didn't like the pay and living conditions. They weren't worried about Mexicans taking their carnival jobs. They could have them.

A film played on a big screen TV but ended mid-movie when the lights went out at 9 p.m. More than a hundred of us lay head-to-toe and side-by-side on floor mats. Sometime during the night, I wondered what these men were dreaming.

I wanted to hear the Rev. Al Green singing gospel. I wanted to hear Memphis blues songs about men falling apart. Any sign. Any comfort. I visited nobody's dreams. I already knew that nobody was dreaming about summer Ferris wheels, easy marks, and state fairs.

The wake-up call was at 5:30 a.m. Volunteers served a breakfast of cereal and bagels at 6 a.m. The main requirement for lunch and dinner was attendance at sermons. The sermons were not about the people I was following. I bolted because I was the only one who'd spent the night dreaming of the next great American traveling carnival.

TAKING out a long screwdriver from his vest pocket, the young man used his lips and tongue to wet the shaft. He leaned his head back and twisted the screwdriver down his nostril into his skull. He pulled the screwdriver out of his nose, then shrugged and smiled like the sweet-faced boy he was born.

"My name is Mess, Kid Gypsy," he said. "I'm a traveling show. An original freak act."

Petting his shepherd-collie mix named Bo, Mess might have performed his whole routine if given the time.

"I hammer six-inch nails up my nose. I put screwdrivers up my nose...scissors. I swing bar stools from my plugs. I hang weighted objects from my plugs. I hang weighted objects from my septum ring.

I walk on glass, jump on glass, allow people to walk on my face, and back on glass. I swallow fire, and that's about it, I think."

We met along I-81 in the Shenandoah Valley between the Allegheny and Blue Ridge mountains. He was a thin, tattooed man sitting in the grass with his dog, guitar, backpack, and a cardboard sign saying "Charlottesville."

His hair was cut in a Mohawk style. Rings pierced his earlobes, nose, lips, and chin. Tattoos adorned his chin and nose. His skin was a tattoo shop creation. Some of his tattoos may have come at a discount because his parents owned a tattoo shop. Yet his face was still a work in progress.

"Omi is a great inspiration to me," he said.

The Great Omi was a famous painted man and freak-show performer who died in 1969.

"I want to be totally covered head-to-toe in tattoos," he said. "I want horns."

At twenty-five-years-old, he'd already been drifting for years. He claimed his home was "nowhere." When he reached "a cool town," he went into local bars offering his freak show. Bars could barter with beer or pay fifty to one hundred dollars for his act.

At sixteen, he took the summers off to travel. By eighteen, he was out on the road full time. He drove a soup kitchen bus for a while following Rainbow Festivals before meeting up with the freak show Mr. Blank's Weird and Wandering Sideshow and Carnivale of Black Hearts.

"Before I knew it, I had ten tricks," he said. "I could snort floss, condoms, and jewelry up my nose and out my mouth."

He grew up in Staunton and was hitchhiking to Charlottesville, where the previous year he took part in the Occupy movement. He was arrested for public disobedience while in support of affordable housing for the working poor.

As I walked back to my own hitchhiking spot, I looked back at Mess playing with Bo beside the highway. Vehicles filled with normies drove by as he sat at the corner of freak and normal.

With 7.5 billion people living on Earth and so many doppelgangers, he nakedly sought to be the only one of his kind. A bright, painted trickster and his hobo dog rolling nowhere.

I later looked up his website and saw how he poured himself out for all to see. If you're the only one in the world, are you all alone?

"I realize that I can't depend on people," he wrote, "to make my life interesting or not lonely."

MATTHEW WAS RETURNING from chasing Tiger Swallowtails around the Great Dismal Swamp. A budding lepidopterist, he studied climate change on the genetics of butterflies. He assured me lepidopterists are serious scientists who only sometimes look silly.

"We run around fields swinging nets in the air," he said.

A Ph.D. candidate at Princeton, Matthew picked me up in Delaware on his way back from the swamp on the North Carolina-Virginia border.

One of my favorite authors, I told him, was Vladimir Nabokov. The author of *Lolita* also was a world-class lepidopterist. As a lark, I asked him how lepidopterists party. He assured me they were intellectuals who loved the outdoors. They spent most of their time analyzing computer models.

"If I committed a murder," I said, "how would I fool the cops by passing myself off as a lepidopterist?"

"The ovum, not the sperm," he said, "determines the sex of the butterfly. Also, a group of butterflies is a kaleidoscope."

"Thanks, I'll need that cover story for my murder," I said. "I'll tell everyone you were so helpful."

I was messing with the butterfly boy genius, but he got to me when he talked about global warming's effects on butterflies. We're so interconnected. Separateness is just another illusion.

About forty drivers picked me up on my Pacific-to-Atlantic, 3,200-mile trip across America. Drivers included truckers, factory workers, real estate agents, a plumber, an inventor, two Army combat medics, a former Army intelligence officer, a fruit tree nursery owner, a

Mayflower mover, a longshoreman, an international environmentalist, a hang glider, a pizza delivery man, a Scottish Highland Games wrestling coach, a Protestant pastor, a retired oilman, three state troopers, a meth cook, a Chinese cook, a retired cleaning lady, an ex-Beale Street musician, a Navajo lineman, traveling drug dealers/grifters, and one wild and crazy lepidopterist.

People were at turning points in their lives. Even those with good jobs wanted to change their lives. They were people helping another soul in need. They shared stories even their best friends didn't know. In the right truck, in the right car, hitchhiking is arguably the greatest show on earth.

PART III
NEW JERSEY & NEW YORK

APRIL, MAY

KING OF THE MISFITS

PASSAIC & NEW MILFORD, NEW JERSEY

I have spent my life judging the distance between American reality and the American dream.

— NEW JERSEY-BORN BRUCE SPRINGSTEEN

A big black dog growled as I walked into the McDaniel Brothers warehouse on 10th Street along the Passaic River. "Watch out," Jason said, "that dog bites."

The rides, equipment, and tools in the warehouse seemed old and out of order to the untrained eye. The Passaic office was a cluttered, alive museum. Freddie and Richie McDaniel sat at their desks a few feet from each other, two huge men leaning back in their swivel chairs.

Freddie McDaniel questioned me a bit about drugs and whether I could drive a truck. He wanted to know which carnivals I worked.

Freddie and Richie were tall, forty-ish, with thick Jersey accents. They both smoked, and their bellies suggested strong appetites for both food and drink. I liked them. The job paid $250 a week. Freddie welcomed me aboard and told me to load my packs into a van with Jason, a veteran in their unit.

I found the McDaniel brothers after a carnival internet search of the New York-New Jersey area. I began calling all twenty-three carnivals I found online. Roseanna was the owner of Ace Amusements. Her carnival was full, so she suggested her husband Freddie might have an open hole.

Jason brought me across the street to a beat-up van, and we drove to the New Milford-Teaneck Elks Annual Carnival on the Elks lodge grounds. The McDaniel brothers had already set up eleven rides in a tight parking lot.

The Elks ran their own games and the grills. Traveling carnivals have partnered from the start with business and social clubs like the Elks, Kiwanis, and Moose lodges.

On the first night, I ran a kiddy ride called the Apples. Cars shaped like happy ladybugs revolved around a large center apple, with another ladybug tunneling out. It was the perfect ride for younger children and my newest routine.

Strapping the kids into their ride, I whispered the secret word "applesauce."

"What's the secret word, kids?" I yelled.

"Applesauce," they yelled.

"What's the secret word?"

"Applesauce," they yelled louder.

"I can't hear you."

"Applesaaauce!"

Before they fully blurted out the magic word for the third time, I turned on the ride. The kids squealed as they lurched forward.

Few people showed up the first two rainy, cold nights. The brothers fumed.

The New Jersey customers didn't look my California customers. Grade school kids wore their hats backward, like little rappers or working-class heroes. The carnies were different, too. The differences were the reason I wanted to work around the country.

Young Puerto Rican women ran several games. When business was slow, someone turned up Bon Jovi music. The Puerto Rican women jumped on top of the game counters and danced. Ride jockeys and food vendors danced along with them. It was a New Jersey music video. Everybody screamed the song lyrics across the carnival – "Wanted, dead or alive."

THAT PEACEFUL MAY MORNING, Dana sat on a trailer bed wearing shorts and a blouse off her shoulders. Her head was bowed, and her hair hung over her face like a black storm. When she raised her head to greet me, the hair fell away from her face.

"Hi, Mike," she said.

Her left eye was swollen shut. Her right eye was so black and blue she could have been wearing a Halloween mask. Her nose ring was ripped out. Her nineteen-year-old prettiness was pulverized.

The Dana I knew was a lively white teen with jet-black hair and deep blue eyes. Lou was her black boyfriend, a great carny and the chief suspect to our carnival of Sherlocks. Richie, Freddie, and the rest of the crew huddled a few feet away, wondering what to do next.

When Richie saw her, he said, "I wanted to throw up."

The brothers prided themselves on being in carnivals thirty years, but this was a new one for them. Women in the crew urged them to fire Lou. The two Jamaican brothers in my bunkhouse heard Lou and Dana yelling at each other the night before.

"I like Lou too," one of the crew said, "but if he did this, I don't see how you can ignore this."

Dana said she was "jumped" at a local bar. Lou was innocent.

"Who sees his girlfriend beaten up like that and doesn't go out after the guys?" said another crew member.

A dozen solutions were floated. The McDaniel brothers were reluctant to bring Dana to the hospital, where there would be questions. I wanted someone to pay for what was done to this young woman. I suggested they report the incident to the police station next to the carnival lot.

All at once, the group blurted out, "Ooooohh!"

"We're in a carnival. We never call the cops," one of the crew said.

Angry and incredulous, some of them didn't know what to do with their hands. They shook their heads and paced back and forth, staring directly at me. Their deep, primal disgust somehow shifted to me. Had I learned nothing since the armed robbery in Bay Point? Carnivals don't call cops.

Dana went to the hospital anyway. I talked in private with Lou, who denied everything. He gave me an alternate scenario. He didn't have a scratch on his face or hands. He hinted at drug or alcohol abuse the previous evening.

"Dana was so far gone," he said, "she didn't know who did it."

Dana never spoke to the police. Nobody on the crew talked about it again, and Lou stayed. Dana wasn't allowed on the midway until she healed. She nursed her wounds and kept her mouth shut. I'm sure the Elks were clueless about the woman hiding behind the clubhouse. Dana became another carnival secret.

The crowds stayed away again as it rained another straight night. The McDaniel brothers paced back and forth. At closing time, Richie and Freddie called us over for a meeting.

"Come closer, youz, so I don't have to yell," Freddie yelled.

We were about to get the first of many speeches from the management. Freddie stepped forward to speak his mind.

"In this business, you have three strikes against you," Freddie said. "You're in a carnival. You're black. And you're Puerto Rican. And I'm not even prejudiced. I hate all of you. But you know as well as I do, if someone gets robbed three miles from here, who do they come looking for? Us."

Freddie and Richie stood shoulder to shoulder. Richie drank a beer and smoked a cigarette. He stepped in front of Freddie when it was his turn to hurl a warning at us.

"Clean up. If I smell you, the customer can smell you. No punching each other either. No matter how much they deserve it. Even if they don't deserve it. Don't punch nobody. You're not that big of a badass."

The rain and cold kept customers away, but someone had to take the blame.

"I'm going to start docking you twenty dollars for talking on the cell phone or talking to this guy or that girl, or this guy talking to that guy, or this girl talking to that girl. And some of these food joints are filthy. I hate to see how you live at home."

Nobody likes getting a dressing down for a job that underpays. Yet some of Freddie's speeches reflected common owner concerns.

"Look around you. Ninety percent of you will be here tomorrow. Then, look around in a week and they'll be gone. Then at the end of the season, ninety percent won't be here. Some of you we trust, and some of you are drifters."

I believe he meant me when he mentioned drifters.

Freddie appealed for everyone to pull together.

"People say someone is getting rich off this stuff. Don't worry about us. You do your work. We work all week fixing rides and painting, and then we have these short hours to make our money. Wednesday night. Thursday night. Friday and Saturday nights."

One morning I asked Jimmy Tattoos what he thought of the speeches. His tattoos ranged from NY Yankee tattoos to "Death without Dishonor," "Concrete Jungle," and "Goon." On his chest was a map of New Jersey.

"They act like they aren't making money. I've worked for carnivals. I've seen them make money every time. They act like we're taking advantage of them. They are taking advantage of us. Nobody can live on $275 a week. Nobody. I just bought a TV and a DVD set. That was two weeks' pay."

In another speech the next night, Freddie talked about our abuse of the welfare system.

"We all like free stuff. I love free stuff. I'd like to eat free like all of you. So don't go up to our windows to get free food. Pay half price or whatever we charge."

It seemed like everybody received government food cards except me. They acquired them by saying they were unemployed. It's one of the many benefits of being paid in cash. Carny John bragged his wallet was packed with government food cards from Colorado to New Jersey.

On the night of slough, Freddie regaled us with his favorite speech.

"Ever see *Rudolf the Red-Nosed Reindeer?* Remember the Land of the Misfit Toys? Well, this is like that, and I'm the head misfit."

When we locked up the last of the rides, I hitched a lift with a trucker to the next jump. We were headed to Marlboro, about fifty miles south along I-95, the New Jersey Turnpike. The misfits were on a southbound convoy to a new jump, carrying with us the secrets of a battered young woman in hiding.

APPLESAUCE OF A HARD LIFE

MARLBORO, NEW JERSEY

*S*teve the Mechanic yelled up to me up on the scaffold, "Don't fall." Almost simultaneously, I fell over the end of the scaffold.

We were setting up on the grounds of the Church of Saint Gabriel in Marlboro. I was high on a platform helping set up a Gravitron, a spinning ride whose centrifugal force holds riders in place as the floor drops from under them.

I was told to kick a panel the last few inches into place, but I was wearing sneakers. Even boots wouldn't have worked. It was my first setup with McDaniel Brothers, and I wanted to prove myself. Instead, I proved myself reckless.

As I fell from a height of about twenty feet, I reached out my arms and grabbed on to shoulder-high bars. My legs swung back and forth like a pendulum. Using a swinging motion, I swung both feet back up on the scaffold and climbed to safety. It was a careless mistake. The crew and I laughed it off.

Blood streamed down inside my right pants leg, pooling in my shoes. The impact of the kick severely bruised my knee. The extent of my injuries went unnoticed. I was sure the open wound wasn't serious, but hiding the blood was important. There's an old saying about carnival injuries, "If you fall, you're fired before you hit the ground."

WE SPENT the days leading up to the show painting and freshening up the carnival for the weekend. The carnival was setting up on a long entrance driveway. Our bunkhouse trailer was hidden in the background near the Catholic grade school. It was during those setup days that people opened up about their lives.

"This is a hard life," said Wayne, while we painted a swing ride. "This is a haaard life."

Wayne and Devon were brothers from the violent and crime-ridden neighborhoods of Saint Catherine, Jamaica. Devon was tall and thin, while Wayne clocked in at well over three hundred clicks. Wayne was working American carnivals to save for his old age at $250 a week.

"My mama said some people have it hard in life when they are young, and some people have it hard when they are old. I said to myself, I want to have it soft when I'm old."

While setting up a swing ride, I told Wayne I met President Obama back in Chicago.

"He said, Michael, if you ever meet a big Jamaican who likes to eat ahi and jerk pork, you better watch out because he will be trouble."

"I think Mike hates Jamaica," he told the crew. "If he comes to Jamaica, we won't let him in."

Jimmy Tattoos often talked about his messy custody battle with his ex-wife. Then one morning, he was gone from his bunkroom. He was in a Marlboro jail, having surrendered himself on a child custody warrant. He owed $12,000 in child support payments for his two-year-old daughter. He was never going to make that kind of money as a ride jockey in a carnival.

Lou and Dana lived in their storage room on the church grounds. As directed, Dana stayed away from the midway.

The bunkhouse heater blew up one night and smoked us out of

our rooms. We slept the rest of the week in unheated rooms while temperatures overnight dipped to near freezing.

A water hose from the Saint Gabriel grade-school tap fed the shower in our bunkhouse. Most of us showered in a frantic soapy silence, but not Lou. He screamed bloody murder, pleading with the shower, "No, oh no, nooo. Please. Not again!"

Carny John, forty-two, lived at the Passaic headquarters and commuted to the Marlboro lot. He was born and raised in carnivals. He worked in so many carnivals he could rattle off the list like an auctioneer. Butch Butler once gave Carny John's mother a loan to start her carnival. Carny John helped her run it for a while.

Just a teenager when his first son was born, John was a widower and a grandfather, but he partied like a teenager. His girlfriend was a local Passaic bartender. He drank a twelve-pack of beer and a bottle of liquor at night. He bragged that his mother drank more than him.

When I mentioned I worked for Butler too, he told me that when he worked for Butler, he'd prepare for every slough by driving all night to his drug connection in Sacramento. Everybody in those days, he said, worked the slough twisted, high on one drug or another.

His carnival life took a detour in Denver, where he sank into homelessness and crack addiction. He returned to carnivals because he was so good, he said, he was the best there is.

Carny John was a rowdy crew supervisor and a heretic in the church of the politically correct. He had a lip beard and gave everyone lip. His excesses and wild behavior were a source of pride to him. He patrolled the grounds shouting to carnies, regardless of race, "Myyy, niggas." I never learned the proper response to that greeting.

Charlie was a tall toothpick of a black man around thirty years old. His arms were steel wire. A child of the Bronx, he wore his hair in cornrows. He was the best-dressed man in the crew, showing up for shows with new hats and neon shoes. He loved to bust chops. He bounced around on his tiptoes, mocking fellow carnies and the owners. Mostly it was just clowning around and not serious.

Several of us one day were hauling heavy lead lines over our shoulders across the grass. Charlie felt miserable. All this for a rip-off paycheck? We should elect him union president. "Union. Union. Union," he chanted. Every one of us hauling the lead lines fell silent. Then we all laughed. Charlie loved to clown, right?

STEVE THE MECHANIC vouched for pals in the old neighborhood and drove them out to help us with the setup. The new hires asked me who I was, so I pointed to the church.

"I'm the priest here, boys," I said.

"Oh, I'm sorry, Father," one new guy said, "we thought you were one of the guys."

I smiled and told them I was kidding.

"Oh, man, I thought we were in trouble because we were swearing like crazy."

"You are in trouble," I said, "because I really am the priest."

They believed me again, profusely apologizing. When I gave up the ruse, half the crew kept calling me The Priest. The other half called me Cowboy because I wore a safari hat.

Setting up and tearing down carnivals, there is always a task that stumps someone. That's when carnies love to bark clichés. This isn't rocket science, you know. This isn't brain surgery. Work smarter, not harder. You have to be smarter than the hammer. Is this your first rodeo?

Carny John asked me why I worked so fast.

"You want a quick work bonus? Nobody earned more money by working faster."

Steve the Mechanic came by during setup and showed us cell phone pictures of the devastation from the previous summer's Hurricane Sandy. The hurricane slammed into the East Coast, flattening carnivals for hundreds of miles. His pictures of the Seaside Heights boardwalk made it look like a ravaged childhood psyche.

He compared the post-hurricane rebuilding of the carnivals to the ancient Egyptians' building of the pyramids.

"How did those guys do it?" he said of the ancient Egyptians. "They didn't have forklifts or nothing like we have."

The carnival life is always precarious, and global warming will make weather disasters more frequent and devastating. Sandy was gone, but there'll be more ahead.

The rain kicked in as we finished cleaning, painting, and putting up fifteen rides and nine game joints. The McDaniel Brothers carnival glistened on the church lawn. With the church in the background, it looked like a carnival Brigadoon.

FREDDIE GATHERED us around after the first Marlboro show night, another frustrating, rainy affair. This time the speech was about drugs, drink, and tools.

"No more smoking pot. For Christ's sake. You walk around here like zombies. People think the inspectors are dumb, but they're not dumb no more. They'll get a piece of your hair, and they'll test you. There's a $5,000 fine, and you'll have to go to Albany."

I loved those speeches accusing us of being knuckleheads. When he was finished, I realized I'd missed some gossip about misbehavior.

"You can drink. My brother and I drink. But you can't drink on rides. And pay your child support because they will fine you."

It was nice to hear Freddie, paying us what he was, tell us to pay our bills.

We spent the week putting local kids on rides between the rain showers. Jimmy Tattoos returned from his child-support incarceration and was put in charge of running the teacup ride.

Kiddy rides get little respect. Bald, tattooed ex-cons sometimes don't feel kiddyland fits their tough-guy image. Steve the Mechanic saw this and walked by Jimmy singing, "I'm a little teapot short and stout, here is my handle, here is my spout."

Local musicians played during breaks in the rain all weekend. Lines were short. Carnies mulled around under tarp awnings. Newly painted rides stood still for hours. It was a grand carnival for ducks.

SHARON APPROACHED me in the Church of Saint Gabriel asking why I was looking at the church's artwork. She was a devout, active parishioner. She followed up with a few questions about carnival life. What are carnival people are really like?

It was Pentecost Sunday, and I hoped the priest's sermon mentioned carnivals. I was there listening for a connection. Sharon was fishing for a soul.

Slough that evening seemed like an eternity in a cold, drizzly, muddy hell. Out of the mist, across the grassy field of half-torn-down rides, materialized the vision of Sharon and her lovely teenage daughter.

"Hey, Cowboy," Freddie yelled. "Someone here to see you."

I was working on the carousel in the muck and the rain. I turned around to see Sharon and her daughter in pristine, warm rain gear. In my mind, an ethereal glow surrounded them, and I was mudman.

Work on the rides stopped. In front of the tough, wise-cracking, streetwise New York/New Jersey carnival crew, the ladies handed me a Bible, a prayer book, prayer cards, two rosaries, and a bottle of holy water.

"I'm giving you these," Sharon said, "because carnivals can be hard places to keep God in mind."

Thanking them for their kindness, I didn't mention I was at the church for the artwork. As if immune to the rain and wind, they walked back to Saint Gabriel's past a jungle of rides and a score of speechless carnies.

Turning around to face the McDaniel brothers and the crew was not easy. They folded their arms and waited for an explanation.

"Yes, I was at church this morning," I said, "and I didn't see any of you guys there. Including you, Freddie."

"I went to my own church this morning," Freddie said. "There is a carny priest, you know. Father Mac up in Watertown (New York)."

It was the first I'd heard of anything like a ministry to carnival workers. Msgr. Robert McCarthy was turning ninety-five years old that summer. Appointed by the Vatican to minister to carnivals, he was revered throughout carnivals. I later saw him quoted in an internet article.

"I always carry my entire church with me, the chalice, vestments, etcetera," Father Mac said. "I just set up the church on Sunday on a ride like the Ferris wheel or anyplace I can find."

Pentecost is called the birthday of the church by Christians because the disciples of Jesus left their gathering room for a traveling ministry.

On that Sunday, I became determined to seek out traveling ministries in carnivals. Not for evidence of the divine, but for people searching for meaning in their lives.

AFTER SLOUGH, a bunch of us piled into Connie's car at 1 a.m. on our way to the next jump, in Westchester County, New York. Hitched up behind was a battered fifteen-foot Skyline RV trailer with a busted-out window.

"I once had a teenage crush on a girl named Connie," I said. "You ain't her, are you?"

Connie was my age, and it didn't take much to see she once turned heads on the midway.

During the ride, a young man named Osi bragged about cheating on "bitches."

"Don't talk about breaking a young girl's heart," Connie said. "You don't know what I've seen."

Carnival people often meet locals ready for love and adventure. It seems like the traveling life is better with someone to love. The aloneness is the beast.

Connie joined the carnival when a handsome young carny gave her a ride. She fell madly in love. Still in high school and on the verge of her big break as a competitive roller-skater, Connie became pregnant. All of her plans for the future changed. She found new dreams and was whisked away on the road with her carnival man.

She didn't discuss the specifics of her heartbreak, only that she felt she was finally bouncing back. She worked in carnivals during the season. In the off-season, she helped kids at her local community center with their art projects.

One of her four children was working with us. Dizzy, age twenty-one, was big, strong, and full of good humor. Connie was proud to say that Dizzy worked in carnivals since the age of five. She raised all her kids in the whirlwind of carnivals.

Dizzy's girlfriend, Amber, worked a grab wagon. She was about to make Connie a grandmother. If the family tradition continued, Dizzy Jr. could expect carnival routes in his future.

At one toll booth on the way to Jefferson Valley, Connie couldn't pay the twenty-dollar toll.

"Fourteen dollars is all I have in the world," she said.

I hoped that wasn't true. She collected money from the riders, money the McDaniels should have paid to bring their crew to the new jump.

Jimmy Tattoos looked out the window when we passed Hackensack. He pointed to what he called his "home away from home," the Bergen County Jail.

We took the Taconic State Parkway through the hills and small towns of the Taconic Mountains and the eastern Hudson Valley. Trees and the early-morning fog hugged the road. Connie and I talked in hushed voices as people slept in the back seats. We weaved through the woody, haunted 4 a.m. roads of Westchester County.

She told stories of being a love-struck girl excited about the adventurous carnival life and of being a single mom barely scraping by. Connie thanked me for keeping her awake and listening to her life story. Thank me?

Connie was the carnival mother of a soon-to-be three generation carnival family. Thank me? Connie, you're the kind of person I came to find.

A SUCKER FOR RED TAIL LIGHTS

YORKTOWN, NEW YORK

More than a dozen of us were setting up rides in the Jefferson Valley Mall parking lot in Yorktown, a wooded area of Westchester County. The bunkhouse parked on the lot had no access to water, but we were working fast and were finishing up by the second day.

Then I received an email from my ex-mother-in-law, saying my daughter wanted me home for her eighth birthday. I knew it was true because her school therapist said she was suffering from separation anxiety.

Her birthday was on Friday. I became obsessed with making it back for her birthday party.

I searched the internet for traveling carnivals based in the Chicago area. Calling Modern Midways, I told them I was "clean-cut and drug free." I heard they were based somewhere on Chicago's Southside. They agreed to hire me, sight unseen.

Freddie wasn't surprised when I called him to say I was hitch-hiking back to Chicago. He promised to send me my pay.

"You're a good guy," he said. "If you're ever back this way again, come work for us."

To the crew, this sounded like a sucker move. If I was turning from a carny into an easy mark, they wanted to take advantage of me too.

"You should buy us all a round of beer," said eighteen-year-old Osi.

"Give your check to me and Devon," Wayne said with a wink. "We'll make sure you get it."

Connie puffed her cigarette, looked into the sun, and asked me one question. "Why?"

"My daughter's eighth birthday is this weekend," I said.

Freddie never sent me my check. His disparaging speeches accusing us of stealing and not paying our child support took on a new meaning. He had no intention of paying me.

In carnival parlance, it's akin to being "red lighted." All you see when you finish your job are the red tail lights as the carnival drives away. Outside carnivals, it's called wage theft.

Almost every veteran carny I spoke to told stories of being cheated out of money by an owner. It is the number one issue among carnival workers.

With no union or money for a lawyer, no carnival worker was safe from wage theft. Not only were wages crushingly low, but beatings were a time-honored way to keep discipline. What other job is like that? Deep down, I knew before I left that this might happen. Such was the chance I had to take.

I packed my bags and embarked on the great New York-to-Chicago race to a little girl's birthday party.

A DIRTY, SMELLY GIFT FOR A LITTLE ANGEL

HITCHHIKING NEW YORK TO CHICAGO

*H*itchhiking is illegal in New York and more so around Fishkill Correctional Facility. I had 800 miles to go to Chicago and four days to get there. The parkway has no shoulders for a vehicle to pull over for hitchhikers. I might not make it to Chicago on time or at all.

My first ride drove me to the Clarence Fahnestock State Park and dropped me off on a connection ramp with no shoulder. A state trooper pulled up and parked in the middle of the ramp. A line of traffic backed up behind her.

"Don't you know hitchhiking is dangerous?" she said. "Don't you know you could get killed? I ought to take you in."

People are more likely to stumble and kill themselves than die hitchhiking. Reports of violence are rare. The myths are based on exceptions.

As she checked my license on her computer, a driver behind her honked his horn. She stopped her license search, exited the squad car, went back to the driver, and yelled at him from outside his driver's side window.

"You got a problem? You got a problem you want to talk about? Then you better stop honking that horn."

Another police car soon followed and drove onto the grass. The two officers stood there with their emergency lights whirling, interviewing me as the traffic stood still. Frustrated and still furious, the first state trooper drove me about twenty miles down the road to the next exit.

"Stop looking out the window. I know you're looking for another spot. Hitchhiking is illegal in New York. If I catch you again, I'm arresting you."

She dropped me off at a small gas station on Route 52. As I exited the squad car, she kept demeaning me. I bet she continued her rant while driving away.

I'm a respectful dude. I'm the type of guy who listens. I walked behind the gas station to a dumpster, found a box, tore off the lip and wrote I-84. Hitchhiking at the front of the gas station is okay because that is private property. The inner hitchhiker attorney in me discovered a loophole.

A local cop pulled up within minutes. According to the internet, I told him, hitchhiking was legal off the road in the good state of New York.

Being a young policeman, he still remembered the exact code number making it illegal. "If I see you again," he said. "I'm arresting you."

He described hellish jailhouse conditions. I hate when a policeman threatens a person with prison rape. They should be embarrassed that they can't control their own facilities. I kept my jokey mouth shut. He promised to patrol the area periodically, so I better not even think about it.

My luggage rollers wore out long ago, so I picked up my red suitcase and carried it against my chest. I slung my laptop backpack on my back and began hobbling toward the interstate. This time I'm never going to make it.

Still, I'm a respectful dude. I'm the type of guy who listens. After five miles of walking, my inner hitchhiker attorney thought of another loophole. Side streets.

This time three police cars pulled up, red and blue lights on full tilt. Six officers of the law stopped me within two hours. I was hitch-hiking along a police gantlet. Three officers exited their vehicle and walked toward me. Do not joke with the police. It's one of my top hitchhiker rules, but this was an extreme case.

"What am I, public enemy number one, fellas?"

Facing six heavily armed policemen, I argued that the internet told me it is okay to hitchhike on side streets. Their lights kept flashing. My impromptu hitchhiker lawyering wasn't working. After a long conversation, they suggested I return to New York City by train and take a bus to Chicago.

"I don't have the money for that," I said.

The most senior state patrolman's face was a mix of surprise and anger. We were at a standoff. Adopting a faraway look, he adopted a now-I-have-heard-it-all attitude.

"I'll walk then," I said, pointing westward. "How far is it to Pennsylvania?"

I'd won. The senior patrolman never heard that one before.

"About sixty miles," he said, "but hitchhiking might be illegal there, too."

In a world-weary tone, the senior patrolman told the youngest cop to drive me to Fishkill. He gave me a stern warning and drove away. I sat and thought about the last few hours.

On the surface, it looked like I was having a very bad day, and it could be getting worse. Yet I was pretty sure I just talked my way out of jail three times. I was having a very good day, and it could be getting better.

I'm a respectful dude. I'm the type of guy who listens. Then my inner hitchhiking lawyer came upon another plan. I put my I-84 sign on the back of my computer backpack and walked along the road. I'm not hitchhiking if my thumb is not out. Yet drivers could see where I was headed. Wink. Wink.

After I walked a couple of long, nerve-wracking miles, a pickup truck veered across the lanes to pick me up. I ran up to the truck and saw a young father, his son, and the family dog. Peter told me to hop in the flatbed. The young boy looked at me like I was a work of fiction. He seemed more confused than the dog.

Throwing my bags into the flatbed, I leaped in next to a ladder and lawnmower. The truck peeled away from the curb, and we sped down the on-ramp to I-84. We passed cars like they were standing still on our way to America's Rhine, the Hudson River.

I wanted to whoop and sing. Peter gave me a ten-dollar bill and pulled away fast from the last exit before the Newburgh-Beacon Bridge over the Hudson River. The onramp there was in full view of the toll booths. It was too dark anyway, so I walked to the nearby well-lit Mobil station. I found a traveler's cardboard in the grass behind the bushes and fell asleep.

In the morning, I walked across the 1.5-mile steel beam bridge toward Newburgh. The Hudson is wide at that point, which makes it feel like the crossing means something.

About halfway across, I met a tall black man walking the other way. D.J. was forty-two years old, and wearing the clothes he wore the day before. He told me how to make it on the streets with no money, giving me advice about shelters in Connecticut, Delaware, New York, and Rhode Island.

He was the first person I heard call a government food card a "homeless visa." A $200 card is easily sold for $100 in cash, so you can buy beer. Hitchhiking on trains is easy. Get on and tell the conductor you have no money. If he kicks you off, hop on the next one, and then onto the next one until you get to where you're going.

D.J. was living at his girlfriend's home, but he predicted that he would be kicked out that day for staying out all night, "checking out some ass." At one time, D.J. ran a carousel at a carnival. He loved traveling carnivals. He'd have reminisced all day about his glory days in traveling carnivals if I let him. I told him I needed to get to Chicago. We stood shoulder-to-shoulder for a moment, watching the river below in silence.

"Isn't it interesting," he said. "Here we are halfway across a bridge, and we're both at a crossroads in our lives."

NEVER STOP HITCHHIKING, even when eating at a restaurant.

My "I-80 West" cardboard sign was propped up next to me at a Subway shop inside the Pilot Flying J truck stop west of Scranton, Pennsylvania.

A truck driver named Mesud Cevra was working on his laptop at the next table. I was bold enough to strike up a conversation with him, and before long, I was hoisting myself up into the cab of his eighteen-wheeler truck.

We began the ride talking about our pasts, and a bridge opened up between us. A bridge was the most architecturally distinct feature of Mesud's hometown, Mostar, Bosnia. Croat forces destroyed the sixteenth-century Ottoman bridge spanning the Neretva River in the Bosnian war in the 1990s.

An estimated one hundred thousand people died during the breakup of the former Yugoslavia. Mesud and his family were among the two million people displaced during the war. Mesud and his father, mother, siblings, and cousins were imprisoned in concentration camps.

"I heard a lot of screaming going on in the next room," he said, speculating people were tortured.

Mesud survived two murder attempts, swam the Neretva River to safety, and survived the concentration camp. A Muslim, he disguised himself as a Catholic priest to escape the country. At times during our ride, he couldn't speak without tears for Mostar.

He immigrated to the United States in 1997 with two thousand dollars in his pocket. In fewer than twenty years, he'd bought a truck and was planning on purchasing two more. He offered me a job driving for him after my year in carnivals.

We drove more than six hundred miles together from eastern Pennsylvania to Kalamazoo, Michigan. We spent the night in his cab, him in the bottom bunk and me on the top. I filled two notebooks with his stories.

When he dropped me off at an I-90 truck stop, Mesud gave me his views on his adopted country. After two million miles of driving across America, he could confidently say he admired the American people.

"I love the freedom," he said. "Ninety percent of the Americans I meet are honest people. I think people are very happy. I see people with no money, but they are happy."

JOHN LEE SCHNEIDER was an ordinary truck driver by profession. By inclination, he was a traveling showman.

We met in line for fast food at the truck stop outside Kalamazoo. Waiting in line for his order to be taken, he agreed to drive me to Chicago. When I opened the door to his eighteen-wheeler truck, an avalanche of colored inflatable balloons fell out into the parking lot. The truck cab proved to be full of surprises.

Schneider drove more than one hundred thousand miles a year, giving him plenty of time for truck stops across the country to eat, rest, and entertain. He made balloon giraffes, elephants, and other animals for kids and waitresses.

"If I see a family in a truck stop, I'll go up to the parents and ask if the kids can have a balloon. A waitress might sit down next to me, and I'll make her a puppy. Then they'll show it around. I've had a family buy me a meal."

Before he became a trucker, he made his living as Gimmick the Clown and David Lee the Magician.

"I love entertaining people," he said.

Schneider gained unwanted notoriety in the 1970s when one of his fiery escape tricks set him on fire on national TV. He was devastated. His magical dreams were crushed. He tossed his magic tricks into his garage. He moved out of Sheboygan, Wisconsin, and earned his trucker's license.

"Now, I'm known as the balloon man in a lot of truck stops."

Schneider dropped me off just short of Chicago, between the TA and the Pilot truck stops near Gary, Indiana. It was too dark to hitch-hike, so I found an empty Subway table to write all night.

The TA and Pilot signs loomed over truck stops like neon palm trees. Tired after three days of near-constant hitchhiking, I slipped in and out of dreams with my eyes open. Lou Rawls sang, "Late in the midnight hour, you're gonna miss my loving."

About twenty trucks and cars picked me up on the New York to Chicago trip. Most drivers weren't finished talking when it came time to drop me off.

When the sun came up, I arranged for my family to give me a ride to Chicago's South Loop. The race to Grace was won. I made it in time for her birthday, but there was a twist.

I wanted to surprise Grace, so I never mentioned I was coming. And she never mentioned she'd be out of town visiting her grandparents. I wished her a happy birthday on the phone. We laughed about the mix-up, I thought. I realized later that she hung up the phone near tears.

After a week of hitchhiking, I expected to show up a dirty, smelly gift for a little angel. Instead, the next morning, I reported to the grittiest, purest urban carnival in all of American traveling carnivals. Not a little angel among them.

PART IV
CHICAGO

JUNE

CARNIVALS THE CHICAGO WAY

GAGE PARK

Never play cards with a man called Doc. Never eat at a place called Mom's.
Never sleep with a woman whose troubles are worse than your own.

— CHICAGO WRITER NELSON ALGREN

*W*ith my sleeping bag and backpack in hand, I walked onto the hurly-burly carnival lot of Modern Midways.

Workers at half-finished rides and joints were setting up on Chicago's West Side along a street known locally at the time as a dividing line between Latino and black gangs.

Owner Robert Briggs told me to show up on the lot and look for a short guy in charge. He gave no other description. I spotted a short black man talking to a local middle-aged man. The local looked like he needed a break.

"Is that right?" Shorty said to the man. "I don't think so. We're not hiring."

"Are you Shorty?" I asked, "Robert Briggs told me to ask for you."

The local man backed up, dejected. He knew the score. Somebody sent me. Nobody sent him.

"We don't want nobody nobody sent," is an old political saying in Chicago.

I acted as if I was hired, but I knew Shorty had veto power. Shorty took his time looking me over. My heart pounded. Finally, he asked me if I knew how to drive.

"Can I drive? If it takes an hour to get there, I can get there in ten minutes. I don't worry about the people in the way. Nuttin'. They get hurt, that's their fault. I drive like a bat out of hell. Put me behind the wheel and hold on."

I didn't know it at the time, but I was talking to one of the toughest, most volatile carnival bosses on the circuit. He took forever to respond. I realized my mistake. Oh no. Oh no.

"I like you," he said. "You're funny. You're a funny guy."

There was no reasonable reason I would lead with a joke on a new carnival lot. In carnivals, as is true everywhere, comedy is dangerous.

"Can you climb?" he said.

"You're younger than me, Shorty."

"Ya, but you're in shape. You're going to climb."

Boy howdy, he wasn't kidding. Shorty was no jokester.

The carnival shut down a side boulevard in Gage Park next to Western Avenue. It was an annual carnival spot. Carnivals played that neighborhood for years. Struggling parents saved their money to go to the carnival they went to as kids.

The Chicago-side of our crew ate hot dogs at a place named Maxwell Street, chicken at Harold's Chicken Shack, and ribs from any joint serving from behind bulletproof glass. It's a Southside thing.

~⁓

SOMEONE AT MODERN MIDWAYS was a genius at lot design. The Fire Ball, Orbiter, Spider, Grand Carrousel, Giant Wheel, and bumper cars were as tight as a Rubik's Cube.

That first afternoon, I set up and ran the Flying Dumbos. In the cartoons, Dumbo's ears flap like wings giving him flight. In carnivals, the ride's arms rise up so that the kids feel they are flying on Dumbo's back.

On the Gage Park spot, the Dumbo didn't fly because we were too close to the Fire Ball's swinging arm. Yet it was still close enough for stray cell phones to come flying from the Fire Ball. If it was raining cell phones, it wouldn't scare those Chicago kids. They were used to worse.

Dumbo's glassy eyes and half-witted smile makes him look very high. Or as they say on the midway, "Dumbo looks like he's flying twisted." It's not an unfamiliar look in that neighborhood.

My routine on the Lolly Swing in California was "Up I say, up I say, and awaaay I say." In New Jersey, my routine on the Apple's ride was the magic word "Applesauce." In Chicago, I went with the magic words "Mumbo Jumbo" for Dumbo.

"What are the magic words, kids?"

"Mumbo Jumbo."

"I can't hear you."

"Mumbo Jumbo."

"What?"

"Mumbo Jumbooooooo!"

I'd hit the switch, jerking the kids forward. Kids loved the mumbo-jumbo routine so much they shouted it to me as they passed by all ten turns, "Mumbo Jumbo. Mumbo Jumbo. Mumbo Jumbo." They came back all night long breathlessly saying, "I already know the magic words."

Little black girls wore beads in their braided hair. Their braids looked like colorful candied strings when they ran. Boys ran in groups of best friends. Other kids stayed close to their mothers but broke away when they saw a ride they liked. Single moms, couples, gang-bangers, and West Side preachers all came by my Flying Dumbos.

In the middle of their tough Chicago neighborhood, the carnival landed like a spaceship. The kids felt like they were flying away from it all. The children loved going in flat ride circles as if the spinning might change something. They wanted to imagine themselves far away.

The next day, all the smiling, happy kids woke up right back in their shoot-'em-up neighborhoods. The carnival feeling wears off, but some kids walked away with something extra in their backpack of tricks.

"IEEE!" Peanut yelled. "This is my hometown. I've been gone too long. My homeys are waiting for me. If you don't see me tomorrow, it's because I've been having fun or I've been killed."

It was payday for the crew. The Chicagoans who traveled to Southern states that winter were wildly happy to be home sweet home in Chicago. It was Friday night, and everyone was lined up outside the main-office trailer to get paid.

Peanut was a tall, thin black man born and raised in Chicago. He was not wrong about the dangers of partying it up on Chicago's West Side. Five people were killed and twenty-five shot in twelve hours one night.

The security guard in charge looked like he was going to battle. He wore a bulletproof vest with a baton in his utility belt along with three visible guns and another gun hid on his leg. A tall veteran MP, he taught martial arts and walked the carnival lot as if it were ready to blow up any minute.

Most of the carnival workers hated the security people and kept away from them. I made the mistake of talking to the former MP. Shorty shut down the fraternization. Security guards were too much like cops.

Modern Midways traveled almost year-round, working the summer in its home-base Chicago and the rest of the year in warmer climates in Alabama, Florida, and Georgia. In Chicago, Modern Midways played both some of the swankiest spots and the most violent, poverty-prone neighborhoods.

Modern Midways, Windy City Amusements, and North American Midway Entertainment (NAME) dominated the once-crowded carnival scene in Chicago.

At the end of the day, I helped lift the ATM box into the office trailer and waited outside with the rest of the crew to get paid. Owner Robert Briggs sat at a desk inside the trailer handing out cash.

When it was my turn, I walked up behind him and waited for him to acknowledge me. He swiveled around and shook my hand.

Payday was also my first day, so I wasn't sure if I'd get a penny. Briggs welcomed me to the crew and handed me a few bucks as a draw.

"Everyone is talking about you on the Dumbos," he said. "We care about those things here. Great work."

Briggs was a husky, strong, compact man whose handshake could crush clay bricks. He was a carnival owner who could, if he felt justified, rule by force. Yet he once dreamed of being a veterinarian and attended vet college for a while.

When his carnival-owning dad died, Robert took over with his two brothers. Employing eighty carnies during the peak season, the former veterinary student learned to handle a different variety of animal, *et Carny Americanus.*

I like carnival owners. They are wildcat entrepreneurs. They place high-stakes bets on highly leveraged rides and trust in their own cunning to make it all back on the road.

His two brothers were involved with the carnival, but I only met Eddie. He was another big man in his thirties or forties. Eddie walked the midway like a carnival pirate with his bulldog, Hercules, at his side and his parrot, Louie, on his shoulder.

Overseeing games, Eddie bragged about being a vicious street fighter. He smoked pot with his friends on the crew and hid that vice from his brothers. Potheads are fine, but lushes cause accidents. Drinkers had reason to worry about their personal safety if caught drinking on the job.

After being paid that first night, we made our way to the filthy, rusted patchwork wreck they called a van. It was the #1 sticky, bug-infested, body-odor van in all of carnivals. Eighteen people packed into the van every night after a full day of work. I was the newest on the crew, so I sat on the floor with my knees at my chin.

They shut the van shades, so cops couldn't see the crush inside. Everyone could fit in if we squirmed for a few minutes. Then almost every sardine in the van lit up cigarettes. Each ride was an atomic bomb of concentrated mentholated smoke and sweaty bodies. Marine Eric called those rides limbo because we were so close to hell, and it felt like an eternity.

Marine Eric may have known a thing or two about hell. He was a tall, heavy black man in his thirties, a veteran of the Iraq War. People said he suffered horrific nightmares, shouting in Arabic in his sleep.

Talk in the van rides was funny and fast until the driver, Peanut, cranked up the gangster rap on WPWX Power 92, "Number One in the Streets." Every head bobbed. Marine Eric led the van in raps. The music of our inner-city carnival was rap music. Modern Midways was no relic of a bygone era.

Our crew included Angel, Asia, Biggin, Boogie, Cockroach, Chico, Chunk of Cheese, Confederate Max, Cosmo, Curley, Darko, Dre, Fireball Pete, Ghost, J.C., John the Horse Walker, La La, Lewis, Louisiana Brian, Marine Eric, Muscles, One Shot Carl, Pork Chop, Robert the Killer, Rachel, Raúl, Roger the Artist, Sis, Smalls, and Uncle Fester.

The carnival quarters were on the edge of Chicago Heights, a southern Chicago suburb. I spent my first night sleeping in that God-forsaken carnival van. When I awoke, I felt a pair of huge, dull eyes watching me. Looking up from the seat, I saw a big dumb cow face questioning my existence on her turf.

I crawled out of the van and walked around the curious cow. Little by little, I saw a herd of cows in a junkyard of bunkhouses, rusted-out rides, and abandoned joints. I knew the owners owned cows. I just didn't realize we'd be living in a junkyard pasture with forty Black Angus cows.

Pork Chop was on his way to the donniker when he saw me in awe of the cows and the widespread decrepitude.

"Welcome to The 30," he said. "When it rains, it's The Dirty 30."

Our carnival quarters were on US Route 30, the coast-to-coast highway called the Lincoln Highway in Illinois. The Lincoln Highway was the first bicoastal highway in the country. Next to US Route 66, it is the most fabled road I had traveled to date.

One morning, a carny pointed at the rising sun.

"My house is right on this highway out that way," he said, "in Ohio."

It was a rainy June, so the Dirty 30 became an obstacle course. The crew was forced to make its way through deep traps of fecal mud and piles of fresh manure. I slept in the van my entire first week on the Dirty 30, suffering so many bites that my skin felt like a scratchy overcoat.

When a few carnies quit, rooms opened up in the bunkhouses but no rooms with working doors. Every room was open to mosquitoes, bugs, and a curious cow.

Showers were at the far end of the field, across minefields of manure and mud. Red graffiti was scrawled across one broken shower door.

"The girls don't like seeing your hairy ass so close the door."

We had time to work on the lot between jumps one week. I helped build a new bathroom and shower. I didn't finish the work, but the plan was to charge two dollars for a clean shower and sink. They should have paid us two dollars to take showers.

The donnikers were more than one hundred yards away through an obstacle course of mud, wood planks, junked rides, abandoned grab wagons, and a metal cow gate. If you were in a hurry, cows standing in the way could slow the frantic run to the donniker.

That was Marine Eric's nightmare scenario, and he'd fought in the Middle East.

"If you have diarrhea, you'll never make it," he said. "You'll have to do it next to the cows."

The cows were a great source of humor for everyone. Cows operated rides while we slept. They snuck into bed with us to keep warm. Cows outsmarted us. Cows were guilty of the seven deadly sins. Cows were endowed with super cow powers. Cows were hot-tempered, but they showed more common sense than any of us.

Carnivals concoct stories every day to make money. Our crew

turned our pathetic pasture into a magical traveling cow show. It was cow genius.

Father's Day can send a chill down the back of some carnivals.

Childhood and parenting are central to the carnival experience. It's the main challenge for the working poor, as carnival workers are generally away from home for six months or more.

Many carnival workers were happy kids raised in struggling but happy families. Many more grew up in unhappy families, as orphans, foster kids, juvenile delinquents, and victims of abusive parents.

Carnival children sometimes travel with the carnival or stay with their extended families back in their hometowns. Smartphones close the distance, but online time isn't the same.

Forty-year-old Dre told me he was a grandfather to seven grandchildren.

"I was raised real ghetto," he said.

He became a dad when he was twelve years old, and his daughter became a mom when she was twelve years old. Another carny showed me his text to his newest grandchild on Father's Day. He was thirty-six years old.

Carnival workers aren't all lonely parents longing to be with their kids. Deadbeats work off the books to avoid child-support payments. They declare themselves homeless, with no income, to avoid detection by authorities.

Lewis bragged about his girlfriend in Florida being pregnant. He couldn't wait to get his new fiancée pregnant in Chicago, too, because pregnant girls are sexy. He expressed no wish for fatherhood other than the period of pregnancy.

Before coming to Chicago, I made nightly cell-phone calls to my daughter. She loved to play in the dogwood tree outside her apartment. I asked her what she thought about at the top of the tree.

"I climbed trees when I was your age," I said, "and daydreamed all afternoon."

Her school district encouraged diary keeping. I told her to write about her treetop thoughts. Silly thoughts. Funny thoughts. Pretend thoughts. It was her idea to call me from the tree. I worried she might fall, but she assured me, "I'm an expert."

"What are you thinking about?" I said.

Long pause.

"I'm thinking about what I'm thinking about," she giggled.

"It's not so silly. Writers always watch themselves think. That's what you are doing."

"I'm thinking about what it would be like to be a dolphin trainer. Would the training be hard?"

Somehow, I was on the other end of the phone and yet on the ground staring up into the tree at my sparkling, darling girl.

After the carnival teardown in Gage Park, I took buses directly over to see her. A week late, I showed up a dirty, smelly gift for an angel. I gave her presents I bought at the carnival—a blow-up pink beach dolphin and a dolphin necklace that flashed bright colors. She named the necklace dolphin "Colorful." My parents said she received better presents, but she raved about her carnival dolphins.

"Dad's hat was so dirty . . . He says I've grown."

Perhaps the most shining example of parent-child empathy was an older Sinaloan man working with me back at Butler in California. Jesus saw a mother with three crying children being turned away at the ticket office because they did not have enough money for tickets. Jesus left the Shrek gym, opened his wallet, and paid the seventy-five dollars for all-you-can-ride wristbands.

It was almost two days of his wages. He never mentioned the gesture to me. I heard it from the ticket lady. She teared up when she handed over the tickets to the kids.

I failed my first test of generosity to kids in carnivals. A couple of ten-year-old best friends in Gage Park were hustling up free rides. One child could muster up tears. The other wiped his eyes as if he were crying.

"Mister, we don't have any money. Can we have a free ride?"

Tears. Sad faces. More tears. For fear of being fired, I said no. Even though I knew it was a con, I felt like a crumb. The real carnies knew they were being conned, too, but they let the kids ride every ride.

The tears were fake, but the kids were genuinely poor. They just wanted to scam rides so they could be like the other kids with money. I vowed never again to let a chance to be kind slip away.

When kids asked for free rides, I found I could credibly ask myself, "What would Jesus do?" That is, Jesus of Sinaloa.

BIRTHPLACE OF TRAVELING CARNIVALS

MIDWAY PLAISANCE, WASHINGTON PARK

*S*horty never told us where we were going next. I couldn't believe my eyes one morning when our trucks drove up along Midway Plaisance.

Running a traveling carnival on Midway Plaisance is like playing a Major League Baseball game in Cooperstown, New York. Midway Plaisance is the birthplace of traveling carnivals, which trace their lineage to the 1893 World's Columbian Exposition in Chicago.

We were setting up on the same midway. In traveling carnivals, that is as close as it gets to sacred ground.

The University of Chicago's Victorian Gothic architecture lines the north and south sides of the street. The midway that once featured low-brow entertainment evolved into a high-brow boulevard known for cranking out Nobel laureates as casually as Modern Midways cranked out corn dogs.

A couple blocks off the university campus were low-income neighborhoods with gang violence worse than the days of Al Capone. They were our people. Our carnival drew few U of C intellectuals. That week, Midway Plaisance returned to its roots, entertaining the people from the streets of Chicago.

AFTER THE GREAT Chicago Fire of 1871, pollution in the city was so out of control that it could turn day into soupy night. The stench of the stockyard slaughterhouses fouled the air. Sanitation was a nightmare.

It was a city on the make, with rampant political corruption, seven thousand bars, and by some estimates ten thousand prostitutes. Chicago was widely seen as a red-hot mess.

The Nobel Prize-winning British writer Rudyard Kipling visited in the 1890s and wrote, "I have struck a city – a real city – and they call it Chicago. . . I urgently desire never to see it again. It is inhabited by savages."

Kipling was a King Kong-sized asshole for saying that, for about a million savage reasons living in Chicago at the time.

There was plenty to recommend Chicago, but the city's leaders knew the score. They vied for the world's fair to show that Chicago was on the comeback trail. Architect Daniel Burnham and a circle of philanthropists and builders went to work.

In a bloody, polluted, blackened city, they envisioned a "White City," a bonfire of lights, a shining example for cities of the future.

The world never witnessed anything like it. It was a paradigm of the world in technology, entertainment, and forward thinking. Burnham's favorite quote was, "Make no little plan. They have no magic to stir men's blood."

On 690 acres of lagoon and swampland, a cadre of Chicago's best and brightest began building a fair with neoclassical buildings and public spaces. The fair lasted six months, from May to October. To this day, that's still the traditional carnival season.

As with carnivals, many of the structures at the fair were temporary. About two hundred temporary buildings, representing people and cultures from 46 countries, sprung up in record time. Most were made of plaster, cement, and fiber. The buildings were covered in stucco and spray-painted white. The original midway was a mile long and six hundred feet wide.

Midway Plaisance wowed the public with freak shows, medicine shows, thrill shows, water shows, animal shows, magic lantern shows, comedies, and fan-dancing "girly" shows.

The original Ferris wheel was a colossus meant to rival the Eiffel Tower in Paris. It was the size of a twenty-six-story building, and it held two thousand people. Passenger cars could hold 60 people and had waiters.

The fair introduced the country to the zipper, Juicy Fruit gum, Quaker Oats, and Aunt Jemima "instant" pancake mix. The beer that won first prize at the fair is still named Pabst Blue Ribbon. Vienna Sausage began selling frankfurters that later became the prototype of the Chicago-style hot dog.

The crowds saw a moving walkway, phosphorescent lamps, and third-rail-powered elevated trains. The first all-electric kitchen unveiled the first dishwasher.

The newspapers called the fair the "Battle of the Currents" because it was the most visible battleground for the future of America's electrical power grid. Alternating electrical currents backed by Nicholas Tesla and George Westinghouse vied for placement at the fair with Thomas Edison's direct current system.

Tesla performed lighting and electricity shows at the fair. His AC currents powered most of the boulevards and shows. Most notably, Edison's DC electricity powered the lights on the original Ferris Wheel.

Westinghouse was an engineer and industrialist who bet on his scientist, Tesla, and AC current. Edison was a prolific, adaptive inventor who once employed Tesla. Their spectacular rivalry was a version of Microsoft's Bill Gates versus Apple's Steve Jobs for the future of PCs and the internet.

Tesla's AC became the dominant current, but DC is making a comeback, powering electric cars, LEDs, and solar panels.

The birth of American carnivals happened at the dawn of a new technological age. What followed was a boom in railroad lines for freight trains and roads for gas-powered trucks.

Cities began putting in outdoor lighting, but traveling carnivals brought outdoor lighting to small and big cities alike. New York City's Coney Island followed by turning night into day with millions of lights.

The White City may have been the inspiration for the Emerald City in the novel *The Wonderful Wizard of Oz,* published seven years later. Chicago-born Walt Disney's father, Elias, worked at the fair. Many aspects of Disneyland may have also been highly influenced by the fair's concepts.

In the six months that it lasted, a mind-blowing 27 million visits were recorded to the exhibition. The entire population of the United States at the time was just 63 million people, versus today's 330 million.

When the fair ended, wildcat entrepreneurs capitalized on its momentum by combining traveling minstrel, medicine, burlesque, and freak shows.

The supernova energy of the White City gave birth to American traveling carnivals. Soon a never-before-seen concept was orbiting the country.

While European carnivals focused on religious holidays, a new breed of American carnivals became brightly lit movable feasts on wheels going anywhere, any time.

PEANUT'S GIRLFRIEND, Asia, approached me one morning as the ride jockeys were pretesting the rides. She was a young black woman about twenty years old with a mile-wide smile and even bigger daring streak.

"Hey, Michael, you want to come on the Fire Ball with me?"

The Fire Ball is a giant Dutch-made ride with a long arm that has a spinning circle of seats at the end. Twenty-four seats swing sixty feet high and spin. The arm swings up 120 degrees before diving back toward the ground.

Roger the Artist and Fireball Pete laughed like evil villains while locking us into our seats. Ride jockeys need to test the ride's limits every day before the show, so the wildest ride of the day is the first ride. Roger and Pete wanted to test our limits.

When the Fire Ball's arm reached its maximum height, I looked over at Asia to see if she was scared. No. She was thrilled.

We saw the Northside, the Southside, the West Side, and Lake Michigan. The ride jockeys tried to make us puke, but we loved every g-force inducing second. When we came off the ride, they were sure they had turned us into milkshakes.

I asked Asia if she felt nauseous.

"No, it was cool," she said. "I saw Chicago upside down."

The Illinois Department of Labor oversaw 530 amusement companies in 2013-14, which included tracks, ski lifts, and "bounce houses." Its four inspectors checked the safety of 2,800 rides.

The Outdoor Amusement Business Association estimated that about twenty thousand people worked in the industry across the country. In Illinois that year, twenty traveling carnival companies were listed on websites. I never witnessed an unsafe ride.

Asia walked away from the Fire Ball as chill as a young woman can get. She brimmed with good health and smiled all the way back to her kiddie rides. I didn't know it, but among her carnival secrets was morning sickness. Another little Peanut special was on its way, having ridden its first Fire Ball before being born.

BORN AND RAISED IN CHICAGO, Boogie was a proud black man running the Eli Wheel on the original midway. Standing high on the launching platform, wearing a flashy, baggy jacket, Boogie controlled the neighborhood crowds lining up below. He held a lofty position and felt it.

Carnies were drawn over to the Eli Wheel to talk to Boogie. There was something about him. I didn't know him well, but I'd talk to him about the carnival. He knew the original Ferris wheel was crazy huge.

He knew Midway Plaisance was the site of the first real midway.

Boogie's presence meant inner-city kids in Chicago grew up knowing something about the city's past.

Midway Plaisance inspired the names of Chicago's major landmarks and gathering places. There's Midway Airport, Midway Airlines, and the Monsters of the Midway, the nickname of the Chicago Bears football team. Restaurants, bars, and churches have midway in their names. We worked for Modern Midways.

Boogie knew the importance of being a wheelman in the tradition of wheelmen on Midway Plaisance.

During a rain break, I told Boogie a cow woke me up the previous night when she poked her head through the van window. He told me cows are part of Chicago's history.

"Remember, a cow is responsible for all the good shit we have around over there," he said, pointing to the Southside of Chicago.

He could have been referring to the legend of Mrs. O'Leary's cow, blamed for knocking over a lamp and starting the 1871 Great Chicago Fire. The city revitalized after the fire and has been doing so ever since.

Boogie was probably talking about the Chicago stockyards, just blocks away in the Back of the Yards neighborhood. At its peak, Chicago's Union Stockyards district was the busiest meat-producing square mile in the world. About 400 million animals were slaughtered on its killing floors every year. It employed forty thousand people. Meatpacking names like Swift and Armour still thrive.

Upton Sinclair's 1906 novel *The Jungle* was partly about the unsanitary conditions in the stockyards. Sinclair felt he had to work seven weeks in the stockyards before writing the book. His scenes about the work conditions and the sanitary practices he witnessed caused such a public outcry Congress passed new food-safety laws.

Sinclair thought he was writing about bigger societal issues, but his immersion into the life of stockyard workers moved people at a gut level. Living the life made writing about the life come to life.

At the head of Midway Plaisance is the grandly named Fountain of Time. The fountain resembles a sandstorm, with a variety of people walking on a march of time. A robed and hooded Father Time stands outside the sandstorm, watching the people pass by.

During the carnival, the reflecting pool in front of the Fountain of Time turned the old, forgotten sculpture into a living piece of art. Young boys took off their shirts, rolled up their pants, and jumped into the pool. Girls and boys played dodge ball, diving into the shallow water to escape the ball. Kids ran from the Fountain of Time to the carnival and back again.

It may be that time and demographics have made Chicagoans different from those who built the world's fair and worked the stockyards. Yet there we were on Midway Plaisance with a Ferris wheel and carousels surrounded by Chicago street kids. And that night the crew of Modern Midways slept with the cows.

In New Jersey, I heard a ghost story that echoed in Chicago.

The New Jersey carnies were talking while setting up the Ferris wheel on the Saint Gabriel church lot. The stories turned to bar fights, crazy prostitutes, and a shooting.

Jason was high up on the Ferris wheel, talking to the rest of us on the ground. He was so covered in axle grease that it looked deliberate. From up above, like a grease monkey with the gift of speech, Jason told the story of a carny named Ghost as if he was telling a joke.

"Ghost got his money and started flashing it around at the bar saying, 'Look what I got,'" Jason said. "Somebody shot him in the shoulder. Nobody's seen him since. Now he's a real ghost. Ha, ha, ha."

Jason felt no sympathy for Ghost. "If you have money," he seemed to say, "of course people will want to take it from you," which also seemed like a basic lesson of carnivals.

On the Gage Park lot one night, I heard someone yell, "Ghost." I didn't see anyone or hear an answer. Before the evening lines formed, I waved Marine Eric over to my Dumbos ride. I asked him if the carny running the balloon game was named Ghost.

"Oh, that's really Bobo the Clown. He the funniest guy here.

Anything he say make you laugh. He walk by you and say something – you laugh. He all kinds of laughs."

Ghost was known as Bobo the Clown when he worked the dunk tank. He was an insult clown, and the crew of Modern Midways admired his wit. Bobo knew the right verbal slap to get people to throw the ball and sink the hated clown. He was outrage in a cage.

Bobo the Clown was his show name, a persona he put on when he worked, which for a carny was almost all the time. Nicknames in traveling carnivals are sticky. They say something about a person, making the real name sound strange. They also can be ongoing insults. I didn't know them personally, but I'm sure Sugar Lips and Dum Dum were plagued by their nicknames.

Nicknames usually refer to a person's worst day. Never stand next to a guy named Sparky. At Butler, Huey wanted to stick me with the nickname High Street because I was foolish enough to wander into danger at the laundromat and get my bicycle stolen.

Ghost's girlfriend was Angel, a quick-witted white woman in her twenties. Angel rolled a souvenir cart around the carnival, selling cheap, loud items. I bought the dolphin necklace for my daughter's birthday from her.

"I wanted to be a veterinarian. Now look at me, right?" Angel said. "I'm going back to get my GED. I'm going to college. I'll major in business so I can open my own joint in a carnival. I'll put in all my own stuff."

Carnival workers like to dream of making it big and coming back to the carnival as an owner. Where were the dreams of hitting it big and never working again? Deep down, many carnival workers didn't want to quit carnival life. They wanted a better carnival life.

Ghost and Angel wore shirts with the Hatchet Man, the logo of the rap group Insane Clown Posse. The t-shirts bear the outline of a wild-haired man running with a butcher knife. Known as ICP, the band's founding myth involves a dark carnival with a ride called the murder-go-round.

Ghost and Angel were talking to each other when I approached them.

"I heard about a Ghost on the East Coast," I said. "Is that you?"

"I don't think so," Ghost said.

"I heard there's another Ghost on the East Coast," Angel said.

Ghost lifted his low-brimmed hat and took a short breath.

"Wait a minute. What did you hear about this Ghost?"

"I heard he was shot in the shoulder," I said.

"Well, I wasn't shot in the shoulder," he said, as if it couldn't be him. "I was shot in the chest."

A while back at a Tennessee carnival, Bobo the Clown was taunting people from the dunk tank when a "hillbilly" took offense. The hillbilly drew his gun and blasted away. I had an image of a clown dodging bullets in the water.

If I'd been there, I might have thought it funny because even frightened insult clowns make people laugh. Right? But Bobo was hit in the chest, which bleeds out fast. The water must have turned bloody. I imagined the ambulance and stretcher. Surgery. Recuperation. No insurance. Nightmares for life.

I wanted to ask both Ghost and Angel more, but they disappeared one night after collecting their pay.

Marine Eric didn't know why they left.

"When people quit carnivals, they don't say where they're going. They just not there the next day."

Bobo disappeared like a Ghost in the night. Ha. Ha. Ha.

~~

DARKO JOINED the carnival with his best friend, Curley. They were twenty-something white guys from the same central Illinois town. They were rural, awkward young men living on the edge. Darko showed me his arm, tattooed to appear bloody and ripped to shreds as if a zombie tore at his flesh. He planned to ink more of his body in the same horrifying way. Darko was turning himself inside out.

While helping us set up along Midway Plaisance, Darko told Shorty his father suffered a heart attack. He wanted to go home to be with his dad. Carnivals don't have sabbaticals. Leaving during a show is a firing offense, and so it was for Darko. He swore to return, but nobody believed him.

Darko was paid and returned to the lot for his clothes and electronics. Stuck at the lot without transportation, he paid Shorty forty dollars to drive him to the Greyhound bus station in Chicago. Darko sat in the station all night, waiting for the next day's bus.

Shorty fired Darko, kicked him out, overcharged him for the ride, and dropped a few choice words on his head. Shorty was a Bronx-born leader of unruly men, and Darko wasn't one of his men.

Sis was the daughter of a renowned carnival boss and a gypsy mother. She spoke fluent Carny, or ciazarn, a secret carnival language.

I've heard it compared to pig Latin. Ciazarn is a language that inserts sounds into words so only carnival people understand. A "mark" might become "meazark."

Sis was trying to teach it to younger carnies, but the only other place I heard it spoken fluently was on YouTube. Rappers use versions of the "izzle" style. Speaking Carny is more of a novelty these days on midways.

A large, black-haired, attractive woman, Sis said the Gage Park lot held special significance for her. She shot her ex-husband four times in the legs there years earlier. She flew into a rage after discovering he was sleeping with her teenage daughter.

Another time, she went into labor while working a Gage Park joint. And her father's carnival wake was held outdoors on the midway just the previous year. She shot a man, went into labor, and memorialized her father along the same midway that rises up every year at 55th Street and Western Avenue.

Sis was pushing a souvenir cart around the carnival. She owned souvenir joints touring at the time in Southern states, but she was back up north for personal reasons she didn't care to share.

She grew up in Chicago and was bright enough to be accepted by Northwestern University in Evanston, Illinois. She was going to be the first in her family to graduate from college. But she loved carnivals, so she dropped out of Northwestern and never looked back.

Sis wasn't the happiest person when I met her, but she was at peace about leaving Northwestern. She associated traveling carnivals with her happy childhood. She didn't quit college so much as return to the only life she'd ever known.

People say carnival workers don't have better options, but the career world didn't fire her imagination. People who love traveling carnivals understand.

MY ANTICS on the Dumbos impressed Robert Briggs and Shorty, so they made me foreman of the Grand Carrousel.

When the word spread, the crew came over to shake my hand. "When you're the boss, you can yell at anybody," one carny said. It's true. Some foremen yelled from sundown to sunup during a slough.

Shorty wanted me to run the biggest carousel for the rest of the season. He started calling me "family."

"You're family now. You're one of us. How many times do I have to tell you that? You're family."

It was the single most moving exchange on the carnival circuit. I didn't expect articulate, kind words from a fiery, hot-tempered tough guy like Shorty. I think it would have shocked his mother. Maybe that's why I was surprised and cynical.

"Until I quit," I said. "Then, I'm nobody."

I said it more than once. I expected fury. Instead, Shorty acted like I was joking. I meant don't make me your favorite, Shorty.

DO YOU KNOW WHO THIS KID'S DAD IS?

PUERTO RICAN FEST, HUMBOLDT PARK

*M*y meteoric rise to the carnival elite came as we set up at Chicago's largest annual carnival, the Puerto Rican Festival in Humboldt Park. As foreman for the Grand Carrousel, I ran an ornate, classic, vintage 1954 carousel. No more Dumbos for me.

We moved more than thirty rides to the 207-acre park. Rides, games, grab wagons and food tents spanned half a mile.

The Chicago newspaperman L. Frank Baum wrote *The Wonderful Wizard of Oz* while living in the Humboldt Park neighborhood. The city put a yellow brick sidewalk outside his apartment building to commemorate the work.

The park is named after Alexander Von Humboldt, the Prussian polymath geographer, naturalist, explorer, philosopher, and most famous scientist of the nineteenth century. Humboldt Park was steeped in history and a new, rich, lively Puerto Rican culture.

When I stepped out onto the Grand Carrousel platform there, I was a proud traveling carnival man. The carousel has thirty wild-eyed horses and two chariots featuring women in Greek robes with harps and cherubs.

"Ladies and gentlemen, you're riding the Grand Carrousel made by the storied Allan Herschell Co. of Tonawanda, New York," I yelled. "Hold on to your horses and ride."

The Puerto Rican People's Parade stepped off on Division Street along a strip known as Paseo Boricua. On both sides of the strip are fifty-nine-foot-tall steel depictions of Puerto Rico's flag. Supporters claim the neighborhood is the capital of Puerto Rican culture in the Midwest. Organizers expected thirty thousand people in four days.

Most people wore their everyday clothes to the fest, but many women wore traditional frilly dresses. Traditional musicians played maracas, bongos, and trumpets. Foods from the best Hispanic restaurants in the city were served on paper plates. Beef on skewers, yellow rice and beans, roast pork, sweet and fried green plantains competed with Modern Midway's sausages and pizzas.

Clothes, hats, and bandanas featured Puerto Rican red, white, and blue flags. The park flooded with people in bright tricolored clothing dancing, singing, and eating. On the surface, the festival seemed wholesome and passionate. Yet it was arguably the most violent festival in Chicago. High gates surrounded the park, and scores of Chicago police racked up overtime working the weekend.

Three people threatened Louisiana Brian, saying they were going home to get their knives to kill him. Uncle Fester saw a woman walk out of a donniker and collapse on the grass. People weren't sure what was wrong at first, but EMTs later said she was stabbed.

A lovely young mother became infuriated with me when I told her to pay extra if she wanted to stand next to her son on the carousel. Her son was the right age and height to ride alone.

"Do you know who this kid's dad is?" she said.

I didn't clearly hear the name of the gang or the kid's father, but the mere mention of the father's name was supposed to terrify me. I knew better than to ask her to pronounce it one more time.

It was clear this was a gangster's woman and their child. I kept my joking mouth shut. Still feeling insulted and furious, she put her boy on the ride and walked behind the perimeter gate.

On the second turn of the carousel, she couldn't help herself. She jumped the fence and ran onto the carousel as it was moving. She slipped and fell onto her stomach, screaming, with one leg on the ride and one leg off. Her son began crying as he rode a horse up and down.

I hit the emergency switch and ran onto the carousel. The carousel was slowing down, but still spinning when I pulled her onto the platform. She jumped up and held her son until the ride came to a stop.

"You see what happened?" she said. "I told you. I told you this would happen."

She vowed to get the boy's father and return for revenge. The day went without further problems, but I heard her threats in my head.

That night in my bunkhouse bed, I dreamt I was hiding behind a carousel horse like Ghost had tried to hide in the dunk tank. Automatic gunfire sprayed the carousel. I ran hiding behind horses. Every time a horse head exploded, I ran behind another horse. I woke before I was gunned down.

Lying in bed, I thought it would have been funny if my last words on this earth were, "On second thought, lady, maybe you should ride with your child." But the dream wasn't funny.

I was credibly threatened with death on a Chicago carousel and a second time in my dreams.

RANDY THE HAT, Robert the Toup, and I drove off the lot to pick up supplies. The topic of the morning was the people who hide out in traveling carnivals.

They'd traveled with a serial killer for a while and only found out about him by watching the news after he left. He'd seemed like a nice guy. They couldn't remember his name.

Another time, a cop pulled over their carnival van and asked to see everyone's identification. A member of their crew turned out to be a member of a billionaire industrial family. The Hat and the Toup wouldn't have known a Du Pont from a Mellon. They didn't remember the carny's real name.

The scion to a family empire quit when the carnival discovered his real identity. He was afraid for his life. He claimed his family might want to kill him for his inheritance.

By the time his mother and a private investigator turned up on the carnival lot in a stretch limousine, the young prince of carnivals had disappeared.

There were more stories, but they all ended the same way. You don't really know anybody in carnivals.

SOMEONE STOLE MY PANTS.

Smalls was furious when I told him about the theft. A carny once stole his clothes too. A handsome, middle-aged Floridian, Smalls was an easygoing carny until you brought up clothes theft.

"Bastards. That's so common. If you find him, let me know who he is. I'll beat the fuck out of him for you."

A beating over old, stinky pants? Not even his pants? I was slightly insulted that he thought I couldn't do my own fighting. I also was surprised that, even for a brief second, I thought I should do my own fighting over a pair of pants. I was thinking like a carny.

In the end, there was no thief. I'd mistakenly left my black jeans in the bug-infested van.

Tempers flare for countless reasons at carnivals. People are too hot or too cold, hungry or thirsty, hungover, or just in pain. Tempers flare brightest when so little means so much.

We all fight for our bit of colored ribbon, for what we want, however trivial or important to us. How strange then is it that people who work with their hands fight with their fists?

WORKERS SAT around in the grass during a slough break at the Puerto Rican Fest. The electrician Sparky was convinced he was working with cultural idiots.

To prove it, he quizzed us on American history. Electricians are considered the smart ones on the crew, so a quiz from the electrician was Carny Jeopardy. Sparky was our furious host.

"Do any of you even know where Sherwood Forest is?"

It wasn't a question. It was an accusation.

The story of Robin Hood is a legend in which a highwayman and his "merry men" live in a forest and rob from the rich and give to the poor. The story dates back so far that it's unclear if any of it was ever true. American movies set the Robin Hood adventures in Sherwood Forest, Nottingham, England.

Our small crew guessed places in both the United States and Continental Europe. People guessed Italy and New York. Every wrong answer made Sparky angrier.

"How is this country going to go anywhere if we don't even know where Robin Hood came from? You don't know your own history."

I held my tongue but couldn't stop myself in the end.

"Nottingham, England?" I said.

"Wrong," Sparky said in triumph. "Virginia. Sherwood Forest is in Virginia."

Sparky stared at us, just shaking his head at the depths of our ignorance.

There is a Sherwood Forest in Virginia but no American version of Robin Hood. Sparky was wrong and may have sensed it from my answer. He tried to recover.

"He might have come from England," he said, "but he was here robbing the rich to help the poor."

These days, America could use a man like Robin Hood, an immigrant robbing the rich and helping the poor like us.

CHICAGO'S INNER-CITY streets were the talk of the sloughs. I heard about girls trading sexual favors for rides. I watched two carnies argue over who knew the most feared gangsters on the West Side. I didn't belong in their crowd, but I worked the sloughs, so I belonged to their carnival tribe.

At the Puerto Rican Fest, I helped tear down the Grand Carrousel, another smaller carousel, a rollercoaster, and several kiddie rides. It was two straight days of work without sleep.

Peanut and I worked together on the Grand Carrousel. He talked freely about his rap sheet, which was longer than the Lincoln Highway.

He spent half the year working for Modern Midways carnival and the other half on unemployment. In Chicago, he was near his children by two mothers. Asia was overjoyed that she was late, too. She couldn't wait to be a mother.

At one point, Peanut was loading the truck trailer, and I was standing on top of the Grand Carrousel pole. I told Peanut I was leaving in the morning. He took a moment. Then he told me I was making a monster mistake.

"You will miss us. We have the best crew. You want to kill them sometimes, but they're the best crew there ever was. You might even miss the cows."

I left the next morning from The 30, but not before Shorty expressed his sense of betrayal.

"I don't get it," he said. "The man offers you a good job, and you just leave it."

I took one last look at the carnival bunkhouses, junkyard rides, and cows. Peanut was right to link our crew with the cows. I did love the Modern Midways crew and even The 30 on sunny mornings. I just didn't know how much I loved it while I was shin-high in bullshit.

MODERN MIDWAYS WITHHOLDS the first week's pay and promises to pay it back when you leave. Many workers quit on impulse without the back pay. Shorty praised the practice, saying it forces people to save money for the end of the season. Without it, most carnies would go home broke.

I waited a week to collect my pay at the jump at a Northside immigrant Polish church. Robert Briggs pulled out a wad of cash and peeled off small bills faster than any ATM.

"I thought you weren't going to pay me," I said.

"Me? I'll work you, but I won't cheat you."

He put my number in his cell phone, saying he might be able to use me again someday.

While waiting for the pay, I took a week off and spent it with Grace. I read her bedtime stories. We walked by the 18th Street beach. We didn't have swimsuits on, so we went swimming in our street clothes. She was the happiest I'd seen her in a long time. Then I kissed her goodbye and vanished.

PART V
CHICAGO TO ALASKA

HITCHHIKING

WRITE ON CARDBOARD - ALASKA

The hobo never knows what is going to happen the next moment; hence, he lives only in the present moment. He has learned the futility of telic endeavor, and knows the delight of drifting along with the whimsicalities of Chance.

— JACK LONDON, THE ROAD

*I*t didn't seem real. Out of the corner of my eye, I saw a little man with a red beard and red hair running across a parking lot. He leaped high to the top of an industrial-sized dumpster and reached inside with the concentration of a fanatic. The Electric Leprechaun was in Chicago, dumpster diving.

I saw a kindred spirit. I knew I could hitchhike with him. The trip to Alaska began at that moment, at the O'Hare Oasis along I-94.

"You want a ride?" he asked. "We're going to Montana."

The Electric Leprechaun led me to Apocalypse Julie and Rainbow Eric, each of them thirty-something from a commune outside Burlington, Vermont. They were bound for the Rainbow Gathering in

Montana's Rocky Mountains. A magic caravan of merry pranksters was making history and heading west.

The Electric Leprechaun was my sponsor. I think Apocalypse Julie and Rainbow Eric saw me as an ancient stranger, an old hitchhiker who might mess with the far-out vibe of the ride. Julie wore a flowered sundress and colorfully tinted sunglasses. She was the car owner, trip planner, and flower-power driver. Rainbow Eric also wore tinted glasses and came off as smart, earnest, and hungry for whatever comes next.

"We're all pretty out there," he said.

I laid on the blarney until I won their unanimous consent to ride along with them. I was riding to Big Sky with a new generation of American hippies. We peeled out of the fast-food oasis, hell-on-wheels in a faded red 1998 Subaru Outback.

A Hawaiian hula doll in a green grass skirt bobbled wildly on the dashboard. Don't worry, green-grass-skirt girl. We're on a rainbow ride to the Rockies.

The Electric Leprechaun began the ride with a restaurant review of the oasis dumpster. A gourmand of garbage, he commented on the food from Sbarro, McDonald's, Panda Express, and Subway. All tasted as expected, but the meatball sandwich with Parmesan "tasted a bit corporate."

Hitchhiking to Alaska is the mother of all hitchhikes in North America. I was headed four thousand miles to the sole traveling carnival in the state, Golden Wheel Amusements. I called Golden Wheel ahead of time but got no promises. I could apply for a job like everyone else when I arrived. Hitchhiking to Alaska with no job guarantee seemed like madness to everyone I knew, both inside and outside carnivals.

In California, I wanted to work traveling carnivals from the Pacific to the Atlantic. In Chicago, it occurred to me that I should also crisscross the country north to south. I aimed to hitchhike to the heart of Canada's oil and gas country, the so-called Patch in Alberta and British Columbia. Then north on the entire 2,700 miles of the Alaska-Canadian Highway from Dawson Creek, British Columbia, to Delta

Junction, Alaska.

Ahead lay North America's highest mountains, meanest grizzlies, and the traveling carnivals of the frontier.

~⌒

DRIVING INTO THE SETTING SUN, my new friends told me about their pink polka-dot commune house. The Electric Leprechaun said their motto was, "Cut consumption, not foreskin." About a dozen people at their commune eked out their living there. Some fixed bikes and sold them. Their mascot was a tattered cat named Fan Belt, named after a fan-belt accident.

Their car's name was Carina-Carina. It wasn't supposed to be Ken Kesey's Magic Bus, but my hosts shared a "merry prankster" DNA. They called themselves hippies and lived solidly inside a counterculture still alive in America.

Rainbow Gatherings attract tens of thousands of people from around the world focused on peace, love, and harmony. They're anticapitalism, consumerism, dirty energy, mass media, and popular culture. They are pro-people like Julie.

Julie earned her apocalyptic nickname from volunteering for two years in post-Katrina New Orleans, much of the time as a FEMA mechanic. She'd spent about a decade of her thirty-one years on the road following Rainbows.

She was unemployed at the time but showed me a stack of business cards promoting herself as a pet taxidermist, hairdresser, underwater investigator, licensed private investigator, licensed motorcycle courier, gymnastics coach, home douche provider, mechanic, zipper fixer, and more. She apologized for all the cards.

"I probably have a short attention span," she said.

Her worst career choice was setting up a hair salon under a tree at the Rainbow Festival. Hippies don't like haircuts, she discovered.

We drove for long stretches, stopping only for gas, dumpster diving, and hippie-dippy humor. In a hardware-store parking lot in

Sparta, Wisconsin, the four of us rushed across the lot to form a circle in the center.

"Insanity workout," Eric yelled. "Insanity workout. Insanity. If you're not insane before the workout, you will be after."

The Electric Leprechaun knew his cue. He touched his nose. We touched our noses. He touched his toes. We touched our toes. He sat in the parking lot. We did, too. "Meditate," he said. We sat in lotus positions as commuters drove home from work.

Then Electric Leprechaun stood up and walked away with a blank expression on his face. What did it all mean? Nothing. It was just insane. The normies drove past gawking at the roadside spectacle. It all made sense to us.

WE STAYED the night in Great Bluffs State Park overlooking the Mississippi River, telling stories around the campfire before going to bed in our tents.

The Electric Leprechaun's first dumpster dive was an epiphany. He was in his early teens when he found high-end stereo speakers. Ever since that day, he's been on a never-ending trashy treasure hunt.

He never bought a morsel. He dashed off to dumpsters at rest stops and gas stations along the way. He came back sharing broccoli, cauliflower, donuts, cookies, pork sandwiches, and dried-out pizza slices. The rest of us joined in on some late-night dumpster runs.

Among his many exploits was panning for gold in Alaska. He took thousands of dollars of gold out of the rivers. He wasn't sure. The Electric Leprechaun's pot of gold financed a trip to Hawaii.

RAINBOW ERIC OBJECTED to being called a hippie until Julie chided him.

"Don't betray your people," she said. "If you're not a hippie, then everything I know about you is wrong."

Eric liked Julie, so he recanted. Hippie or no hippie, he was a lover.

Wearing a t-shirt made of hemp, he told us about having written the perfect reggae song. It's so good nobody has been able to sing it.

"I can't sing it. It's too good. It's in a pitch I can't reach. I don't know where it came from, but it just came to me. It's really good though."

Then he smiled and said in a singsong voice, "Yaaa."

Julie was right. He probably was a hippie.

We crossed Wisconsin, Minnesota, South Dakota, and Wyoming on our way to Montana. Julie turned the driving over to me much of the way. I was in hippie heaven listening to their stories and looking out the window. Suddenly, out of nowhere, a singing competition began. Julie and the Electric Leprechaun each sang verses to the Broadway song *Tomorrow* from the musical *Annie*. Then I belted out the final line.

> *Tomorrow, tomorrow I love ya tomorrow*
> *You're always a daaay, aaaawaaaaaaaay!*

That shut those hippies up. They didn't know they were dealing with the singing hitchhiker.

They were counterculturists who didn't know what they wanted, but they wanted more than rivers and mountains flashing past on a cross-country road trip. More than anything ordinary, they wanted something too deep and powerful for words. Like Rainbow Eric's song, they wanted something too beautiful to be sung. They wanted more.

Goodbyes were made at a McDonald's in Butte, Montana, and then we hugged.

"You're our friend now," Eric said, "You're one of us."

After 1,500 miles riding with the young idealists, I stood and watched them head off without me to a rainbow Shangri-La in Big Sky. They beat it out of town, melting into their dream-soaked mountains. I walked out to the on-ramp and flew the sign, "**ALASKA**."

UGLY, Apache, and their pit bull Molly the Dog walked up the long I-15 on-ramp toward me. The pit bull was by far the cleanest. They carried Slurpee and Pepsi cups filled with Johnny-jump-up and all kinds of trouble. Ugly and Apache achieved their sticky, dust-of-ages filth from freight trains. I remembered the look from my own time riding freight trains in the 1980s. It comes from boxcar floors, oil-covered trackside patches, and airborne freight-train soot.

As they walked toward me, I braced for violence. It might start with a friendly greeting. Then a second later, a comment or a misunderstanding could touch off holy hell and a pit bull. Once again, I vowed to watch my jokey mouth. They introduced themselves. Then mid-sentence, we each instinctually ducked.

Woooooosh.

A half dozen fast-food bags flew by our heads. A car filled with teenagers drove away, cursing at us. Ugly and Apache were out-of-their minds angry, but I think Apache was too snabble-d-dabbled to run. Ugly and Molly the Dog ran, but Ugly ran at a bit of an angle. He too was snoozamarooed. A filthy rainbow of profanity came from Ugly as he ran after the car. It wasn't for show. He genuinely wanted a pit-bull-versus-assholes showdown.

Kids throw debris at hobos, hitchhikers, and bicyclists. It's practically a time-honored juvenile tradition. The hobo term for it is "getting rocked."

Ugly and Apache weren't the lovable tramps in movies. They were on a years-long loop of brutal freight yards and wandering. Walking back to Apache and me, Ugly identified himself as a hobo. I told them I once went to the National Hobo Convention.

"In Britt, Iowa?" both men asked at the same time.

Pressing my luck, I asked them if they go town-to-town across the country until the money runs out, getting waa-zzoo wholloped on tub-thumping gargle wash, or words to that effect.

"Pretty much," Ugly said.

Blond, with defined arms, Apache was stinkoparalytico. Tall and road strong, Ugly was stinkoprofundo. Both young men were thin from hard travel and the liquid diet.

Apache yelled at me. He was angry that I didn't praise them as the stars of the open road.

"Carnivals ain't shit compared to what we live every day."

Hopping freight trains is a subculture of its own. They knew everyone who rode the rails. They met each other in hobo jungles, sharing a brotherhood of sorts.

"Are you a cop?" Apache asked.

Pointing at my backpack, Apache then accused me of being a thief.

"Is that Jack's backpack?" Apache asked.

Ugly turned to Apache, letting it rip with a full-throttle tirade.

"Shut the fuck up, Apache, You're fucking drunk. I'm taking your fucking drink. I will punch you in the fucking face. We're trying to have a conversation. He's asking how we make money every day. That's not Jack's backpack. He's not a cop. We just walked up to him hitchhiking on the road. That's why they call you Apache. You're Irish, but you have the tolerance of a mosquito."

Ugly was crazy angry at Apache for being more snoozled than him. I tried to relate to their wandering, but Apache took another sip of disdain and spat it back.

"You're what we call a Summer Bunny," Apache said.

Ugly took Apache's bug juice and poured it into his own.

"I am this close to punching you in the face," he said to Apache.

Each time Ugly yelled at Apache, it was a verbal version of unleashing the hounds. Apache gave me a what-else-do-you-want-to-know look. He once was a "professional." He didn't have to be homeless and wandering. He worked for more than a year on the film crew of the movie, *The Avengers* during filming in Prague.

Ugly let me know he hated the square life and loved the life he was living.

"We do this to see the country. I don't need to do this. I have a profession. I'm a stage rigger. I build concert stages. I'm not a roadie. A roadie moves shit and screws in shit. A rigger anchors the lighting and climbs and dangles himself on little beams."

Neither Ugly nor Apache wanted jobs anymore. They wanted to ride the rails, hitchhike, and see America. Family life held Ugly back for years.

"I didn't tour with any bands. I had kids. I was in their life. I still have kids. But . . . Apache, you are so fucking drunk. We're going now."

"In my experience," I said, "hitchhiking between train rides is fun when tipsy or high."

"Not when nobody's picking you up, only when you get a ride," Ugly said. "This asshole will pass out walking half a mile down the road."

They believed hitchhiking and living on the rails was heroic. No subjugation. No conformity. No money. No cares. Liberation. Rebellion. Freedom. Escape. Then repeat. They were not so much broke as going for broke. Many of those same words came from Lone Wolf, Don and Sancho, and Ru and Bear. Ugly and Apache lived by their own road rules.

"We aren't stabbing anybody," Ugly said. "That's not right. But if they fuck with us, we'll stab them. Oh, ya. We'll fucking stab you if you fucking take our shit or something."

Whoooooosh.

A full can of soda flew by our heads.

"Get a job," a teen yelled from a car full of his friends.

Ugly and Molly the Dog took off running again. Ugly kept yelling at the car as it drove out of earshot.

"That's what turns us into stabbing hobos," Ugly said. "Come here and say that to me, you assholes. You don't know me. I could make more than you in a day. That is so fucked, just because we chose to live the life we chose."

Life on the road, they said, was still giving them more thrills than ordinary life. The straight life was slow death to them. They were choosing life and living their dream.

The two men turned and walked back down the onramp toward town. They sat by a single leafless tree in the distance.

Hours past. The interstate was quiet. The tangerine sun dipped down over the horizon, bathing the mountains in sunset hues. When the breeze shifted, two men swearing echoed up the on-ramp toward a hitchhiker and across the Continental Divide.

OVER THE ROCKY Mountains and into the Flathead National Forest, drivers took me along creeks named Bison, Beaverton, and Prickly Pear. We drove alongside the Missouri River past people hiking, fishing, and boating. A glorious Big Sky sun was lighting up the rivers, creeks, and the mountains. I was lost in an epic Western spell.

The retired head of the FBI for the northwest territory told thrilling stories of outsmarting the outlaws. The West makes legends of its lawmen like him.

A retired naval nuclear engineer talked about operating a nuclear control panel in his active-duty days. He knew the secret nuclear launch codes. Those were dangerous and bawdy days in ports around the world, but they made him world-weary. He'd needed to settle down somewhere far from the sea, so he settled in Montana.

The old sailor quoted advice given to the legendary Greek sailor Odysseus.

"I needed to go 'where there are men living who know nothing of the sea,' and 'never saw an oar,'" he said. "It's from *The Odyssey*. Look it up."

A Homer-quoting Navy nuclear engineer in the middle of Montana. The stories were just starting. I didn't want to get out of the car.

A WHITE PICKUP truck hauling a horse trailer pulled to the side of the road to pick me up near Shelby. Rancher Everett Morton was hauling Red Dog, his prize quarter horse. Everett, sixty-ish, owned 1,800 acres of land and one hundred head of cattle. He said he rode bulls for twelve years before his body broke down. He was riding in about twenty-five senior rodeos a year when I met him. A real rancher and prize bull rider, he was the stuff of Hollywood westerns and Frederic Remington paintings.

He saw another rodeo rider as he dropped me off at the last gas station before the Canadian border. He introduced me to the Canadian rancher and vouched for me.

"This guy tells the greatest stories," he said. "It'll be fun."

The other rancher and his wife felt pressured to take me. They were too Canadian-nice to leave me there, but only barely. They were hauling their own rodeo horse. They didn't like the situation one bit, and I didn't blame them.

Sweet Grass station is usually a low-traffic border crossing, but Canadian Independence Day weekend made it a small madhouse. The guard at the border-station booth seemed ready to wave us on through, but he asked one last question.

"How do you know each other?"

The Canadian rancher wasn't about to let me turn him into a human trafficker.

"We're Canadian," he said, "but we never met this guy in our life."

"You're kidding, right?" the guard asked.

"No, it's true. We picked him up at the gas station back there. He's a hitchhiker. We don't know him at all."

The guard must have hit an alarm button under the desk. Guards came out of the main building and kept an eye on me for five hours. The rancher and his wife waited for me to clear customs. If the ranching couple left me behind, the guards might not have allowed me into Canada.

The guards X-rayed my backpack and questioned me in an isolation room. I told them I was a writer with a blog about carnivals. They asked to examine my laptop. A guard later came out of the back room and handed back my computer.

We were allowed to go but not before the guard commented on our ordeal at the border.

"I liked your blog," he said. "I think I'll follow you."

My INTRODUCTION to Canada's universal health care system came when Westley drove up in his White Chevy Blazer on the outskirts of Calgary. A tool and die maker, Westley began talking about himself with the zeal of a new convert.

He'd suffered two heart attacks. They scared him enough to undertake "cognitive restructuring." His new diet consisted of small portions of food, including beans in emptied Gerber bottles. He began running barefoot marathons. In his sixties, he was proud to say his girlfriend was thirty-three years old.

We talked about his diabetes as he chain-smoked Pall Malls and drank tall cups of caffeinated coffee. Instead of driving me north, he drove to a free health clinic on a Sunday morning. A line formed outside the front door. I couldn't believe my eyes. Doctors were working on a Sunday.

While waiting, Westley railed against the lack of universal health care in America.

"We have similar cultures, but we don't let our people suffer like that."

Westley spoke to his doctor for a while, received his medicine, and went back to Pall Malls and high-octane coffee. We talked about the recent flooding in Alberta. Men were volunteering for flood rescues and sandbag relays across the province.

Perfect. The Calgary Stampede was starting in a couple of days. The flood would dry up the labor pool. They'd need me.

The Calgary Stampede is ten days of rodeos, parades, concerts, exhibitions, and carnival rides. Calling itself *The Greatest Outdoor Show on Earth*, it draws ten million people or more every year. Westley dropped me off near the lot, and I walked past security onto the fairgrounds as if I'd done this a million times.

Up walked a tall, bulky South African with his shirt sleeves rolled above his biceps. His yellow hard hat was cocked to the right side. After a few questions, he brought me to the office trailer for work papers. I tried to hide my lack of a work visa, but the office turned me down.

As I walked off the lot, I took pictures of the rides. Managers grew suspicious. The head of North American Midway Entertainment (NAME) in Canada drove up in a golf cart. I never caught his name.

I told him I was hitchhiking up to Alaska to work at Golden Wheel, but I could spare three days to set up rides. I wanted to work for cash and be on my way. The front office turned me down because I'm American.

He sat in his golf cart thinking about ways to get around the law. He gave up. But he knew the woman who founded Golden Wheel.

"Say hello to Claire Morton for me," he said. "She's a great woman."

I STOOD beside the road and watched one of the biggest boom times in history. The Patch at the time contained a third of the world's natural oil reserves. Alberta and British Columbia were rich in gold, diamonds, tar sands, oil shale, lumber, and other resources. It's back-country work until it makes its way to the highway.

I watched rigs with thirty wheels hauling logs, oil, gas, water, drills, pipes, cranes, engines, and generators all roll by in a boom-time parade.

My first two rides out of Calgary came from men employed in work camps. A diamond miner and a tar-sands worker both lived in luxurious modular trailers with free food, a gym, and a pool. Both said they couldn't turn down the money, but the isolation from loved ones was a high price to pay. A twenty-four-year-old mechanic told me he made forty dollars an hour. He didn't have a wife or family, but he was investing in mini-mansions on vast plots of land.

When I told drivers that I was hitchhiking to traveling carnivals, they told their own stories of hitchhiking and carnivals. A mining trucker named John talked about his cousin who hitchhiked around Canada blind. His blind hitchhiking cousin was infamous in family lore for getting swizzled and picking bar fights with his cane.

A bulked-up, oil-patch trucker named Aaron said Charles Dickens set some of his books in his hometown of Gravesend, England. Dickens should have written about traveling carnivals, he said, and turned the Artful Dodger into a fast-talking jointee.

A BUTTERFLY FLEW past me on the road to Pink Mountain. That part of Canada has dozens of butterfly species. I saw them, but I couldn't identify them. Matthew the Lepidopterist said butterflies can see ultraviolet light. Some butterflies' eyes have five times more color receptors than human eyes. Think of what a butterfly sees flying down the center of the midway. Jointees say it's bad luck to shoo away a butterfly.

Not a single vehicle passed me for hours. I was still lost in daydreams when a kaleidoscope of butterflies surrounded me beside the road. For a fleeting moment along the deserted Alcan highway, I stood in a butterfly glitter globe.

Moments later, Leonard Nietupski stopped in his old pickup truck next to me and told me to hop in. Part-myth, part-legend around Pink Mountain, he drove down the road a while before veering off onto an unmarked dirt road into the woods. This might be a convenient place to murder me. Beautiful day for it.

Leonard promised the woods hid something I must see to believe. A hidden castle? A gold mine? The road widened into a clearing with a 1979 yellow school bus, with an adjacent white tarp tent. A one-eyed black Belgian Shepherd mix named Zena came leaping and hopping out of the bushes to greet us. A cat named Casper prowled behind.

Leonard, sixty-three, and wife Stephanie, thirty-four, began living in the bus around 2003. The bus cost him one thousand dollars. He gutted the bus, leaving the driver's seat and one original seat row. The couple built or installed the rest. It was tricked out with a bed, kitchen, sink, dinner table, propane oven, refrigerator, and an iron wood-burning stove with a chimney protruding from the bus roof. They owned no cell phones, television, or computer.

"The stove works great," he said. "It can be fifty-two below zero outside and we'll have to open windows and doors to cool down."

They spent most of their time outdoors. Their living room was the area around the bus.

"We get all sorts of wildlife walking through our living room, including moose, deer, elk, bear, bobcats, and lynx."

There was a separate woodworking shop at the back of the bus with saws and tools. For hard currency, Leonard made jewelry boxes. Stephanie worked at a convenience store in Pink Mountain. Their expenses were small. They lived on about $750 a month, most of which went to buy gas for the bus and generator.

Leonard hunted in the mountains for big game that he later skinned and grilled on the open pit next to the bus. They lived on raspberries, strawberries, gooseberries, and loganberries. Living off the land and bartering was their way of life.

"If I have to pay for it in cash, I don't need it. I don't want it. When you barter and trade, you don't use cash, so there are no taxes. When the government says you have to pay taxes on that, I can say, 'Kiss my ass, I traded for that.'"

Leonard was once a dairy farmer, but he'd wanted to live on a bus since grade school. The bus still worked. They intended to change location someday and move farther back off the grid. I helped him change a tire, and he returned the favor with some hermit advice. I should live like him. Writers don't make much money. He recommended I buy a bus and write from the road.

"It's the cheapest way of living you can find. If you don't care for too many people around you, this is the way to live because you'll be left alone. That's what I like about it. It's peaceful. Tranquil."

Leonard dropped me off at the next brake-check turnoff. He peeled away, kicking up mountain gravel and dirt. Out from behind a curtain of dust, bouncing by on an updraft came another unknowable butterfly.

THE NEXT RIDE was Fast Eddie, a full-blooded Cree carny who in his youth was quick with his fists and handy with the ladies. Driving up in an old station wagon packed with bags, Fast Eddie was seventy years old and in frail health. We were headed 250 miles to Fort Nelson, but I had to earn my way. I helped him rummage through the trash for cans and bottles at eight stops. He made about thirty dollars in recyclables on our ride.

Fast Eddie was his name back when he worked for British Columbia's West Coast Carnivals.

"They named me that because they said, 'You can knock a guy down, and we don't even see you hitting him.' I hit a guy so hard one time, his tooth stuck in my knuckle."

Did you give the tooth back to him?

"No, I just pulled the tooth out of my knuckle and threw it away."

Fast Eddie was on a fixed income and was financing his trip by picking up recyclables in roadside trash cans and dumpsters. Wearing a blue flannel shirt open down across his chest, he wore gardening gloves while sifting for bottles and cans.

He spent a half-dozen years on the carnival circuit, traveling throughout the Northwest Territories and eastward. He was part of a group of Cree carnies who stuck together on the road. Conditions were raw. He slept under rides, inside vans, and outside on the ground. He used a bucket of water to clean himself up in the morning.

"I partied all night and came staggering out the next day."

If there was a fight with the townies, "everybody looked out for each other." He knew not to go into town because the cops used any excuse to throw them in jail. If anybody went to jail, the owners usually left them there. Only the top hands were bailed out.

Fast Eddie rose from running a kiddy ride to being the boss of all kiddyland. There he met plenty of young, single mothers.

How did you get them alone if you were sleeping under a ride?

"The girls, if they liked you, they'd drop the kids off and come back after. We'd go under the truck or into the bushes."

A few local girls traveled back to Fast Eddie's hometown in Fort Nelson in the off-season, but it never worked out. Fast Eddie "barely had money for the bus home at the end" of the season, much less bus fare for the girls. When the relationships didn't work out, the women were forced to find their own way home.

I noticed a heart-shaped two-sided tag hanging from his rearview mirror. It read "Party with Sluts" on one side and "Big Booty Bitches" on the other.

Fast Eddie painted a nightmarish picture of his childhood.

"My dad was an out-of-work alcoholic. There were twelve of us kids. When I was growing up, I never had much fun at all because of my drunken dad. I never learned to be young."

Fast Eddie dropped out of school when he was in fourth grade. On his recent driver's license exam, he needed someone to read the questions to him because he couldn't read or write. After carnivals, he began mining on the Patch. He worked as a gold miner, a trucker, a heavy equipment operator, and a firefighter.

His drinking worsened after his carnival days. He didn't have to go to any counselor to quit drinking. All he needed to hear were his daughter's heartbreaking words of almost thirty years earlier.

"Daddy quit drinking. I want to come home."

He quit, and she came back to live with him. He held back tears as he spoke. The thought of those words still made him sick.

Addictions haunted his family. Several of his grandchildren were in foster care, living their own childhood traumas.

Yet in Fast Eddie's story bag of ups and downs was the carnival of his youth. A Cree man who grew up in an unhappy place was appointed the king of kiddyland, the happiest place in carnivals for kids.

ON THE FAR WESTERN edge of Fort Nelson was a giant pig-iron welcome sign in the shape of a grizzly bear.

"Welcome to Resource Full Fort Nelson," it said on the front.

On the backside, someone wrote graffiti in white chalk.

"Hitchhikers Are Bear Food."

I stood hitchhiking across from the sign, alone at the top of a long hill outside town. Viewed from a distance, I imagined, I looked like a scarecrow dressed in black and quietly singing to himself. It was the Fourth of July weekend. Daylight lasted until about midnight. The sun was gone, but it was just darkish. It came back around 3 a.m. I squeezed in every bit of sunlight to hitchhike.

Thinking it might rain overnight, I slept for a few short hours in an old baseball field scorer's box. Giant mosquitoes buzzed around my head, making the scorer's box sound like a beehive. If a bear wandered into that scorer's box in search of garbage, I'd have been man tartare.

Smokestacks and energy plants dotted the outskirts of Fort Nelson, an industrial patch surrounded by pristine rivers, mountains, and provincial parks. I was on the northern edge of the Rocky Mountains and the Patch.

On the third day of being skunked, I approached drivers with American license plates at the tourist center. The aggressive plan worked, and I landed a ride with Robert "Shacky" Shackelford and his girlfriend Vanessa Runs.

We headed through the northern Rocky Mountains and Muncho Lake provincial parks, past the Muskwa, Toad, Liard, Coal, and Hyland rivers toward Watson Lake. We saw bears, bison, goats, and sheep. We cruised by snow-capped mountains and rivers made high by recent downpours. Shacky drove, and Vanessa made snacks while talking about living their dream life.

Their nomadic magic carpet was a twenty-two-foot Winnebago Realta camper with solar panels on the roof and an Aloha Hawaii, four-inch, green-skirted bobble doll on the dash.

Vanessa was a thirty-one-year-old Canadian health editor, blogger, and author before she hit the road with Shacky. He was a forty-three-year-old former Navy petty officer and electrical engineer for a San Diego DNA firm.

They shut off the lights, gave the house to the bank, and beat it out of town in their van. They were both bloggers and ultra-marathon trail runners. Vanessa was the author of a self-published bestseller, *Summit Seeker*, which started as a popular blog.

They believed earnings from Vanessa's blog and e-books could keep them perpetually driving around the world. If all else failed, they could live another two years on savings alone. They were always on the lookout for ultra-marathon races and willing driving long distances to get to them.

Shacky foresaw endless travel ahead.

"I want to be on the road for the rest of my life. There's a lot to see still."

As for hitchhikers, Vanessa later wrote this on her blog:

"Every hitchhiker we pick up confirms my suspicion that strangers are inherently awesome, trustworthy, and good human beings . . . dangerous men are more of a minority than we believe."

We drove 320 miles on our seven-hour trip to Watson Lake in the Yukon Territory. The small town is known for its Sign Post Forest. Carl K. Lindley started the "forest" when he worked on the Alaska Highway in 1942. He put up a signpost pointing to his hometown, Danville, Illinois.

Travelers have joined in on the fun ever since. There are an estimated seventy-six thousand signs in the town center. The Sign Post Forest was thick with messages, each with a similar theme. Home is far from here.

Vanessa and Shacky drove into a parking lot and pulled the shades down to sleep. They didn't need a Watson Lake road sign. Their van was their home. It was still light, so I stood across the street from their camper and thought of the two runners inside, so sure of great adventures ahead and so surely in love.

UP DROVE A BRAND-NEW, white twenty-two-wheel Mack Pinnacle truck with a polished silver bulldog on the hood. The driver poked his head out the window and asked if I could keep him awake all the way to Whitehorse, 270 miles and six hours away.

The real answer was no. I couldn't stay awake for another marathon Alaskan night.

"Why else would you ever pick up a hitchhiker," I asked instead, "in the middle of a sunny night?"

After two days and nights stuck in Fort Nelson, I was putting together a six-hundred-mile hitchhiking day. Riding high in a powerful new Mack truck out of Watson Lake, I launched into my best hitchhiking stories. Ray taught me a bit of Newfie and how treacherous Yukon roads were in winter. We squared off in a joke-telling contest that veered into the X-rated. Naughty carny.

We drove through Canada's Yukon Territory in its midnight light past mountains, glaciers, ice fields, tundra, and boreal forests. I imagined the forest teeming with arctic foxes, snowy owls, lynxes, bison, grizzlies, wolves, and bald eagles. Its human population was a mere thirty-six thousand. The Yukon is geographically larger than the combined countries of Belgium, Denmark, Germany, and the Netherlands.

"I never miss a hitchhiker. But just one at a time. I only have one seat. I picked up some real down-and-outers. I'd reach into my pocket and give them twenty dollars to buy them a meal. But there are all those bears and bobcats out there. I don't know how you have the courage to hitchhike."

"It's easy," I said. "Ignorance."

Ray was born to a big family in Stephenville, a former farming and fishing village on the west coast of Newfoundland. He was seven years old when his father fell thirty-five feet to his death in the local limestone quarry. The family fell into poverty. He went off to join the Army, spending seventeen years in Cyprus and Germany.

Divorced from his first wife, he had a longtime girlfriend who was the great, great, great-granddaughter of Sitting Bull. He loved her Indian warrior lineage and went to powwows with her.

There's a compliment among truck drivers, "He's driven more

miles backward than some drivers have driven forward." Ray's best guess was that he drove 275,000 miles a year.

I asked him about his most sublime moments as a trucker.

"Sometimes you come to up from a valley through a cloud," he said, "and come out at the top of the hill above the clouds like an airplane."

As we drew close to the town of Whitehorse, my eyes were open but I was in a dream state, babbling. Ray grew angry. The deal was that I keep him awake. When I stepped down from the cab in White-horse, I said goodbye and thanks. Ray did not reply and drove away.

PAT PICKED me up on the outskirts of Whitehorse in his utility van on his way to work laying sewer and water lines. I called him my tour guide because of his encyclopedic knowledge of his town.

Whitehorse is named after the White Horse Rapids on the Yukon River flowing through town. The rapids were compared to the manes of charging white horses. It lays claim to the cleanest air of any city in the world and one of the best places to view the aurora borealis.

Pat was an outdoorsman and a good one. He'd won money and prizes at the Kluane Lake Fishing Derby.

"The water is fresh and clean, coming off a glacier somewhere . . . I take pictures of the scenery and wildlife. There are eagles everywhere and ducks and cranes."

When the subject turned to carnivals, he prided himself on being one of those ringers jointees hate to see coming. He waited every year for the carnival to come to town.

"I like winning prizes for the people I'm with. I like beating the system. I like winning the big bear."

FOR SEVEN HOURS, I stood watching the Saint Elias Mountains at the edge of Haines Junction until up ahead drove a red Hyundai Accent.

An attractive, brown-haired woman with a Québécois accent leaned her head out the car window.

"I'm sorry I can't pick you up. I'm coming home from work," she said, pointing down a dirt road. "That is my house."

She asked me a couple of questions until I realized she was skipping a breath. She was rambling. I made her nervous. Chicago writer Saul Bellow once wrote that telling a woman you're a writer is an aphrodisiac.

"I'm a writer," I said.

I told her about the carnivals, hitchhiking, blogs, and my past as a handsome, international journalist. I was shameless.

"Maybe I'll see you later," she said, "when I walk my dog."

She drove down the driveway to her new Alpine-style pine home. I stood at the front of the driveway, pretending to hitchhike. But never did a hitchhiker want a ride less. I kept turning my head to see her through the tall front windows.

Haines Junction faces the Saint Elias Mountains, the highest coastal mountain range on Earth. It contains the top five highest peaks in Canada, and Mount Saint Elias is the second-highest in America after Mount Denali in Alaska.

Fifteen minutes later, she walked down the dirt driveway toward me.

"I have extra food around the house."

Putting my hand on her back, I thanked her. We walked back to the house together. Her home was an art gallery of her bright watercolor paintings. First and foremost, she considered herself an artist. One portrait was of windblown flowers and watercolor butterflies.

Her kitchen table was fully set. While I was outside hoping to be invisible to every passing car, she must have spent the entire time racing around changing clothes, making salads, and cooking meats.

I felt like a bedraggled guttersnipe. I asked to shower before eating. Months on the road and thirty-hour workdays slinging iron whipped me into the best shape since my twenties.

After the shower, I put on a pair of clean jeans. Still wet and bare-chested, I walked out of the bathroom to get a clean shirt from my pack. She stopped cooking to watch from the kitchen.

Our meal began with fingerbowls of fish, onions, and black olives. Fresh salads followed with hamburgers from the grill. She talked about being an outpost nurse in town. Outpost nurses in Canada are all the doctor most people get in the outback. They handle births, injuries, and sicknesses. Patients in need of complicated surgery are evacuated to Whitehorse.

Outpost nurses often serve an aboriginal population, the term used in Canada for indigenous people. Haines Junction is an administrative center for the Champagne and Aishihik First Nations. Fewer than six hundred people lived in town.

After her husband left her for one of her best friends, she became an outpost nurse. She was so devastated by the divorce she moved away to the Yukon. She lived at first in a cabin by herself in the bush. Her new home was part of her comeback. She felt life restarting.

Her Shih Tzu, Angel, stood watch at the front window. Buddha owned a Shih Tzu who once shape-shifted into a lion to scare away robbers. Siddhartha brought his Shih Tzu on all his travels.

I stood next to Angel, looking out the window at the snow-capped mountains of summer. At any second the aurora borealis might roar and wave across the sky above the Saint Elias Mountains. The outpost nurse and her Angel had a front-row seats to the greatest show on earth.

Growing up in a French-speaking household in the small town of Wellington, Ontario, she had a happy childhood. Her life stories mixed with French expressions sounding sweet to me.

In the background, Nina Simone sang *My Baby Just Cares About Me*. Billie Holiday begged *Lover Come Back to Me*.

I stopped her from talking in circles.

"I think you're attracted to me," I said.

Before she could say yes or no, I leaned across the table for the first kiss. Soon we were turning her home into the bounce house of the Yukon.

When I came downstairs the next morning, the kitchen table was set with fried eggs, bacon, and coffee. The outpost nurse was a healer. I worried she might regret sleeping with a hitchhiker. Then I remembered I'm not really a hitchhiker. I'm really a writer. Thanks, Saul Bellow.

"I like your bandana," she said, "and your dimple."

She asked about my height. She was still flirting.

Angel and I peered out the front window. I asked how to sneak away from the house without sparking small-town gossip.

With full knowledge I would write about our night, she shrugged.

"I don't care who knows," she said.

We kissed goodbye. I praised her gutsy choice in lovers.

The hitchhiking was no better that morning. I was still there when she returned from lunch with her girlfriends. She drove toward me fast, sliding the car to a stop close to my feet. The tires spit gravel and dust up around me.

"Hop in. I bought you a cookie. I'll drive you to Destruction Bay."

She was dog-sitting for a girlfriend. I sat in the front while Angel and a German Shepherd sat in the back. The outpost nurse and her merry band hurtled down the Alaska Highway toward Kluane National Park and Reserve. We pulled over to the rocky shore of Kluane Lake, the biggest lake in the Yukon.

Walking together along the shore, we threw branches out into the turquoise-colored glacier lake. The German Shepherd jumped into fetch. Angel wanted to do the same but waded in only a few inches before the freezing glacial water turned her back.

A young boy came by playing with his dog. He was on vacation with his grandparents in their RV. I noticed their RV brand name was the Hitchhiker, but they drove past me earlier in the day. The boy said his grandparents wanted to stop for me, but the little stinker talked them out of it.

"I said the border is ahead," he said, half laughing. "He'll be too much trouble."

"You made a big mistake then because he's a great storyteller and a writer," my outpost artist said, "you made a real mistake."

We gathered up the dogs and drove to Destruction Bay, a town with little more than a hotel, small shop, and restaurant/bar.

Destruction Bay, population thirty-five, was named by the U.S. Army Corps of Engineers building the Alaska Highway because the high winds off Kluane Lake blew down their tents.

I exited the car and looked around at Kluane Lake and the Saint Elias Mountains. The outpost nurse rolled down her window, and I leaned in for a final kiss. She drove away, leaving me alone in Destruction Bay with a giant chocolate chip cookie in my hand.

When a friend of mine learned she was dying of amyotrophic lateral sclerosis (ALS), she came to this area to see the aurora borealis before she died. Local Eskimo tribes believed they could summon the northern lights to talk to the spirits of the dead.

Susan Spencer-Wendel never saw the lights before she died. She wrote beautifully about her trip up to this area in her book *Until I Say Good-Bye: My Year of Living with Joy.* I wish I could have summoned her spirit. What a profound place if you wish it.

My own private Yukon was a hedonistic, gastronomic, scenic place. Dog-friendly too. Ack. I ate a giant cookie.

IN THE PARKING lot of Destruction Bay's only restaurant, I saw Alaska plates as big as billboards. Gene was walking out of the Talbot Arms Motel restaurant toward those Alaska plates when I waylaid him. He was as reluctant as a Canadian rodeo bronc. I would not let him go. I could be stuck at the border for days. Gene gave in, and we easily crossed the border back to the United States.

He was sure we'd have nothing to talk about because he was boring. He was just a sixty-three-year-old, third-grade schoolteacher on his way home to Fort Yukon in the Arctic Circle.

Most of the six hundred people up there are Gwich'in people. The chief employer is the government. Essential foods are flown in, making milk fifteen dollars a gallon. Japanese couples visit Fort Yukon believing the northern lights help fertility.

Since leaving the Navy in his twenties, Gene made a career of teaching on reservations for Native American children, from South Dakota to the Navajo Nation. He liked my story of Navajo Mike in New Mexico, the child of the dust-devil air.

Gene's goal in life was to help as many kids as he could to finish high school and college. During the seventeen years that he worked in the Fort Yukon school district, just two kids graduated from college. One graduated from the University of Alaska and the other from Dartmouth College. He said the problem wasn't their intelligence. It was their sense of belonging.

"Most get homesick and want to come home. Most of the kids I teach don't even know they are part of the United States. They think Alaska is a country. A lot of their parents wish it was."

Gene took me to Tok. A sign on the edge of town touts that it once registered sixty-three degrees below zero, the coldest temperature in the United States. I spent two nights sleeping in the woods around Tok. An older man with a long white beard walked by one day with his dog. He once worked at Golden Wheel but claimed he was fired for pointing out a rigged game.

"Forget Golden Wheel," he said. "Go to Chicken."

Give up your crazy carnival scheme. Buy a sluice and go prospecting for gold in Chicken, a former gold rush town with a current population of seven people. Hitchhike up there and watch the creek.

"When you see a good spot for gold," he said, "jump out of the car right there and go to work."

The eccentric old prospector was my introduction to how gold fever was still alive in Alaska, even if gold wasn't doing much for Chicken.

～

THE WAITRESS at Fast Eddie's restaurant told me the forecast called for three days of heavy rain. I sat down at a table and propped up my cardboard sign, "Anchorage."

After a couple of hours watching the rain outside, I finished my hot oatmeal and walked to the front door. I was prepared to hitchhike in the rain for hours, if not days.

At a table near the door, an older woman sitting with her husband asked me where I was going.

Oh God, don't blow this. Not saying a word, I held up my sign.

"We are too," she said.

Then her husband doubled down on their kind offer.

"Have you eaten enough breakfast?"

I was hungry, but I didn't want to drop my momentum, so I told them I'd eaten enough.

Rick and Jinny were a hard-driving trucking couple on their first trip to Anchorage.

I stepped up into their eighteen-wheel Freightliner with a Caterpillar 550 horsepower engine and a thirteen-speed transmission. I stepped up and swung myself into that big rig.

"It ain't good for hills," Rick said, "but it can fly on the flat country."

Rick and Jinny logged an average of 350,000 thousand miles a year together. Rick estimated he drove more than 3.5 million miles in his career.

Jinny and Rick believed their life was the only way to live.

"You've seen this country," Rick said to me. "Why in the world would anyone want to work in a factory?"

THE ANCHORAGE GOSPEL Rescue Mission was my refuge for a couple nights. On those nights in the mission bunks, I heard to every noise that can come out of old men's bodies.

Each morning we were given plastic trays for a feast of day-old Dunkin' donuts and blueberry pancakes.

In my shelter bunk bed, I stared at the ceiling imagining the relative comfort of a carnival bunkhouse. If Golden Wheel Amusements turned me down after four thousand miles of hitchhiking, I could always go prospecting in Chicken.

PART VI
ALASKA

JULY, AUGUST

JESUS GUIDES A GOLDEN WHEEL

ANCHORAGE

We really are becoming gods in the most literal sense possible. We are acquiring abilities that have always been thought to be divine abilities – in particular, the ability to create life. And we can do with that whatever we want.

— AUTHOR/HISTORIAN YUVAL NOAH HARARI

*E*agle River's Bear Paw Festival was already set up, but I was just in time for hiring. Jacqueline Leavitt somehow snuck up on me. A lovely younger woman, she looked up at me as if she didn't believe what she was seeing.

"I'm Jackie. I'm the owner. Are you the one who hitchhiked up here?"

I told her I was delightfully surprised how blessed Golden Wheel was to have such a lovely owner.

She wasn't falling for my blarney.

"Have you ever run games?" she asked.

A dart game, I said, one weekend years ago.

"Don't tell that to my husband. We have a saying around here. We don't care how they do things in the lower forty-eight. We have our own ways. We don't want any bad habits."

She meant this was a Christian carnival. No racket show. No cop balls, ten-pointing, walk money, Chicago set spindles, G-wheels, flat joints, jam joints, alibi stores, nut mobs, out counts, punk robbers, put n' takes, fairbanks, shell games, montes, fast and loose, fast counts, gaffs, gig artists, or grifters.

Stumbling over my words, I told her I wanted to be a ride jockey. I didn't have bad habits because I didn't know jointee tricks. Oh, I wanted to learn all the dirty tricks, but I thought it wiser to leave that part out.

Jackie asked me why I wanted to work in their carnival.

"Because I love carnivals," I said.

She brightened up. I knew we had a love connection, the love of carnivals. It was the perfect answer. Jackie enjoyed pointing out that she was raised behind the counter of a floss wagon, selling cotton candy and other confections. Her husband, Joe, ran away from home and across a farm field to jump on a carnival truck as if it were a rocket ship to adventure.

They were evangelicals believing in a literal, scriptural interpretation of how Jesus Christ might want a carnival run. I'd never met anyone like Jackie in carnivals. She was the personification of why it is so difficult to generalize about carnival people. Genuine carnival people hide surprises inside.

I was hired during that conversation, but I still needed to pass the drug test. I have an irrational fear of drug tests. I always think someone will come back and say, "You're drug-free, but you'll be dead within the hour."

They handed us t-shirts, a W-2 form, and the employee handbook. The handbook was unlike any other in carnivals. The Golden Wheel handbook cited the Bible and advised on how to live for the rest of your life. Mercifully, the advice began with Saint Paul's letters to the Philippians.

Do nothing out of selfish ambition or vain conceit, but in humility consider others more important than yourself. Philippians 2:3.

The handbook explained that the carnival's pastor and his wife, Bill and Patsy Root, were given professional and spiritual oversight of us. It went on to explain the carnival's history.

Our company began in 1967 when Jacqueline's mother Claire Morton came to Alaska with her family to buy an octopus ride.

Claire was a pioneering carnival owner with a national reputation. She was a leader at the Outdoor Amusement Business Association and in the Showmen's clubs in the American Northwest and Hawaii. She was the first female president of the Showmen's League of America. The former Western Indian scout and showman Buffalo Bill Cody once held the same job.

During the carnival season, Golden Wheel traveled from Ketchikan to Fairbanks, reaching eighty percent of the population of Alaska.

It's famous the world around for its Fur Rendezvous in Anchorage in February and early March. The Rendezvous gets its name from the winter swap meets of the early fur traders. It is the largest winter festival in North America and ends with the Anchorage-to-Nome Iditarod Trail Sled Dog Race.

Claire raised Jackie in this iconic carnival. Jackie grew up spinning candy, popping popcorn, and shucking corn for shows. When Claire gave up day-to-day oversight, Jackie took over the carnival. Jackie made sure I knew she wasn't the one who really ran the Golden Wheel.

"I'm not the real boss," she said.

Then she pointed to the sky. The real boss of Alaska's sole carnival was Jesus.

～⌒◯

THE BEAR PAW Festival is famous for its parade, rodeo, cook-off, talent show, 5K race, stinky-sneaker contest, and a Mr. and Mrs. Bear Claw competition.

During the Slippery Salmon Derby, contestants ran through an obstacle course with a humpy salmon in one hand and a tray with a Red Solo Cup filled with soda.

Alaskans complained about the hot, dry summer, hovering in the eighties. Surrounded by boreal forests, they feared heat-induced fires.

My team leader, Russ, led me to the carnival's Golden Wheel, a sixty-foot-tall Big Eli. The Jacksonville, Illinois-based Eli Bridge Company dated back more than a hundred years, almost back to the Chicago World's Fair.

Russ was a heavyset West Virginia man who wore a white cowboy hat. He knew how to set up and slough every ride on the lot. He gave me control of the wheel for a couple of practice spins. I timed the wheel so each car lined up with the platform and customers could get off and on.

Later that day, Logan came to oversee the wheel. Another big man with a dark cowboy hat, Logan had been the rig's wheelman for several years. He claimed to have a special relationship with her that transcended understanding. I was improving and getting better by the day. On the third day, I almost became infamous.

All morning I shifted up and back to get the car in the right position for the exit/entrance ramp. I was ushering a couple out of their seats when the wheel took off. Russ attempted to turn off the wheel, but it kept going until the scared riders reached the top of the wheel. The Eli Wheel was full of frightened riders.

We jiggled the control lever and worked the wiring. After a couple of long minutes, the wheel sputtered and rocked and worked again. We didn't know what caused the problem or what restarted the ride.

Golden Wheel is named for its wheel, and an accident on its signature ride would be a threat to the carnival's livelihood. My days as a wheelman ended in near disaster, but for three long Alaskan summer days, I operated a Ferris wheel in Alaska.

Logan believed the malfunction was caused by the ghost in the machine.

"She only likes me touching her," he said.

Russ was superstitious, and Logan's theory didn't sound crazy to him. He'd injured himself on the wheel several times. He believed the wheel was temperamental about who handled her.

I held no such illusions. My guess is that I was over-shifting, but I still don't know. Yet it was strange that a ride at a Christian carnival mysteriously bucked in the hands of an atheist.

THE BEAR PAW slough was unlike any I'd experienced. We ended the last night eating the unsold food and ice cream from the grab joints.

There was no all-night slough. A well-maintained van drove us back to Chugiak. We tore down the remainder of the carnival the next day. It was a livable pace.

My first week's paycheck at Golden Wheel was $303.43, which included tax withholdings. I was square with the IRS.

If I stayed through the state fair in Palmer, I could make more than five hundred dollars a week. It was the best money I made as a ride jockey. With earnings like that, I might make it to Mexico yet.

NESTLED between the Knik Arm and the Chugach Mountains, Chugiak is named after a Dena'ina word for "place of many places." The name was apropos, given the many places represented by the international students and Native Alaskans working at Golden Wheel.

Waking before anyone else, I rose to see clouds tipping off the Chugach Mountains behind the bunkhouse trailers. Across the street were basketball courts, baseball/softball fields, soccer fields, hiking trails, ski areas, and a jogging path.

On cool summer evenings, locals went to the baseball fields to see the collegiate baseball team Chugiak-Eagle River Chinooks. The team's mascot is an angry salmon flipping a baseball with its fin.

Clean bunkhouses were parked in a semicircle surrounding a tent with a grill. Cooking facilities, bathrooms, and a TV room were in the warehouse next door. In California bunkhouses, the bedbugs ate me alive. In a New Jersey bunkhouse, faulty electrical wiring caught fire. In Chicago bunkhouses, we were surrounded by trash piled high and steaming hot cow pies.

I once saw a moose with her calf walking out of the Chugach State Park. They crossed between the sleeping rides on our lot and disappeared into a bank of white birch trees. At times in Alaska, I was so in love with the carnival and the great outdoors that I felt I should pay Golden Wheel.

The Alaskan labor pool dries up in the summer as manual laborers scramble to higher-paying work. Small Native Alaskan villages become a traditional source of low-wage workers. My three roommates in Chugiak were Native Alaskans, describing themselves as Aleutian, Kenaitze, and Dana'ina. All the Native Alaskan men in our crew showed up for work at the Golden Wheel with fresh wounds from bar fights.

Squeezed for labor, Golden Wheel looked abroad for workers. Albanian, Cantonese, Hawaiian, Jamaican Patois, Samoan, and Slovak were spoken in camp.

Foreign students always passed the drug tests. Marijuana use among American carnival workers was almost as common as cigarette smoking. Golden Wheel's international students were future doctors, lawyers, and government bigwigs destined to talk about their youth as carnies in Alaska.

A few veteran carnies around my age worked there, too. Breeze, Dave, and Jimbo knew how to set up rides fast. Russ was younger, in his early thirties but he was a veteran carnie too, having started working in carnivals in his teens.

Bill Root was a pastor of his own congregation in Arizona when he was asked by Jackie and Joe to head north to run games, though he knew nothing about carnivals. He led Bible study classes during the week and held Sunday services at each jump. It was the show before the show.

Tony was the head of rides. He was a forty-year-old immigrant from Beirut, Lebanon, and came to the United States when he was ten years old. A Maronite Christian by upbringing, he too was an evangelical.

Smart, strong, and thin, Tony spent twelve years with RCS, Ray Cammack Shows, based in Arizona. The RCS ownership is related to Jackie's husband, Joe. Tony knew Jesse at Butler Amusements and heard about the robbery in Bay Point, California. He talked on the phone to Jesse while I was there. I worried that word of my blogs might catch up with me.

One afternoon after a long day of working in a food wagon, three Chinese women from Guangzhou province near Hong Kong invited me to share their homemade Chinese dinner.

We ate rice, corn, sausage, and spices. We talked about their dreams for life in Guangzhou. They were young, lovely, college-educated, and ambitious. They were giddy about their bright futures in China. In a place of many places, I felt transported to another.

Carnival people can surprise you that way. They often have hidden talents having nothing to do with the show. A young American woman named Crystal was a novelist writing a romance/sci-fi series. She called it the *Two Worlds* series, featuring aliens among us. She finished a couple of books and wrote titles for twenty more unwritten ones. She was unpublished, but she was looking into self-publishing.

None of us were just carnies.

WE BEGAN SETTING up rides weeks early for the Alaska State Fair in Palmer.

The days were sunny and warm. The Chugach and Talkeetna mountains in the distance were still snow-capped. The fair wasn't until August, but our job was to set up thirty-some rides. We wanted to finish as much as we could before the start of our next state fair, the Tanana Valley State Fair in Fairbanks.

We saw Miss Claire's original cotton candy wagon from the 1960s sitting in the Palmer field. Miss Claire was retired but kept azaleas, petunias, and pansies around rides and the management office. She helped in the office trailer and walked around the rides during shows.

A group of ethnic Samoans worked in the crew. Most of them were from Hawaii and living in Anchorage. The young Samoans were fearless climbers, crawling up poles without a safety line. T

hey taunted Tony about being an old man. To prove he still could climb, Tony put two hands on a support pole and lifted himself up horizontal to the ground. He looked like a human flag in a high wind.

Tempers flared when workers were setting up the Wacky Worm rollercoaster. Tony enforced a strict no-swearing rule. Managers accused the Samoans of wearing gang colors and told them to stop. Without admitting wrongdoing, the Samoans stopped wearing the colors and swore in Samoan.

Resty was a huge twenty-something Samoan carny working on the Wacky Worm. I was carrying a giant Wacky Worm flower stem across the field when Resty demanded that I put it down to work for him. I balked, saying something about Tony being my boss.

Resty had a quick, violent temper.

"How about if I smash all your teeth out," he said.

I was mad at first. I couldn't help it. Then I looked at reality, about three hundred pounds of angry reality.

"Then I won't come over to help you," I said. "I don't want my teeth smashed out."

I walked away chuckling, keeping a bit of pride with my smart-ass remark. For another couple weeks, Resty and his Samoan friends in the camp kept saying Resty would "eat" me.

Louisiana John in Chicago threatened me on the Gage Park slough. Jamaica Wayne threatened me in Marlboro. Rose Dog wanted to kill me in California. Despite my sacred vow to avoid all violent encounters, I was averaging one major confrontation per carnival. I was more pugnacious than I imagined, and I was running out of dodges.

MAYBE LOVE IS A GAFF

FAIRBANKS

*W*e loaded into vans and trucks on a soupy morning in Chugiak. We headed north six hours and 340 miles to Fairbanks along some of the most magnificent miles of highway on earth.

We were a wagon train of game joints, food trailers, and rides along George Parks Highway. More rides followed on the Alaska Railroad.

It was a clear, sunny day as we drove through Matanuska-Susitna Valley up to Denali National Park. Mount McKinley, as it was named at the time, was picture-perfect.

After a couple of days of work in Fairbanks, we finished setting up nineteen rides with a day to spare. Jackie and Joe paid for a daylong canoe and rafting trip down the Chena River.

My Athabaskan/Russian bunkmate, Curtis, was already into the who-hit-Johnny before arriving at the river and was stiff as a cross-eyed mummy. He was poured into a canoe, and the dipso absoluto show began. He sang out of tune, told incoherent jokes, and shouted to me from his canoe. He kept saying I was the only person who understood him.

On soft evenings, standing outside the Chugiak warehouse, Curtis and I stood staring out into the forest while he told his life's story.

His grandparents raised him in a tiny Eskimo fishing village in the bush. His father was "a real winner," who beat him and left the family.

He grew up strong and athletic. He once scored a seven-second pin in wrestling, and another time he blocked a ball to win a basketball game. At the World Eskimo-Indian Olympics, he dominated his wrestling category. He gained a full athletic scholarship to the University of Anchorage. He either dropped out or didn't attend.

He married, had two boys, and divorced. Without the anchor of home life and family, he kept moving through jobs and epic saloon throwdowns.

"I was lost after my divorce," he said.

He was still lost. He disappeared from the Golden Wheel for a week and returned with hands shaking like river rapids. Curtis used Athabaskan references and movie lines to describe his barroom victories. He never lost a fight. Every time, he stood over the vanquished opponent repeating a line from the Western movie *Tombstone*.

"I'm your huckleberry," he'd say.

One night when his stories ran thin, I felt I should chip in with my own. In the spirit of telling tall tales, I too felt unbounded by reality.

Long ago and far away, I was in the Himalayan mountains studying Buddhism outside Kathmandu at Kopan Monastery. I was with the other students sitting around a blind old lama when I asked him to tell us a story with a moral. The holy man told us the story of Joking Buddha.

A Westerner and a Buddhist monk are in an airplane over Mount Everest ready to parachute on to the mountaintop. The monk takes off his parachute and jumps out. Halfway down, he yells, Buddha–aaaa!"

A great hand comes out of the clouds. The monk falls on the hand and is placed gently on the summit of Mount Everest.

The pilot tells the Westerner that the Himalayas are Buddha's country. People need only yell "Buddha–aaaa!" on the way down and Buddha will save them.

"I too shall be saved by the hand of Buddha," the Westerner says.

He takes off his parachute and jumps out of the plane yelling "Buddha–aaaa."

Nothing. Then he yells again.

"Buddha–aaaa!"

Out of the clouds comes a hand, and the Westerner falls into Buddha's palm.

Without thinking, the Westerner says, "Phew. Thank Christ!"

The hand flips over, and splat!

The blind old lama sat there in profound silence.

"But your story has no moral," I said.

"The moral is obvious," the wise old monk said. "Don't fuck with Buddha!"

Curtis liked my jokes, and I listened to his stories, but that day on the Chena River was not his day. I put some distance between us by rowing ahead.

The three young Chinese women on the crew laughed the entire river trip, circling and floating sideways with the current. People gave up rowing properly and used the oars to splash each other.

Deciding to join in on the happy chaos, I sang a nonsensical song. Adopting an opera-star tenor, I began with a *legato* that rose into a crescendo to the tune *O Solo Mio*.

I knew the tune and the Italian words *solo mio*, but I was winging every rhymed line as I confidently sang. Loudly and without a plan, I began my disastrous song.

> *O solo mio, San Francisco,*
> *O solo mio, where do we go,*
> *We're on the Chena River,*
> *We've no idea, where it goooo hither.*

There were more verses, but why keep adding to the pain?

When I met Jackie back on the fairgrounds, she claimed I was a hit with the managers. Rave reviews were pouring in.

"I won't let you leave us before I hear you sing," she said. "Before I hear you serenade me."

My ridiculous singing display sparked a renewed interest in my past. Jackie began interrogating me. It was time to leave. I already put in a month with Golden Wheel.

The Minnesota State Fair was on my mind. It's the largest state fair in the country by daily attendance. To guarantee I arrived there on time, I needed ten days to two weeks of hitchhiking.

Tony asked me to stay. Without explaining my reason, I said I must go. The follow-up came when Patsy Root walked over to my new ride.

I was working the Cliff Hanger, a simulated hang-gliding experience. She visited me twice asking me to stay through the state fair in Palmer. The second time she offered me a new tent and a free bus ticket to the lower 48, the Alaskan term for the forty-eight contiguous states to the south.

By that time, my coworker on the Cliff Hanger was a young Iraq War veteran named Ken. I told Patsy that Ken was doing a great job. They didn't need me. I'm nothing special.

"That's not true," she said. "You have something special. Everybody can feel it."

I stuck to my plan until Jackie walked over and called in a favor. She reminded me that she gave me a job after I hitchhiked four thousand miles. And it's against the code to setup a show and leave.

I felt an obligation, even if it meant missing the Minnesota State Fair. I agreed to stay and hoped the questions about my background would die down. They only grew more intense. My evasive answers only superpowered my mysterious drifter status.

"I'll find out," Jackie said. "I'm good at finding things out. I'm doing a background check on you."

KEN WAS a former lance corporal in the Marines who served 2008-2009 in Iraq. Calling himself a tramp miner, he joined the carnival after weeks of working in his father's goldfield.

His father owned the rights on 1,600 acres northwest of Fairbanks. Ken swam along creek bottoms, using a suction dredge to suck and sift through the sand and gravel for gold.

If he ever struck it rich, he planned to pay for an around-the-world trip for himself and his Marine buddies. He always wanted to see Amsterdam's red-light district and the coffeehouses with legal pot.

About six feet tall and wearing his short shirt sleeves high on his bulked-up arms, Ken loved carnivals since he was a kid. He was happy putting people on rides. Women around the carnival were picking up on something else. Ken was the first carnival worker I saw who attracted admirers without trying.

On his first day, a young woman from the carnival rifle range, Sam, walked over with fresh hot coffee. In Alaska, Sam was a Christian singer and a jointee. In Iraq and Afghanistan, she was a bomb squad specialist.

The same day, another tall, thin woman walked past me at the Cliff Hanger and gave a giant hot pretzel to the tramp miner. He was impressed, but I was not.

"Is it a giant cookie?" I asked. "When you get a cookie, she's serious."

Ken suspected that the women at the Susitna Street Taco stand also were giving him the green light. I prayed they didn't come over with tacos.

I called them "Ken's Harem." It made him smile, but all the attention probably was confusing to a guy fresh in from weeks of diving into muddy creeks.

My knee hadn't healed since my scaffold accident in New Jersey, but that didn't stop me from trying to be the most energetic carny at the Cliff Hanger.

I tried to out-hop Ken from customer to customer. When the ride ended, I asked the riders if they had fun. If a rider didn't have fun, I gave them another ride for free. Ride free. Feel free. It's Alaska.

I asked Ken what he thought about America. He was worried American freedoms were being eroded. A gun advocate and hunter, he was sure politicians in Washington were "selling out the country."

I once met President Obama, I told Ken. When Obama was still a state senator in Chicago.

"What did he say?" Ken asked.

"If you ever meet a Marine tramp miner, tell him the gold he seeks is within and stop being such a heartbreaker."

THE CARNIVAL RIDES for the Tanana Valley State Fair lined up in a rectangle, with management trailers in the middle. The carny bunkhouse trailers were parked by a bank of trees at the back of the lot.

We brought the Big Eli, Zipper, Apollo, Super Slide, Oriental, Gravitron, Tornado, Sizzler, Cliff Hanger, and bumper cars.

The anchor attractions of the agricultural fair were the animal barn, livestock areas, and agricultural exhibits. The music hall drew country-western acts. Alaskan food and boutique stores lined the paved walkways.

Imagine Dragons' "Radioactive," Katy Perry's "Firework," and Macklemore's "Can't Hold Us," played in loops along the midway. Military airplanes and helicopters from Fort Wainwright and Eielson Air Force Base flew overhead.

The Fairbanks crowd tended to include fewer black and Hispanic attendees and far more bearded white men. A substantial minority of customers were Native Alaskans.

The Tanana Valley State Fair was a regional draw in the middle of Alaska and expected to top 130,000 visits in a city of about 32,000 residents. The warm, dry weather helped. Temperatures rose above eighty degrees every day for more than a month. The heat was igniting fires outside of town.

THE WORDS 'I LOVE YOU' aren't what you expect to hear from your boss in a carnival.

As Jackie and Joe's minister, Bill was also the titular head of the carnival's spiritual direction. Once in a while, I called him the carny preacher.

As the preacher's wife and carnival's personnel manager, Patsy was responsible for much of the human resources management of the crew. Bill, Patsy, and the Leavitts practiced what I called "management theology."

At a sermon in Fairbanks, Bill addressed a group of twenty carnival workers.

"I love you," he said.

It seemed natural in Fairbanks, but the contrast with Chicago was striking.

Modern Midways owner Robert Briggs gathered us in workshop one morning on The 30. A Catholic church official complained to him about the foul language the crew used on setup. Briggs had no intention of managing with love.

"I got complaints that you guys were swearing on setup," he said. "I got a call from the church. They said kids at the school could hear you. The church! People ask me why I hire Americans. Should I fine you all one hundred dollars? Or would a beating be better? Would a beating be better?"

Boom!

Briggs slammed the palm of his hand against the workshop's aluminum wall, making a jarring, loud sound. It was a violent gesture to show he meant business.

"Both," La La yelled.

La La was as profane as any of us. He supported both beatings and fines? You traitor, La La.

About four thousand miles and a world away in Alaska, Bill adopted a different approach.

"You are a marvelous creation of God," he said. "I want to honor you. I work with you. You know me."

On Sundays and mid-week bible studies, we gathered under an open-air carnival tent and thought about mortality and eternity. How should we live? What is our worth?

My favorite sermon was on King David's adulterous affair with Bathsheba. When she became pregnant with his baby, King David sent her husband away to be killed on the battlefront. The steamy sexual drama was relatable to carnies with messy love lives.

"If God can forgive David," Bill said, "he can forgive you."

At a Wednesday Bible study held in a Tanana Valley State Fair eating area, a former prostitute and crack addict told Bill that she was still in love with a bad man. Would reading Ezekiel help? A young Jamaican asked about sexual temptations at parties.

The veteran carny Breeze wanted to know what to do about his carnival love affair with an Eskimo woman on the crew.

Tall, thin, and about my age, Breeze never went anywhere without his black four-beaver Stetson cowboy hat. He nicknamed himself after a Lynyrd Skynyrd song, *Call Me the Breeze*.

He was another millionaire carny. His mother left him more than two million dollars in her will. He didn't have to work, but he loved carnivals. Miss Claire and Jackie were his new family. Breeze's femme fatale was a twenty-something Native Alaskan named Wanita.

Wanita was short, with glasses, and Breeze called her the cutest girl on the crew. More than twenty-five years Breeze's junior, she came from Emmonak, a Yup'ik village in western Alaska with a population of fewer than eight hundred people. I heard she left her child with family to follow Breeze and the carnival.

A Jamaican pre-med student also thought Wanita was the prettiest woman in camp. Breeze found out about their affair on karaoke night at the Arctic Bar in Fairbanks.

The best karaoke singer in the crew, Breeze was singing on stage when he first saw the fireworks between his girlfriend and the Jamaican.

Breeze was ejected from the bar for yelling at Wanita. Another night, he returned from the bar and threw her clothes out into the middle of the bunkhouse common area.

Breeze was justifying his actions one afternoon to a group of us seated around the bunkhouses when Dakota came up to him voicing his sympathy. Dakota was a year out of high school when he fell hopelessly in love with a married woman. She left him to go back to her husband. Dakota and Breeze agreed they wanted to beat up their rivals in romance.

Citing Dakota's age and lack of sexual experience, carny men told him more-fish-in-the-sea stories. One carny loudly told Dakota to "get some ancient pussy" from some "dirty whores" before he entered the holy sacrament of marriage.

All the talk about sex prompted a member of our crew to offer his solution. Two Native Alaskan women he knew were coming to the state fair.

"They sleep with me," he said. "Why wouldn't they sleep with you?"

Around the same time, my Native Alaskan bunkhouse neighbor confided to me that his girlfriend wanted to charge him with rape.

They lived in the same bunkhouse and had children together. The previous night, he was drunk and forced himself on her.

The next morning, he asked me what he should do. I was surprised he came to me for advice instead of preacher Bill. I gave non-biblical advice that seemed to settle him down. They were a loving couple by that evening. But the next night warfare broke out again.

Someone complained to Patsy about the love triangles, loud music, and the late-night parties. Patsy gathered us together.

She reminded us that we were a Christian carnival. Management threatened to fire us if we continued to live like hedonists. Live a Christian life, she said. Do it for yourselves.

~⌒◯

THE NEXT DAY, Breeze kept running from his Apollo ride to a secret area behind the management trailers. I saw him running back and forth all day, but I didn't know what was up.

When the Golden Wheel shut down, Breeze invited the entire crew for a giant pot of his mother's famous Irish stew. Wanita helped him with the shopping list, which called for corned beef, potatoes, cabbage, and spices. Breeze held court that late Alaskan night, the emperor of Irish stew.

"My Irish mother passed away, so I had to ask an Eskimo how to do this," he said. "I had to do this from my heart. I just had to do this."

We stood around slurping our soup from plastic spoons and cups. Laughter and talk broke out among friends. Faint beams of sunlight broke through the smoke from the forest fires outside town, surrounding us in refracted light.

When I finished my stew and stepped away to leave, I turned around again for one last look at the crew. I imagined faint vectors on the smokey air connecting us.

Later that night, we drove in a van to Walmart. Someone shouted from the back of the van for the driver to turn up the radio. It was Mumford & Sons' hit *I Will Wait*.

> *And I will wait, I will wait for you*
> *And I will wait, I will wait for you.*

We sang the chorus at the top of our lungs. Breeze vowed to memorize the song for the next karaoke night. It reminded me of the rap songs on the Chicago van rides.

The Tanana Valley State Fair ended with a pyrotechnic show. People rushed to get in the final rides as the fireworks blasted away around them. Spectators walking the midway stopped to watch. Their raised faces turned the colors of the sky.

That night I lay in my bunkhouse bed thinking of Breeze sleeping alone. Maybe Wanita liked the pre-med student, but it was a fling. Dakota didn't attack the husband of his Bathsheba. Tramp miner Ken didn't settle on just one woman.

In camps where people work and live so close, love can be explosive. Sunday sermons revolved around love. People searched for love on both sides of the carnival lights.

Maybe love and God are cosmic gaffs, yet I saw them in play at a golden traveling carnival one fiery summer month in Alaska.

A WOLF BECOMES A MAN

HITCHHIKING TO MINNESOTA

*O*n the morning after Golden Wheel paid me, I woke early and vanished.

The first three drivers out of Fairbanks were members of separate apocalyptic communes, which seemed like a lot of apocalyptic communes. Each was sure that only self-sufficient, remote communities like theirs would survive. A Christian apocalyptic carnival may have appealed to this local crowd.

A white man and an Eskimo woman picked me up later in the day and wanted to talk about miracle healings. Lloyd Thomas was a Vietnam veteran suffering from a variety of conditions, including lung cancer and calcification of his liver, kidney, and spleen.

His wife of thirty-two years, Barbara, was a full-blooded Athabaskan from Tetlin. They'd raised three grown children together. They were living a near-subsistence lifestyle in a cabin only recently hooked up to electricity.

Five years previously, in a last-ditch attempt to save her husband's life, Barbara drove him to see a miracle worker she'd heard on the radio. The preacher laid hands on him and healed him. Lloyd still needed to have a lung removed by doctors, but even they were shocked to see the earlier signs of cancer disappeared. After the surgery and the miracle, Lloyd didn't change at all.

"The first day I got out, I walked a quarter of a mile along a creek and got a pack of cigarettes, mint chocolate chip ice cream, and a can of cream of mushroom soup. The doctor told me that my marijuana habit had stopped the cancer spread. The faith healer did the rest."

Cancer-free for five years when I met him, Lloyd still smoked Pall Malls. He and Barbara believed in miracles and were free to live as they wanted from that point forward.

Miracles were more than just proof of God's compassion and existence. They were signs of God's favor. Why should new Lloyd change anything when the old Lloyd was worthy of a miracle?

When they dropped me off, I stood by the road watching the fires in the distance. Shades of smoke filtered the golden nugget sun, melting it into the sunset. Later that night, the Perseid meteor shower lit up the sky above the fires. It was the Alaskan sky as theater.

It was nearly midnight and still light when a state highway construction worker stopped in his pickup truck. He was coming from the Tanana Valley State Fair. His side business was supplying the fair with three hundred vegetable-oil fuel tanks.

Repairing Alaskan roads was the only job he ever held. The permafrost, the ice heaves, and the hot summers will keep him employed for the rest of his life.

Woody brought me to his trailer home outside the Tok Maintenance Center and offered me the couch for the night. The next morning, I walked to the closest gas station expecting a long day ahead, and happened upon what I call a miracle.

I NOTICED a one-ton truck's Indiana plates. To a hitchhiker, a three-thousand-mile ride is a miracle ride. After a short conversation, Larry Stout and I were on a five-day drive to Minnesota.

That Pall Mall Reds-smoking, complicated, rural Indiana man

took me on the longest single hitchhike ride of my life and one of the most thrilling.

Larry drove a 1994 Chevrolet Ram 3500, 6.5 diesel with 250,000 miles on the clock. He'd added a cabin in the back for sleeping. Among his many talents, Larry knew every inch of the vehicle and kept the one-ton humming like new.

We took turns driving through Alaska, Yukon, British Columbia, Alberta, Saskatchewan, North Dakota, and Minnesota. We drove the Alaska and Trans-Canada highways. We crossed mountain ranges and rivers on the way to the Mississippi River.

The grain fields above the Bakken Formation in North Dakota were peppered with hammerhead drills and fiery refinery stacks. We covered territory that was both geographic and personal.

He told stories of vodka-fueled Russian roulette, steamy affairs, attempted murder, miraculous escapes from death, and a wolf bite on the ass that turned a woman into a wife and a wolf into a man. Such are the dynamics of long car rides with a curious stranger.

Larry began the ride by saying he was forty-five or forty-eight years old. He was returning to Indiana from hauling a fiber-optic trailer to Anchorage. He was a truck driver, mechanic, tree trimmer, roofer, concrete worker, handyman, and a widower.

We were not even at the edge of Tok when I realized I was in the presence of an American original. He acted out the stories as he drove. When he was happy, I felt happy. When he was in pain, it hurt me too.

When his wife was dying of cancer, he started losing his grip. He couldn't believe it.

"I thought I was losing my mind," he said. "I yelled. I cried. I cursed. I cursed."

It all started when he moved to her small town south of Indianapolis. His younger self was a clever, high-energy local hardware store clerk.

Renting a place in her mother's apartment building, he'd go to her door and ask her out for a drink. She'd swear at him and slam the door. She was a tiny rebel from Hazard County, Kentucky. She could swear like a sailor.

"She looked like a little doll. Blond, brown-eyed, little titties, and an accent like mine, only even more Southern. She was ninety-five pounds tops, tops. She was thirty-nine years old, but she looked twenty-five. I was twenty-three."

One day he realized she wasn't saying no to him. She was saying no to the drinker.

"I know what's wrong," he said to her, "you don't like to drink."

He was proud of his insight, even in the story's retelling. He asked her out to dinner. No drinks. They talked about carburetors on their first date. She could take them apart and put them back together.

When he walked her up the stairs to her door, he let out a wolf howl. Aooooo! Chomp!

"I bit her on the ass."

Carburetor talk. A wolf howl. An ass bite. It turned out to be the primal, epiphanic moment of Larry's life because she liked it.

He quit drinking, and they married. They were together twenty-some years before cancer took her. He married one of her best friends after she was gone. The jack-of-all-trades was slowly rebuilding himself, but he wasn't there yet.

LARRY LEFT me near an all-night diner in St. Paul. I spent the next two nights at the Union Gospel Mission while I spent days trying get hired at the Minnesota State Fair.

After three days at the back workers gate, a young man I knew from line landed a job by buying beer and pizza for a carnival crew at his motel. He got a pass for me too. He pointed the way to the Mighty Midway and told me to look for the kid who hired him.

I'm good at finding people, so I walked in the gate. But I turned around because I forgot to ask a key question.

"By the way," I said, "what's the kid's name?"

"They call him Batman."

PART VII
MINNESOTA

AUGUST, SEPTEMBER

BATMAN'S DARK KNIGHTS

ST. PAUL

Money won is twice as sweet as money earned.

— FAST EDDIE FELSON IN *THE COLOR OF MONEY*

eople all along the midway were working on rides, games, and food stands. Nothing was ready. Everyone was in a hurry. Adam "Batman" West spoke in fast, clipped sentences, directing his crew on hoisting tarps.

"Can you pass a piss test?" he asked me. "Do you have drug or alcohol problems?"

I'm cool.

"Are you honest?"

I chuckled and hesitated for a moment, which flipped on a switch for him. He grew angry fast.

"Why are you laughing?" he said. "Something funny to you?"

"If I was a liar," I said. "I'd say the same thing."

He took a few moments, trying to read me.

"Ha, I guess you would."

In his twenties, with the frame of a former defensive end, Adam stood akimbo with his hands on his hips. You might have thought he oversaw the whole midway, not merely a traveling crew of about a dozen men and women.

"Can you travel? Because I don't want you if you can't travel."

This was a deal-breaker moment. I was not going with him if he wasn't going to Texas. The State Fair of Texas is the biggest state fair in America.

So I said, "Yes."

Get hired, I thought, and quit if he's not going to Texas.

"I'm going," he said, "to Oklahoma and Texas."

Jackpot! I was switching from a ride jockey to a jointee. I wanted to learn all the tricks of the trade. My Mexico plans required more money than a ride jockey could save. I was in the sweet spot again.

The first crew member I met was Joe, a tall, thin jointee in his thirties.

"You're lucky," he said. "We're all proud to be with this crew."

Sharing the name with the iconic TV actor who played Batman, Adam West painted the black Batman logo on his "Batmobile" golf cart and his "Batcave" office trailer. He gave out Batman rings and t-shirts to crew members who stuck with him for the whole season.

At twenty-eight years old, he was a young star of the midway. He was raised in carnivals by his father, Bob West, a legendary owner of games. Adam was the new generation of owners, making a name for himself as an energetic, ambitious showman.

Not yet divorced from his first wife, Adam was living in a luxury mobile home with his two daughters, fiancée Debraun, and his mother, Miss Trudy.

When he left his trailer each morning, he shot out the door like a bull ready for combat.

"Everybody ready to rock and roll?"

Carnival bosses are often as tough as their toughest crew member. Adam was no exception. In a rare moment, he told me how he'd grown up boxing in carnivals. He brought gloves, mouth guards, and sparring helmets from town to town. He fought locals, but he relished beating up on South African carnies. He believed his father and his generation of showmen were a tougher breed of men than carnival men these days.

"I call it the pussification of America. People aren't as tough as they used to be. People used to fight all the time in carnivals. That's how you settled your problems. Now, you'll get tossed if you fight. When I was seven or eight years old, I used to hang off the rollercoaster and watch the Oklahoma police on their horses clear the fighters off the midway. That was my babysitter."

Proud of his trade, Adam called himself the "best at what I do." He knew how to handle carnival men because he grew up watching his father handle the toughest men. When he walked down the Mighty Midway, carnival owners and state inspectors gave him a shout-out.

He didn't think highly of me at first. I was new to games and old in years. He'd have to carry me until I learned tricks of the trade.

"Alaska?" he said. "You worked in an Alaskan carnival? You hitch-hiked? I never met someone who went up there. I hear that road is kinda . . . lonely. There aren't many people in that state. I bet they (Golden Wheel) didn't make much money."

For three days, we hoisted poles, washed tarp, set up pool tables, and hung stuffed animals. On the last night before opening, Adam told the crew we were all going out for a party to the Cosmic Bowl.

It was a combined celebration. His six-year-old daughter's birthday coincided with the traditional pre-state-fair crew party. About a dozen of us went to the bowling alley, where Adam ordered whiskey shots and pitchers of beer for everybody.

Cake, cupcakes, and presents filled a countertop behind the lanes. The crew toasted with shot glasses. The beefy crew boss, Chango, held a pitcher of beer in one hand and a shot glass in the other.

Men with cigarettes parked behind their ears, some missing teeth, and some with racy tattoos down their arms, gathered around to sing the happy birthday song to Adam's daughter.

Cheers echoed around the bowling alley when the little girl tore into her presents and threw wrapping paper high in the air. Adam dabbed his daughter's nose with a birthday cake. More cheers. More toasts.

These hard men who manipulate illusion every day wanted her sweet illusions to go on a little longer.

"Here's to the best damn crew in America," said Adam, holding a shot glass high.

He was once in China, he said, and it's an insult there not to finish your drink.

"Bottoms up."

The party reminded Adam of his own birthday parties growing up in carnivals.

"Welcome to growing up in a carnival, honey," Adam said to his daughter. "I grew up this way. Now my best friends are roughnecks."

Vouching for his story, Miss Trudy nodded as she held Adam's six-month-old daughter. Miss Trudy was tall and thin, with white tufted hair. She and Debraun were the civilizing influences.

The best jointees understand gamblers because they are gamblers themselves. They gamble on cards, trivia, sports, and anything they can think of. The worst of them don't care about the odds. They love the action. The jointees on the West crew weren't touching a bowling ball without a wager.

Adam walked to a space between our two bowling lanes.

"Quiet. Quiet," he said. "One hundred dollars to the winner."

A wild cheer rose. Everyone headed to the lanes.

Clayton was thin, about my age, and once played semi-pro football. His daughter on the crew was Heidi, a petite woman with a broad Oklahoma laugh. Clayton ran the microphone for a ring-toss game in St. Paul. The all-day nonstop talk on the midway damaged his voice. His signature line was a raspy, "Right here, right now."

He was a thirty-year veteran of the circuit. He wasn't about to lose a hundred bucks to any chumps like us. After every bowl, he walked back to the bench, pumping his fist and talking trash.

Vanil was a twenty-four-year-old black man from California. He became a father at age fifteen. His tally was four kids and counting.

Izzy and Tim were tall, thin black men, and hyper-competitive. The previous day, they bet on who could do the most push-ups.

Roger was a tall, thin white Army veteran of Somalia and Kuwait. He also prided himself on push-up contests. In his forties, Roger wore black-rimmed glasses and closely cropped hair. His arms bore tattoos of guns, pills, and bottles of booze.

His prison record and life told the story of a man in and out of trouble while in the passionate pursuit of pleasure. Roger's parents ran a bowling alley in Neenah-Menasha, Wisconsin. He smelled easy money. Adam's wager was as good as won.

Everyone but me was hell-bent on winning. I bowled but was more interested in taking pictures. Then someone noticed I was the second-highest scorer on the crew. The match was already competitive but turned into a five-alarm fire.

Tim was in first place but losing steam fast. Shots and beer were hurting his game but was fueling the aggressiveness of the former Gangster Disciple gangbanger from Detroit.

On a whim, Adam stood up out of turn. He wasn't playing but wanted to bowl one ball. If this tournament was going to cost him a hundred dollars, he wanted to have some fun.

He ran to the lane like a kid and almost without aiming, he grabbed a ball and bowled a strike. None of us had any idea that it was the last round. The strike scored in my column. Surprised, he turned back and yelled from the lane.

"Hey, Mike. You won. You won the hundred bucks."

Tim blew his stack. He felt betrayed. Adam helped the new guy.

Izzy and Vanil tried to calm Tim down.

"If Adam missed," Izzy said, "You would have won."

Tim thought about punching out both Izzy and Adam, and kicking out the van window on the way back to the fairgrounds.

Sitting next to him in the van, I realized I didn't need an antagonist like Rose Dog on this crew.

"Tim, be cool," I said. "Here."

I slipped him fifty dollars.

CHANGO POINTED to a bullet wound on his head and lifted his shirt to show his champion-sized, blue-ribbon pot belly. A scar curved the length of his abdomen like a question mark with the belly button the dot.

Without a notebook, I couldn't keep track of all his scars. Chango was pleased he'd survived his lethal past.

I needed to trust Chango completely. On the first day of setting up, he asked me to hold a four-foot iron stake with both hands. He swung an iron mallet high above his head and smashed the stake at its head, driving it into the asphalt. The spikes are for grounding the joints.

When holding the spike, I turned my head to avoid the bits of metal coming off it. Turning my head away also meant I wouldn't flinch. One wrong swing, and I might be injured and fired at the same time. I was no good without use of my hands.

Oz was a forty-four-year-old, trim carny with a clean-shaved head. His wounds were the newest and most visible. A deep, long scar traveled from behind his right ear, across his jugular, and up to his Adam's apple. His throat was cut a month and a half earlier. The scar made it look like an attempted beheading. He joked about it.

"I'd forget my head if it wasn't glued on."

He looked at me, anticipating my joke.

"Some people tried to help me with that recently."

People occasionally mentioned his throat scar when they first met him. He'd say a gang of Mexicans jumped him.

"I never went down though," he'd say.

Every time he coughed, he sounded like he was coughing up a carburetor. He was a smoker who stayed in homeless shelters, places rife with infectious diseases.

His cut throat was difficult to look at but hidden were still deeper psychic scars. With the nonchalance of a story told many times, he said he was "just a little boy" when his mother and aunt stripped him naked.

They tied him to a tree and told him coyotes were coming to bite off his penis. Drunk and hiding in the woods, they made noises and laughed as he screamed.

"There was no moon that night," he said. "I couldn't see anything. All I could do was listen to the noises."

He remembered everything from that night, the sights, sounds, and questions.

"Mommy," he shouted, "Why are you doing this to me?"

The scars kept piling up from there.

"That was before," he said, "all the foster homes and juvenile detention homes."

It was a sunny, hot day as I listened to him. In the background were *Despicable Me* minions, sock monkeys, Smurfs, and stuffed giant Rottweilers. Rock 'n' roll and disco boomed around us. Good mothers walked past with their sons.

How could this man function? What sort of world did he see on the midway, with his throat cut so theatrically and his psyche slashed to ribbons?

"Life hasn't been kind to me," he said.

Where is the kindness for Oz and his traveling scars?

As he walked away, he turned with an intense smile.

"I have foster brothers and sisters," he said, "but my carnival family is my real family."

ASSIGNED TO THE POOL TABLES, I worked with Oz and a host of recovering drug and alcohol addicts from a local Christian organization. They made an hourly wage while Oz and I received a percentage of the ticket take.

The Minnesota State Fair sold tickets for the games. Carnies didn't handle any cash. We put our tickets in bread-box-sized metal boxes, which were collected at the end of the night.

When the Ferris wheel lights went out, people yelled, "Down!" We raced to fill kid-sized wagons with the steel boxes. Show people from tents and rides up and down the midway rolled their wagons as fast as they could to the brightly lit main collection tent.

The sooner their tickets were poured into bags by the state staff workers, the sooner people could go home. An automatic counter later told us how much we'd made during the day. There was camaraderie in the tent as people finally were able to talk to each other rather than customers.

Our pay depended on our staying with the traveling crew. If I stayed with the crew through the setup in Oklahoma City, I'd get twenty percent of my take in St. Paul. If I crapped out, I could make ten to fifteen percent. From the start, Oz complained about the bosses, crew members, and me. He rode me nonstop. I lived in the nightmare land of Oz.

We worked four barroom-sized tables, each with three balls. Players broke the rack without having to sink a ball. Every shot after that, they had to sink balls sequentially and without scratches or combinations.

Miss Trudy and Chango showed up each morning to help us replace the flash given away the previous day. The plush hung on every inch of the tent, from the tent poles to the ceiling.

Stuffed Scooby-Doos, Rottweilers, huskies, pink pigs, lemurs, striped sock puppets, and yellow minions from the movie *Despicable Me* made our joint a human Venus flytrap.

Miss Trudy and Chango mixed and matched colors and sizes. They straightened and spaced prizes until we flashed the tightest tents on the Mighty Midway.

Rock 'n' roll boomed from a speaker hung on the edge of an overhead pole. We leveled and brushed the tables every morning. Pool cues were racked. Fresh chalk was on the table. Once people came inside, we owned them.

Miss Trudy knew the tables were magnets in the land of Minnesota Fats. Fats was a pool shark who never existed except in books and the movie *The Hustler*. We were trafficking in another myth. All that mattered was that Minnesotans believed he was real.

"I know Minnesotans," Miss Trudy said. "They love their pool. They come back every year."

Outside the joint, I tried to draw attention by twirling a pool cue like a baton. The pool cue was my guitar while I moved to Bruce Springsteen, the Rolling Stones, and U2.

"Pool man, pool man. I know you are a pool man. It's as easy as one, two, three. I'll give you a free shot. Come here. I'll show you how it's done. Best prizes on the Mighty Midway. Free shot. Free shot."

I'd put a pool ball in a passerby's hand, showing how simple the game was to win. I'd offer tips.

"Here's the money shot," I'd said. "The break. If you get that right, you've got it made."

After they lost, I was ready with a new pitch.

"You can't quit now. You can't go home a loser. You'll think about it all year."

Every first-time loser heard the same pitch.

"You lost that game because you are on the Mighty Midway. You're a better pool player than this, but there are distractions here. Your odds of winning go up every game you play. I can't tell you how many people win on their second game."

The pool game was at the end of the Mighty Midway, near the *World of Wonders* freak show. Few people walked past the Ferris wheel to the end of a midway, so our crowds were thin. But I still swamped Oz and the local attendants, becoming the top earner at the pool tent.

The Minnesota State Fair was another milestone because I was on the circuit long enough to know people from past carnivals.

During setup, a young woman stood waving hello from the middle of the midway.

"Remember me?" she asked.

Then she took out her glass eye, waving it around.

"Now do you remember me?"

She was Steve's wife from Butler Amusements in California. Steve was a fast-talking cocky jointee and one of Butler's best.

"Slim," I heard someone yell. Only one guy called me by that nickname.

Steve was around my age and ran a racing game. Butler fired him for selling drugs to the other carnies, but he was innocent. My routine at the pool tent impressed him.

"Where did you learn to do all that, Slim?"

"By watching you guys in California," I said.

I told him about running rides from Alaska to Chicago to New York.

"Slim, you are a real carny now," he said.

AT THE BEGINNING of the fair, Miss Trudy made us run around the tent with a plush toy yelling, "Winner. Winner. Winner." After a few hot days she let us stop, admitting the foolish running around was too garish.

We worked sixteen-hour days, showing up before 9 a.m., returning to the bunkhouse at 1 a.m. At night, we climbed ladders and restocked the joints around the midway. In the morning, we stocked the pool joint, then cleaned and leveled tables.

The West family operated games in St. Paul for years. That year they ran a ring toss, bottle break, rubber ducky game, balloon game, and a pool tent.

Miss Trudy considered herself an expert at hanging game prizes in a splashy, colorful way. Arranging the right colors and sizes next to each other was called hanging flash. She was a woman possessed when we heavily decorated the tent with flash. We worked like we were in a sped-up time-lapse video. Miss Trudy's mantra was, "No flash, no cash."

ON THE BUSIEST day of the fair, my daughter and parents arrived on a train from Chicago. I'd traveled to Alaska and back since I saw her last. I wondered if this might be one of the seminal moments of Grace's life she'd always remember.

When she saw me at the front gate of the Minnesota State Fair, we ran to each other. I kneeled on one knee, and Grace flung her arms around my neck. She was half laughing, half crying. Over her shoulder, I saw tears welling in my father's eyes.

"It feels like four years," she said, "since I saw you."

We ate at O'Gara's restaurant by the front gate. I told her the words on the wall, *Cead Mile Failte* in Gaelic means "One Hundred Thousand Welcomes." It was her welcome too, into the fantastical world of her first state fair.

At breakfast, she showed the gifts she brought. A watercolor painting of a dog. A postcard of a lion from her visit to the Brookfield Zoo. And her own coloring of a rainbow. I thought of Dorothy, Toto, the Cowardly Lion, and the rainbow from *The Wonderful Wizard of Oz.*

We walked the Mighty Midway around giant rides, fantasy games, and Ward Hall's *World of Wonders.* This "world" billed itself as the last traveling ten-in-one freak show in America. Outside the tent standing on the bally stage was a woman in a black, short skirt. She was the talker. The term carnival barker isn't used inside carnivals.

"Children in strollers get in free because we all know how kids love freak shows," the talker said

I showed Grace the pool table tent, and I introduced her to Oz. I think she saw a bald man with a slit throat. What Oz saw is unknowable. He never said a word to me about Grace.

When Grace left the fair with my parents, I wasn't sure what her impressions were. I told her to write about her trip in her diary. I kissed Grace and my parents, and then I ran away into the midway crowds.

I felt their eyes on my back. I don't know how Grace will feel about all this in years to come. Will she be inspired or hurt? All I truly knew is the part of me she brought and the part she was taking away.

～

WHEN THE MINNESOTA STATE FAIR ended, the teardown involved thousands of people. I found that breaking down our game joints was similar to sloughing rides. Rides were heavier, but both took a long time. At about 4 a.m., the rest of the crew headed back to the bunkhouses.

I walked up the midway to Mel's food concession. Sitting at a picnic table using the Wi-Fi, I stared at the Ferris wheel coming down like a broken spider web. It was a pristine, starry night. The few joints still standing were closed and empty. Big rigs were parked on the Mighty Midway waiting to haul away rides.

The absence of the fair's noises made it feel muffled, tranquil. The midway became the backstage. Workers milled around in the colored carnival shadows. A Zipper operator walked by and waved.

"See you next year," he said.

I thought I was leaving. He thought he was returning. It's the carnival cycle.

I once heard a kid in California ask his mother, "Will they ever be back?"

PART VIII
OKLAHOMA

SEPTEMBER

NEVER LEAVE A DOLLAR ON THE MIDWAY

OKLAHOMA CITY

We don't know what we want, but we're ready to bite someone to get it.

— WILL ROGERS, OKLAHOMAN, HUMORIST

a state fair grew wheels. Trucks hauling the entire Minnesota State Fair joined convoys in almost military fashion driving off the fairgrounds. Our five-car caravan joined in behind Adam, who drove an eighteen-wheeler southbound on I-35.

Deep into the night, we stopped at a small motel. I shared a bed with Chango. His nickname means monkey in Spanish and can be either funny or menacing. Sort of like Chango himself.

I rolled over and noticed one of his tattoos. "Smile now, cry later." The gang symbol 13 was tattooed on the nape of his neck. He repeatedly denied it meant MS-13, the Hispanic gang that originated in his home state of California. He'd deny it either way. He just said it was a dangerous gang.

Chango's hair was shaved short, and he wore a more-clever-than-the-mark smile. He was fond of Marlboro Reds, Tecate beer, caffeinated sodas, and chocolate muffins. He was intelligent and a hard ass.

In his mid-thirties, he'd been a carny for seventeen years. Becoming a carnival worker was his ticket off the streets and out of the gang life. Before carnivals, drugs and violence punctuated his life.

Chango pointed to the question mark scar on his belly as if it answered every question you'd ever have about him.

THE BEAT-UP CARNIVAL van we drove to Oklahoma City wasn't worth stealing. The dashboard was lined with vitamin bottles, twenty-eight-ounce Red Bulls, 12Hour energy drinks, Starbursts, and packs of Newports.

Clayton drove, and Roger rode shotgun through Iowa, Missouri, Kansas, and Oklahoma. We watched other Minnesota carnival caravans heading in the same direction.

Clayton drank sixteen Red Bulls every day. By the end of the day, his eyes were neon red. He let us all know that he'd negotiated an exclusive deal with Adam, including insurance, a bank account, guaranteed salary, and a percentage of his joint's overall take.

"Because," Clayton said. "I'm a fucking powerhouse agent."

The West crew was the best, he said, because we did it the way it should be done.

"We knock shit out. We clean the midway. We don't leave a dollar on the midway. We don't sell slum, and we're drug free."

His mentor was an owner named Fast Eddie who ran games along the Eastern Seaboard. Fast Eddie put a blindfold on him and dropped coins on the counter until Clayton could tell the coin by its ping.

Give Clayton a one-hundred-dollar bill, and he'd take out his pocketknife and pin it to the counter until it was used up. The upfront wager in a carnival game is usually a small fee. The hundred-dollar wager was a way to up the ante fast. Pinning the bill to the counter made sure the debt was paid after Clayton took the mark for his money.

"That's illegal in most states," he said.

Roger wasn't to be bested. He also liked to pin one-hundred-dollar bills to the counter. He knew a guy who took a mark for seventeen thousand dollars on the Tubs of Fun.

The tubs is a game in which a customer throws a softball into a basket. The customer wins if the ball stays in the basket. It appears easy but is a game easily manipulated. Roger wanted it known that he was every bit as rapacious as Clayton.

Roger's career in carnivals began after he was less than honorably discharged from the Army. Facing a marijuana charge while on R&R in Kuwait, he flipped out and told the military judge he'd reveal top-secret military codes to the enemy if he wasn't immediately released.

Broke and unemployed after leaving the Army, Roger went to Milwaukee with friends to a festival, and he joined the carnival that night. Veterans were a sizable minority on the carnival circuit, with varying military records.

Both Clayton and Roger talked about towns like pirates talked about cities they sacked. Remember Raleigh, Inglewood, Bakersfield, and the Meadowlands? Roger could rattle off the names of every major carnival troupe in the country and their owners.

Passing by outside the window was the best farmland outside the Eurasian Steppe. That will change in the coming years. Global warming is creating more droughts, and the water tables are falling in the Midwest. Traveling carnivals survived the Dust Bowl in the 1930s. They'll have to adjust again in the coming decades.

By the time we reached Oklahoma City, there was little doubt I was in the presence of two cocksure showmen ready to take the Oklahoma State Fair by storm.

THE SETUP BEGAN in the fiery-hot parking lot outside the fair. Inside the trucks, the heat was inhuman.

We rearranged stuffed prizes until we could enter the fair and set up our joints. After setup, Adam paid us for Minnesota. I cleared more than one thousand dollars after the cost of my trailer room and motel expenses.

The carnival portion of the fair was run by one of America's biggest carnival companies, Michigan-based Wade Shows Inc. I bought a Wade Shows hat and went to work.

The fair featured the Xtreme Bull Tour, the Kraft Cheese Wheel, free concerts, an agricultural hall, *Disney on Ice*, and a butterfly house. Foods included frosted-flake chickens, chocolate peanut butter fudge puppies with deep-fried butter, and bacon-covered caramel apples.

The real star of the fair, however, wasn't the food, the rodeo cowboys, or even the country stars on stage. In show business, the star attraction gets the marque.

A fifty-foot-long illuminated marque over the main entrance proclaimed the Oklahoma State Fair "The Greatest Carnival in the World."

ADAM THREW another pre-fair party at On the Border restaurant near our Super 8 motel.

Tequilas, margaritas, and Mexican food were all free. Once again it was a family affair, with Miss Trudy and Debraun at the table. At one point, Debraun passed her six-month-old baby around the table. The men held her at arm's length like a ticking bomb.

Two new members joined the crew, Adam's cousin, Greg West, and Patrick White, who was fresh off the bus from the East Coast.

Feeling magnanimous, Adam raised his tequila shot glass high in the air.

"I may be young, but I grew up south of the border (in Mexico). We used to take the crew down there for the end-of-season party, and some of them wouldn't come home for a week. Like they said in that movie *Armageddon*, roughnecks raised me. What do you expect?"

At that meal, I heard the Tub Thug talking about his pimping from the road. In carnivals, he called himself the Tub Thug because he was a mugger on the Tubs of Fun game. He could leave you broke and asking, "Who did this to me?" He was all showman by day and all pimp by night.

Time was the Tub Thug's thief. Running a Dallas-based pimping business from spreadsheets to bedsheets was exhausting. A broad-shouldered, bright-eyed black man in his twenties, Tub Thug smiled with gold-plated teeth. He praised the storytelling of country singers, but he was a world-class freestyle rapper.

He disappeared fast after dinner. The big money was in pimping, and he was off to his not-so-secret life as the #1 pimp in Dallas.

"WINNER, winner, shark for dinner. Free try. Everybody's a winner. Free try!"

Such was my routine at the shark pool. My new joint was a fishing game with blue rubber sharks floating in a shallow plastic pool. Customers paid two to five dollars to use a toy fishing pole for fishing out a toy shark. Everyone hooked a fish. The value of the prize was always worth less than the five dollars paid.

The most popular prizes were the blow-up dolphins and swords, which we blew up during setup until our faces were as blue as the sharks. My favorite prize was a giant-sized blow-up hammer. It was an invitation to mayhem.

"Here, Johnny, you won a hammer. Remember, don't . . ." Wham! ". . . hit your sister with it." Wham!

Oz worked at the long-ball game before being fired for theft. Long ball is a basketball free-throw game. I heard that Oz's earnings were so pathetic that Adam suspected him of pocketing the cash. Oz claimed incompetence. Before I learned the whole truth, Oz was back at work with me at the shark pool.

We worked alongside a host of recovering drug addicts and alcoholics. The addicts worked hourly for room and board at their rehabilitation house.

Adam gave the regular crew a one-hundred-dollar cash bankroll at the beginning of the day. He came by every few hours to collect the take. On a good day, I'd reach into my apron and pull out fistfuls of cash and hand it over to Adam.

None of the crew talked about it with me, but the temptation to steal from Adam was undeniable. I suspected more people than Oz were skimming.

Adam came by the shark tent every evening and gave me an extra five dollars.

"Good job," he'd say. "Go get yourself a dinner."

Those tips made me happy. I didn't skim, but I was working for the stories. Is that more or less virtuous? I went to the local Denny's, ordered all-you-can-eat pancakes, and wrote until early in the morning.

JACK POE WAS the fair's official chaplain and dropped by my shark-fishing game wearing a chaplain badge and a baseball cap that read, "I (*heart*) Jesus."

Every carny received a goody bag from him containing Curel moisturizer, Crest toothpaste, a Colgate toothbrush, a razor, peanut butter crackers, and a pair of white socks.

Chaplain Jack urged me to visit the fair's main tent to talk more about spirituality. All I cared about was taking off my reeking socks and putting on clean white Christian socks.

A member of the Christian drug/alcohol recovery program working with our crew, Carmen, defected from his group and asked to join our traveling crew. He started drinking beer again but asked Adam if he could minister to the crew.

Carmen said Adam was stunned that he wanted to save the souls of the West Crew. According to Carmen, Adam said, "Hell no."

BEHIND THE SCENES, the Oklahoma State Fair was a different show with fights, drugs, strippers, prostitutes, and a robbery.

A microburst flattened part of the fair one day, crushing joints and scattering prizes. It touched off a mad dash for plush strewn down the midway.

Another night, rival gangs savagely attacked each other in front of my shark joint. Inexplicably, a middle-aged local hire named Slippery Pete tried to single-handedly break up the gangs. Oklahoma City's mounted police arrived ready for a riot, causing a reverse microburst of people running away.

America's opioid scourge was often visible at the fair. One night, a man flopped to the ground next to me, attempting to swim down the midway. He undulated, using his arms like fins, barking and roaring like a seal. Unable to stand up, he continued to make seal cackles even after EMTs rolled him onto a stretcher to haul him away.

Adam scheduled a couple of rest days for the crew. The handyman Russ was ready to blow off some steam. He started a drunken donnybrook in my motel room with Chango, which ended in a broken TV and motel lamp. Then he left to wrestle Adam and lost again.

One guy hired a call girl and told everyone he couldn't perform because he was too butt-wasted. Several crew members spent their free day at bars and strip joints.

The next morning, I was in the motel's continental breakfast room eating my Raisin Bran and reading an online *New York Times* story about Elizabeth Gilbert, author of *Eat Pray Love*.

Roger walked in with Candace, a stripper he'd met the night before. He'd been bounced from the strip bar for asking strippers to come on the road with us, but still somehow ended up with Candace.

Candace said she loved the movie *Eat Pray Love*. She flashed an ear-to-ear smile.

"Lots of people say I look like Julia Roberts," she said. "I don't have her big lips, do I?"

There was a resemblance to the movie star. I imagined lots of her strip-show patrons mentioned it to her.

"Your lips are lovely," I said, not realizing how that sounded until I said it.

Earlier that morning, Roger convinced Candace to get into bed with Clayton and fabricate a false story of a *ménage à trois*. When Clayton said he had no memory of a threesome, Candace acted hurt.

Candace was living proof that at least one of Roger's stories was true. He was great at getting strippers. His ex-wife, at the time in prison on a drug conviction, also was a former stripper.

The motel was full of people who worked for the Oklahoma State Fair. Drug dealers and prostitutes hung around in case anyone needed their services. Chango told me that if I ever needed the room for a woman, he'd make sure I got my privacy.

Tim let a drug-addicted woman into his hotel room when his roommates were out. She stole all Patrick White's cash and credit/debit cards. Patrick was outraged at Tim and cited the us-against-the-world carny code. It calls on showmen to protect each other from locals and cops.

"That's a cardinal rule," Patrick said. "You don't let locals in your room."

"What do you want me to say?" Tim asked. "I didn't take your stuff."

Carmen walked to the nearby coffee shop one morning as the sun was rising and met a streetwalker.

"Sister," he said, "you need prayer."

"Mister," she said, "You need fifteen dollars."

Roger bought a new pair of Michael Jordan shoes in Oklahoma City and gave me his old pair. They appeared new and fit perfectly. I thanked him for the shoes but added that they were giving me a wild reputation around Oklahoma City.

"Now when I walk around town," I said, "every stripper and whore in Oklahoma City is waving to me and saying, 'I know those shoes. How are you, baby?'"

The Oklahoma slough was an all-nighter. The Tub Thug and Vanil worked as hard as anyone, despite their nocturnal enterprises.

Patrick White walked up from behind me with a question.

"What's it like to kill people?"

"What are you talking about?" I asked.

"I was told you were Vietnam special ops, with dozens of kills under your belt. What's it like killing people?"

"I don't talk about my past," I said.

Patrick shook his head as if he just couldn't believe the kind of people he meets in carnivals. It took me a while to realize he was joking. He was just keeping in shape with a quick prank. Patrick's favorite line was, "No funny, no money." He wasn't rich, so how funny could he be?

Our crew moved in and out of the spotlight circles, loading plush bags onto a truck. We didn't get paid for the early-morning midway clean-up. Plenty of money was made when the midway was open. We practically vacuumed up money when the midway was rocking.

Clayton predicted it on the ride down from St. Paul. We didn't leave a dollar on the midway.

PART IX
TEXAS!

SEPTEMBER, OCTOBER

WELCOME TO THE BIG TIME

DALLAS

If at first you don't succeed . . . fuck it.

— TEXAS-BORN SHOWMAN WILLIE NELSON

Two million people would pass within the sound of my voice in the next three weeks at the State Fair of Texas. Step back and let me work. I'll juggle. I'll sing. I'll dance. They don't know what they want, and I do.

Chango drove the crew van on to the fairgrounds and gave us the behind-the-scenes tour of the nation's biggest state fair. He pointed out the Texas Star, a Ferris wheel twenty stories tall. About seventy rides were being set up, more than double the rides in St. Paul.

Deep-fried masterpieces make the State Fair of Texas the annual king of heart-attack jokes. Fifty thousand people that year ingested the fair's Thanksgiving meal, a deep-fried ball made of stuffing, turkey, and cream corn.

The King of the pitchmen every year is the fifty-five-foot-tall Big Tex, a rudimentary robot capable of moving its hands, head, and mouth. Standing at the front of the illuminated "Super Midway" sign, Big Tex is a crowd magnet. If I could land a joint near him, I'd be in the honeypot.

"Hoooowdeeee, folks," the voice from Big Tex would say. "Chevrolet is the official vehicle of the State Fair of Texas."

Big Tex is a big, imbecilic, misshapen, awkward moving statue so technologically backward that he is as dearly loved by Texans as a big goofy family dog. Rebuilt after a fire the previous year, the new Big Tex still looked like a Route 66 fireworks store display.

Texas is the home of the Johnson Space Center and some of the best high-tech universities in the world. Anything as outsized as the State Fair of Texas demands a high-tech Big Tex.

At the very least, why not a sixty-foot hologram of a person hawking products? The person could change genders and races. Mrs. Tex. Hispanic Tex. Black Tex. Asian Tex. The possibilities were endless. Is Texas ready for a LBGQ Tex?

I floated my Big Tex ideas with the crew, but their faces screwed up as if to say, "Yankees like you are the reason we execute morons in Texas."

Adam hammered us about keeping our energy levels high. There were only twenty-four days left to make as much money as possible before going home. Dig deep on this final sprint, he said, and the winter will be cushy.

On my first walk down the Super Midway at the Texas fair, I saw Steve working on his game joint. We'd worked carnivals together in California, Minnesota, and Oklahoma. After Texas, he was heading back to California with his lovely one-eyed wife.

"Hey, Slim, you've hit the big time now."

We didn't have to set up joints in Texas because the state-fair joints are permanent structures. We stocked our joints and then stored the rest in a giant warehouse behind the Super Midway.

Our plush was the hottest on the midway, the two most popular prizes being brightly colored, giant stuffed pigs and *Despicable Me* minions.

We stocked our warehouse area by throwing clear plastic bags filled with giant pigs up over the second-story guardrails. We all showed off how easy it was for us to throw the human-sized plush pigs from the first floor over the second-story railing.

I missed a couple of pig throws. Aware I was being laughed at for being too old, I dug deep, throwing the pigs higher and higher in long flying arcs over the rails. Big round pig after pig went flying in ever more ridiculous orbits. I was a feverish madman trying to prove pigs can fly.

SETUP WAS EASIER, but not easy. We scaled ladders. We sat on beams to hang plush from the roofs.

Chango gave Heidi a rag and told her to wipe down a game joint pole. Heidi was dressed in a purple tank top and jean shorts. Her brunette hair with blond streaks was pulled back in a bun. She took the rag, let down her hair, and walked toward the pole.

Heidi was once a stripper for Dallas's most exclusive strip joints. Slowly she climbed twelve feet up the pole. Then she swung around and slid down the pole as the song *Disco Inferno* blasted along the Super Midway.

Her performance drew hoots and whistles from crews along the Super Midway. When she reached the ground, she looked at her captive audience, smiled, and climbed back up again. The second version was even vampier and drew a bigger reaction.

Chango once asked Heidi to be his woman on this route, but she declined. When she finished her midway pole dance, she walked up to Chango and handed him back the rag. What she said next must have disoriented her former suitor.

"Pole's clean," she said, and then let him watch her walk away.

Heidi told me she quit stripping because she was doing "too many eight balls." She didn't specify if the eight balls were made with meth, cocaine, or heroin.

She didn't love carnivals. All she wanted was to get closer to her dad, Clayton. As a child, she saw little of her father. This was another chance for healing. Heidi failed the drug test in Oklahoma, but the testing lady there let her slide.

In St. Paul, Heidi took up with Irish Patrick. He was twenty-something, thin, and struggling with his own drug problems. Irish Patrick was raised in foster homes and thought he might be a father but wasn't sure. His dream was to work in carnivals, quit drugs, find a good woman, and be happy forever. Heidi was in no shape to help anyone.

Her car disappeared from the motel lot in Oklahoma City, and she knew her husband couldn't have taken it because he was in prison on weapons charges. She thought the car was stolen until she realized it was repossessed.

Irish Patrick suggested they have a child together. She was still married to her husband in prison, and I heard there was a child to consider. She told him no marriage was in their future, but she stayed with him for the duration in Dallas.

Tim, the former Gangster Disciple, was another crew member trying to kick his drug habits. He took time off between Oklahoma and the Texas state fairs, supposedly to see one of his children.

When he finally showed up in Dallas, he asked for a separate motel room and locked himself inside. For three days, we heard him puking behind the motel door. He sweated out whatever he was using. On the fourth day, he emerged from his room a shipwrecked man returning to the world.

Tim ran the bottle-up game. Players use a stick with a string and loop at the end to pick up a beer bottle by the neck and set it up straight.

He was so good, Tim could stand up the bottle without using his hands. He tucked the stick into the back of his shirt so that it stuck up above his head. From that position, he could loop the bottleneck and stand the bottle upright.

He was expert at calling in customers. He was always one of the top earning agents in the crew. Yet a master of the bottle-up needs to be a steady hand. He can't have the shakes.

THE TUB THUG, Vanil, and Patrick White were in emergency mode the night before the drug test. They drank gallons of water and too many Red Bulls. They took GNC dietary supplements.

Long lines formed outside the fair's on-site drug-testing facility. It was a pink, one-story, boxy structure behind the rides, with small rooms for medical care.

Adam was there joking with the administrators. They remembered him as a child. Everyone in our line passed the drug tests.

A drug tester commented to Vanil that something strange was going on.

"It's amazing," she said, "how Adam's crew all test a hair below the limit."

I asked Vanil when he and the Tub Thug last smoked pot.

"Last night," he said with a laugh.

During the fair, a random drug tester walked up to Vanil and the Tub Thug while they were working the Tubs of Fun. The drug tester told them to report to the testing facility for a spot check.

They knew the real drill. They packed up their things and knocked off for the day. They never showed up for another test and were never hassled again.

Heidi failed the drug test in Dallas and couldn't work. This was Clayton's chance to make up for lost time by helping his wayward daughter. She needed him.

She'd quit her stripper job to be closer to him. She'd lost her carnival job, her husband, and now was losing her health. Instead, Clayton all but denied she was his daughter.

"You're more family to me than she is," he told Adam.

THE TUB THUG was always drumming up customers, either for the tubs or for his girls. He began working on me, calling me Mike Love.

He saw a "tell" in my eyes. The tell was there every night he went out to his night shift, "selling salmon and peeling bananas." He thought I was just another John, but I lusted for the stories.

The Tub Thug was a magical agent yet as good as he was in carnivals, he was a better pimp. He called himself Sir Tey the Great.

"I will take you out tonight," he said to me. "I will drive by the motel and pick you up and we're going out. You and me."

Half a dozen carnies were watching the exchange. The Tub Thug treated me exactly how he played marks.

"God sends me blessings, and he sent me this Puerto Rican girl. She's not all burned out on the business. She says things to you and your knees go weak."

Playing on people's desires was a game the Tub Thug knew by heart.

"What do you want? Anything you want for one hundred dollars an hour. I've got light-skinned girls. Hour-glass figures. They'll do anything you want. Anything. You like whips, chains, domination?"

As he listed sexual acts, the crew hung up smiling yellow, *Despicable Me* minions. It wasn't a Disney moment.

I declined his offer with a dash of self-deprecation.

"I got no game," I said. "I don't drink. I don't do drugs. I don't sleep with whores. I'm no fun."

What I meant was, I couldn't figure out a way to see his pimping life and still keep my writing life a secret.

During a lightning storm one day, the Tub Thug sat on the game counter, talking to me about becoming an L-7. Then he took his forefinger and thumb on each hand, forming an L and a seven. Put them together and you have a square.

He wanted the L-7 square life. He was living in a fast lane, but he feared being caught and serving a ten-year stint for pandering.

He'd met a woman on the carnival circuit in California. She was a mother with a well-paid job. If he went straight, he'd miss the prostitutes and the clubs. He'd miss being "fresh," with $1,500 in his pocket and driving the streets of Dallas where everybody knew he was a pimp player.

"I'm the greatest at pimping," he said. "What are you the greatest at, Mike Love?"

More than being the greatest, more than the street fame and the money, the Tub Thug wanted what other people find easy. The work-a-day square life was his Mount Everest.

All Tub Thug needed was a commercial driver's license and a clean drug test. He could be a trucker with a California home and a family.

He needed to get out of Dallas, where the game was all around and all the players knew him. Dallas's greatest carnival pimp wanted to settle down with one good woman.

"I need a fresh start with some money and a good woman. That's not bad, is it?"

Walking away from this life would be a neat trick, and yet it was as easy as winning a bright, smiling prize at his impossible tubs.

MY FIRST JOINT in Dallas was a short-ball joint next to the fair's back exit. It was the worst spot on the Super Midway. I worked the joint with Oz and several locals. The short ball is played with a cantaloupe-sized basketball that players shoot at an eye-level hoop.

The Super Midway was an independent, cashless midway. No single carnival company controlled the midway, and a laser gun was used to scan prepaid cards. The fair made us wear long-sleeve shirts to cover tattoos and gave us electric guns so we couldn't pocket the cash. Cashless midways are the reason some showmen won't work Texas's state fair. There's little room for creative cash flow.

I juggled the basketballs. I gave free shots. I danced. I told people they looked like Michael Jordan. I put all my energy into the work. Yet I was still dying by the old real estate adage, "Location, location, location."

I was stuck at the back of the fair. I'd give anything to run a game at the feet of the greatest showman at the State Fair of Texas, that big, dopey, lovable Big Tex.

ADAM HIRED a new guy to help work at the tubs in the joint next to mine. Scott probably was the most unstable and violent man I'd met up to that point.

He had deep, dark rings around his eyes and never seemed to smile. He was in his thirties and stocky. He made extra sure I knew he was not Mexican.

One afternoon, Scott tried to stay on the high-traffic side of the Tubs of Fun joint too long before rotating to the back. When the Tub Thug told him to move to the other side, Scott didn't appreciate the way the black man asked.

Scott told both Adam and Chango that he was going to stab the Tub Thug. Adam fired him, but a nearby joint soon hired him. When the Tub Thug found out Scott wanted to stab him, he laughed and went looking for him.

Scott interested me. I walked over one break and sat with him at the picnic tables next to the Dentzel Carousel. I soon realized I was also once on his hit list. I thanked him for not killing me and asked about his carnival life. The Dentzel Carousel played *My Wild Irish Rose* in the background as he told his wildest stories.

Scott worked his first carnival when he was just twelve years old. He passed himself off as sixteen to get the work. At the end of his first twelve-day spot, he walked away with four hundred dollars.

When he turned sixteen, he was a carnival veteran "banging four girls a week." He'd come out of the storage room covered in white plush stuffing.

He later joined the Army, but when someone said something wrong to him, he jumped across the lunch table and nearly killed the man. He was discharged for "failure to adapt."

When Scott rejoined his former carnival, he found out his girl-friend had an abortion while he was in the Army. With that in mind, he bided his time while working out the rest of the week.

"Then I fucked my girlfriend, ditched her, got a quarter ounce of coke, a liter of whiskey, and I went to Carolina with the carnival. I've been gone ever since. Who wouldn't after that, right?"

He'd worked all over the country and knew hardcore carnies like Nick the Prick, Luke the Puke, and John the Butcher.

Scott's tubs stories were among the most outrageous I'd ever heard. He once clipped a mark for $10,420 on the tubs in Albuquerque, New Mexico.

Scott had regrets. For instance, one mark was an ex-con who did twenty-plus years for a murder he didn't commit. He took most of the man's wrongful conviction money. What he regretted most was that he didn't take it all.

"It depends on what kind of person you are. If you like giving out lots of prizes, balloons are for you. If you like taking someone for all they have and leaving them broke on the midway with no prizes, then tubs are for you."

Scott's stories about carnival owners involved violence against employees. He mentioned owners I knew and gave me advice.

"If you are in deep trouble, never go back to the office alone to get paid. That's where they'll be waiting for you."

He hated that carnivals were not as violent as they once were. Someone once bit off part of Scott's ear in a carnival fight. He superglued it back on and worked the rest of the night. Scott clearly was still violent. He recently had been let out on parole. During his time inside, he threatened to kill the prison psychologist.

His hatred of the Tub Thug also may have stemmed from his racism.

"I told him, 'I'll stab your monkey ass.' Three months ago, if some black guy came up to me and said something like that, I'd have stuck him without thinking about it. I'm on parole, so if I stuck him, I'd get the same time as if I broke his face. By the time I served my time in state prison, my federal time would be up. Getting stuck doesn't make you tough. Sticking someone doesn't make you tough. But that's if he survives. If he doesn't, the world won't miss that asshole."

He carried a derringer wherever he went, and it was helpful when he was running rigged board games "in the hood."

"Those black guys would say, 'I'm going home to get my gun.' Then I'd pull out my gun and say, 'Does it look like this, you monkey bastard?'"

BACK AT THE SHORT BALL, business at the end of the midway was so weak I made slightly more than my daily motel bill. When Adam announced his plan to send half the crew to another carnival south of Houston, I saw an opportunity.

I told him I signed up for Dallas, not Houston. I wanted to quit. There was still time to add another carnival in another state to my year.

"Then we won't send you with the rest," he said. "You'll stay here. You said you'd work Texas. You're a man of your word, aren't you?"

I was so ready to hitchhike out of Dallas I'd packed my clothes.

"Damn," I said. "I was hoping you wouldn't bring that up."

Far from punishing me for my disloyalty, Adam moved me to the honey pot, working with Adam and Clayton at the top of the Super Midway, directly behind Big Tex. They were headed to the next carnival, but Adam must have thought I could use the time with them learning the tubs before they left.

Clayton rode me the whole day, saying I was doing it all wrong. I needed to switch up my cracks and calls. Move people along faster. That first day, four of us worked four tubs. By the end of the day, I'd out-earned Roger, Clayton, and every person on the West crew in every joint.

Every day I worked the honey pot, Adam came by midday and reported that Tim was running ahead of me on the bottle-up game. It was a motivator. By the end of the day, I was the TA, or top agent.

Q transferred with me to the honey pot. He was a big black man with a thick Dallas accent. In his thirties, he pulled back his graying black hair into tiny ponytails on the back of his head. He was friendly, glib, and a strong tubs agent. Adam's dad, Bob West, trained Q, and

Adam told Q to expect his percentage of the take to top three thousand dollars.

He wasn't any better than me at reeling in a passersby, but he was a genius at keeping them at the joint playing game after game. People spent one hundred dollars or more, all for a stuffed minion. Q was the best at giving group deals. He'd have a whole crowd playing at one time, which meant everybody lost at one time. Winners were rare. Cops, celebrities, and pretty women had remarkable luck.

To drum up business, one year Q brought in an Xbox. He told customers they could play for the regular prizes or the grand prize. A part-time local lost the box to a customer, a rookie mistake. Q made the rookie pay him back for the Xbox.

There is no reason to lose at tubs. Adam joked about it.

"If somebody wins one of those big minions, you're fired."

Q danced to the music on the midway. He roamed the outside of the joint during slow times. He'd stand back twenty feet from the tubs and sink every ball. After a while, I did it for the camera.

When crowds were thin, Clayton and Q resorted to funny cracks.

"Ma'am, you have a flat tire on your stroller. No, the other right wheel. No, the other wheel. Just kidding. Come on in here. I'll give you a free try for being such a good sport."

The point was to get people's attention.

"Ma'am, you have gum on your shoe. Not that shoe, the other shoe. Not that shoe, the other shoe. Now you're doing the chicken walk."

Make eye contact. Pressure them to play.

"Why are you texting me, blondie, I'm right here . . . Don't go, blondie, who am I going to flirt with?"

Q added race jokes.

"Free try from the black guy."

"When a black guy gives you something free, you better take it."

"You can trust me. I'm white. No, wait, my bad."

Cracks don't work a majority of the time so even when people are walking away, the crack makes them think of coming back.

"You'll come back later? That's what my ex said. You seen her?"

WITHIN MINUTES of learning the Tubs of Fun, I was the author of a new routine.

"I will hypnotize you. You will throw this ball into this tub. Watch me. Throw the ball to me like a rainbow's arc. I call it Mike's Rainbow. Great. Do it again. Great. Now throw the ball into the tub. You made it. I've hypnotized you with Mike's Rainbow."

I fake-hypnotized the multitudes. The veterans kidded me about "Mike's Rainbow," but they were getting a percentage of the house take. I lived on the illusion of hypnotism. I could make your day or crush your heart. More than one couple walked away arguing because someone didn't stick to "Mike's Rainbow."

The old, the infirm, the unstable, single mothers, kids, and even the dying came by my joint and lost. They played for a *Despicable Me* plush, but they really were playing against despicable me.

On the morning of a peak attendance day, Q looked out at the midway and told me how the day would go.

"I will rob people today. Rob them. Nobody is getting away. When you get a woman in your room, you fuck her."

Peak days were football days at the Cotton Bowl stadium. The Oklahoma-Texas game drew ninety thousand people to the game. Rose Dog's alma mater Grambling State played Prairie View A&M in the State Fair Classic.

Crowd sizes were highly dependent on weather and promotions. The days went by like that, up and down, rainy and dry, long and longer, hot and hotter.

At the end of each day, we filed out the back gate to a people-mover tram. It took us to the parking lots and the Sand Castles RV park, where owners and managers parked their RVs.

From there, we arranged for rides back to the motel. When our crew moved together, Roger said we moved like a platoon on patrol.

The late night tram ride was almost serene. The parking lights shone above us. People on the tram spoke in low voices about their day. Steve sat next to me one night and told me how tired he was. He looked forward to going home and seeing his seven grandchildren after the fair closed.

The last colored lights of the night flashed across his face as he told me a good friend of his was dying of liver disease and was broke.

"That's what happens to old carnies, Slim."

I felt sick.

Patrick White and I took our break one day by the Dentzel Carousel. He spoke in his fast, scattershot rat-a-tat-tat way.

"Who do you think was our best president? What do you think of Spiro Agnew? What do you think will happen to General McCrystal? You look like you can rap. Let's hear a rap."

He asked what I would do after the season.

"I'm worried," I said. "I don't know."

Patrick White held his big dreams close to his big heart.

"I hate this," he said. "I want to change my life. I want to save thirty or forty thousand dollars and buy me a laundromat business."

His fiancée back in Maryland was an assistant store manager. She was pregnant, and he couldn't wait to get home.

He didn't dream of riches and fame. He wanted to save for his laundromat by becoming a union bus driver.

"You can make thirty-five dollars an hour up north with the union," he said.

I talked to him about the joys of growing older.

"I can't eat what I want. I can't drink what I want. I can't dunk a basketball. I can't make love to a woman for three days straight. But there are advantages to growing old," I said, "and when you find them out let me know because I'm stumped."

He laughed. He was young. Not his problem.

IN THE MORNING, our crew made its way to the Sand Castles RV park to meet Adam and start the day. We were still yards away from his RV when we heard the news.

"Patrick is dead," Debraun said.

Patrick White, age twenty-nine, collapsed at 4 a.m. after a marathon day of work. He was sitting on the edge of a bed in a cheap motel room south of Houston when he fell back dead onto the mattress.

He'd been working in Dallas at the break-a-plate joint, a game where customers throw balls to break plates. Then he and half of our crew drove to another carnival. They were still getting settled in at the motel when he died just before sunrise. I imagined his heart breaking like a row of carnival plates.

Patrick White was dead. Where was his family? We were his carnival family, but who loved him off carnival roads? Nobody seemed to know how to get hold of his family in Maryland or Brooklyn or anywhere. The crew stood around in the Dallas parking lot and took drags on their cigarettes.

"Life is too short," someone said.

"He could have had many things wrong with him but not known it," another said.

People began telling stories about death in carnivals. Carnival workers are frequently flat broke. On any given day, they aren't far from a pauper's grave. They face life and death on the road. They are far from people who know them, far from home and love.

The news crippled Q. He found it hard to laugh or work. He'd make a crack to a passerby and then turn to me to talk about Patrick. Sometimes I didn't know if he was talking about Patrick or himself.

Our thoughts were visible to one another. A whisper passed between us, between the sick and the well, "Not Patrick . . . not me."

I thought of Huey in California. He found his dream life in carnivals.

"I'll die in this carnival, on the midway," Huey said. "Many people have."

A veteran showman once told me a horror story about dying alone on the road. He was the driver in a group of cars headed to the next jump when they stopped for gas. A young man went to the bathroom and shot himself up with a lethal dose of heroin. Once back in the car, he drifted off to sleep in the back seat and died.

Not knowing what to do, his carnival family dragged him out and left his body in the high grass of an interstate on-ramp. No money to transport him. No contact numbers. The cops might detain them for questioning or think they did it. Carnival people don't call cops.

The body of the young overdose victim was discovered when a highway groundsman ran him over with a mower.

In Patrick's case, EMTs were called when he collapsed on the bed, and police eventually found Patrick's relatives. I heard his body was transferred back east. I don't know the whole truth. I know Patrick was a carnival man who was cheated, and we all fall down.

THOSE WHO UNDERSTAND carnivals know they are skeins of families.

From the Mexican border town of Laredo, Texas, Gloria was a twenty-ish, raven-haired, bilingual woman with a high-voltage smile. She showed up at the State Fair of Texas to work a water-shooting game and to see Tim in our crew.

Tim was still shaky from detoxing when she arrived in Dallas. Then his infidelities came to light. I was their motel roommate by then and heard her heart breaking. She loved him more than he loved himself.

About the same time, Chango said he was having feelings for his "baby momma." He wanted to see her again. She once was the best-looking girl in carnival games. They were parents of a lively, smart two-year-old daughter.

The woman who showed up at our motel room was pregnant and could barely see out of her black eye. Her assailant was her new husband and the stepfather of Chango's daughter.

That must have cut Chango deep. After his daughter left that afternoon, I saw the man of many scars with a new one opening up.

Adam's cousin, Greg, was dealing with his pregnant ex-girlfriend. Carmen's son was in jail for beating up his mother's abusive boyfriend. Roger was worried about upcoming court dates for being in arrears on child support. The end of the season meant returning to family issues. Even Adam was dealing with a divorce and his blended family.

At a crew dinner with Adam and Debraun, someone asked when they intended to marry. Debraun pointed out that Adam was still married, pending a final divorce. The couple argued throughout dinner at the Red Lobster. At its climax, Adam blurted out that he should have spent his money on Thai strippers rather than on his garlic-soaked shrimp-tailed meal.

Debraun left the restaurant crying so hard that I worried she might leave him that night. Everything was better in the morning. Batman's divorce was still in the works and so too was the wedding.

THE SLOUGH WENT LATE that final night. Crews across the fairgrounds waved goodbye. I gave Q my State Fair of Texas shirt. The crew rode away on the tram for the last time.

The next morning, there was stock to load onto an eighteen-wheeler. When we finished, I jumped into the back of a pickup truck with the crew. Everyone was in high spirits. It was payday for the last fair of the season.

Vanil and the Tub Thug were sitting on the top of the truck bed sidewall when Vanil asked me how the fair went for me. I told them a story of how conflicted I was running the Tubs of Fun.

A young, attractive woman came up to the tubs asking if I could make sure she won a big yellow minion. She had breast cancer and didn't know if she would live or die. She made it sound as if her final request was a free yellow minion.

"Can you help a breast cancer patient, Mr. Mike?" she asked.

I hinted broadly that I could help, but I wouldn't guarantee it. She needed to buy a turn and win it. I'd teach her Mike's Rainbow. But she pleaded with me again and then walked away. None of us knew if I was being played, but I knew she needed a minion bad enough to say she had cancer.

Both Vanil and the Tub Thug worked the tubs, and you'd have to pry a minion out of their cold, dead hands before they gave away a big prize.

"Oh my God," Vanil said. "Mike is going to hell!"

The Tub Thug agreed.

"You are going to hell," he said. "Cancer? You are cold."

I wasn't going to admit regret to Vanil and the Tub Thug. Regret is weak and being cold is strong. I was one of them.

"See you there guys," I said.

ON MOST PAYDAYS, we went to Adam's RV or the office trailer. He met us one-on-one at his desk. He'd quickly run down what we earned. Then he took out a wad of bills and began counting faster than any non-showman can think.

On one such payday, I asked Adam to reminisce about his glory days playing football. Was he really a hometown high school football hero in West Bend, Iowa?

Adam West was a rising star when he tore his meniscus. He racked up more than two hundred tackles and would have gained a scholarship if not for his injuries. He was happy in high school, and his girlfriend was the prettiest in the school. It was as if those tackles happened yesterday. Those victories would never be forgotten.

Adam attended Texas A&M, majoring in business, without an athletic scholarship or even trying out for the team. He was a standout in math class until he realized the square life wasn't for him. Adam dropped out and went back into the family business. His dream was to be the best showman in carnivals, a class they don't teach at Texas A&M.

The last payday at the State Fair of Texas was out of the ordinary. Adam drove his truck to our motel to meet with us in the cab. He was carrying wads of cash as usual, but this time he was selling something he needed us to buy. He was handing out cash and holding out the promise of more where that came from.

We didn't know exactly what we deserved after three weeks of work but we expected a giant lump sum. As usual, we couldn't verify our pay. We had to trust Adam.

Tim met with him first and came back to our room all smiles and with three thousand dollars in cash.

"Adam wants to see you in his truck," he said.

I wanted to hear Adam's views on Mike's Rainbow.

"Great work, Mike, you're our top agent. Only about one in ten, or more like one in twenty, is that good at the tubs. You are and so am I. Playing it well can be taught, but a lot of it can't. It's a natural gift. A lot of it comes down to just standing there and grinding it out. Not spending a lot of time with anyone. Not getting to know anybody. I was one of the best. When I was a teenager, I'd come back to my dad with three thousand dollars and he'd say, 'Boy, what have you been up to?'"

I'd already polled other top earners on what they made. Joe and Tim earned a percentage of the total take in addition to their salary because they were veterans who worked the whole season. Tim told me his total for the year would be around thirty-five thousand dollars. Joe cited a similar number. I made a straight per-click amount.

My pay was on a sheet of paper in Adam's handwriting. Even after spending half the fair at the wrong game and at the wrong end of the midway, I brought in $16,711 by myself. That earned me $3,342 for the fair, or about 20 percent, less the cost of the uniform and motel fees. I bested everyone on the crew in total sales, which made me one of the best at the biggest state fair in America.

Adam started with the flattery, which I loved. He handed over a wad of cash. I loved that, too. But this payday was different because he needed something important from me.

"Come back next season," he said. "If you stay the whole year, I'll give you a free cruise to Mexico with the rest of the crew. It'll be a party."

A veteran showman working with Gloria once asked me if I planned on returning the next season.

"I'm not the real thing," I told Gloria's coworker. "I don't like the, the ... ah ... the ..."

"The larceny?" he laughed.

I told Adam I planned to spend part of the money to go to Veracruz to see my jarocho carny pals. He warned me about the drug cartels and kidnappings.

"No matter what you do, don't go into the mountains. Stay near the resorts."

I told him I was going to the mountains. And I might try to work another carnival when I came back to the states.

"Good luck traveling, man," he said. "The season is over. The rule is, 'No money, no spots, No-vember.'"

CLAYTON MET a woman earlier in the season and was moving her and her kids to his winter quarters. It made me wonder how Heidi felt about her dad offering to father a new family. Heidi and Irish Patrick were headed out with money and active drug habits.

Tim swore off drugs again, and Gloria believed him. Her mother brought their two daughters to the Dallas motel. I met the girls, both younger than six. Their dad was a rock star to them. He was proud of his older, precocious daughter. He never saw any child with more spirit. He and Gloria planned to buy a trailer and spend the winter months as a family.

Roger was packing up his guns and heading back to Milwaukee on the Greyhound. Nobody knew how many guns Roger carried town to town. The Iraq veteran said he packed an arsenal. I once took a picture of Roger sleeping in low grass on a work break. On his stomach was a silver pistol. I assumed the gun was loaded.

Oz's plans were intentionally vague. He said a wealthy couple wanted him to house-sit for them. Having been fired briefly in Oklahoma City for making no money, my guess was he didn't save much during his season. In other years, he'd stayed in homeless shelters.

The West crew was a bacchanalian bunch of erotic, greedy, caring, overindulgent, messed-up, funny individualists. Joe was right about our crew in St. Paul. I was proud to be part of the West crew.

No sense of completion followed the State Fair of Texas. I worked with the West crew for two months and at some of the biggest state fairs in America.

I could still hear Patrick White laughing. Our crew was splitting up without so much as a hug.

Carnival lives never seem complete. They just roll on.

PART X
MEXICO

OCTOBER, NOVEMBER

GHOST TOWN TO MEXICAN SHOW TOWN

TLAPACOYAN, VERACRUZ STATE

The pleasures and riches of this life are but loaned, their substance is vain, their appearance illusory.

— *SONGS OF KING NEZAHUALCOYOTL,* A 15TH CENTURY NAHUATL POET, PHILOSOPHER, RULER

I rode a Tornado to the hottest, meanest, most chaotic place in American carnivals, Mexico.

Taking a Tornado bus from Dallas, I had no idea what to expect in Tlapacoyan, in the eastern state of Veracruz.

"You come in May or June, you'll see this town empty, empty of people," Salvador said back in California.

Out of touch with Salvador and the Butler crew most of the year, I didn't know when they would go home for the winter. I might be heading to a ghost town.

El Chapo's Sinaloa drug cartel was in a savage battle with the Los Zetas drug cartel for control of Veracruz. Their murdered victims included journalists, making Veracruz one of the most dangerous places in the world for reporters. A new cartel rule was no more ransoms for kidnappings, just torture and killing.

The trip to Tlapacoyan was made even riskier because I lost Salvador's address and phone number sometime during the year.

My only clues were pictures of people I worked with back in California. I made paper copies, like missing-person fliers for my lost family. No place to stay the night. No Spanish to speak of. No idea how to survive if attacked.

Most of the Butler ride jockeys in California came from this village nestled in the hill country rolling up to the Sierra Madre Oriental.

The annual return of the carnival men after the season coincides with the migration of the monarch butterflies to the sacred oyamel fir trees of central Mexico.

Mexican carnies are a subculture within the carnival subculture. The Mexican migration to American carnivals began ramping up after 2000. A third to half of the overall carnival workforce in America was Mexican and growing.

Feeder towns are typically rural. Most of the men go north for seasonal work, usually in the agricultural sector. They go together and come back together. Their villages run on a northern clock.

Tlapacoyan is the hub of the carnival migration story. Much of the credit or blame is due to Jim Judkins, a former circus owner whose JKJ Workforce Agency arranged for about half of all Mexican migration to U.S. carnivals.

He estimated that about five thousand workers labored in carnivals the year I worked. He arranged for nearly half of those carnival jobs to draw people from Tlapacoyan and its surrounding towns.

Judkins once owned Circus Chimera and tapped one of his workers, Victor Apolinar, to help him start a migration business. Apolinar soon began running visa operations from Tlapacoyan. The budding industry lifted many families out of abject poverty, where the pay could be as little as five dollars a day.

Apolinar became a local hero. A street was named after him, and he was elected mayor in a landslide. Tlapacoyan became the headwaters keeping American carnivals alive.

Riding the Tornado overnight from Dallas, I headed down I-35 and I-37 before customs in Browning, Texas. I crossed the Rio Grande, entering Mexico at Matamoros.

It's not an arduous journey, but it is long. The Dallas-Veracruz segment was 1,100 miles and took thirty-three hours.

A major port and a naval city, Veracruz is where Spanish Conquistador Hernán Cortés joined forces with the Totonac tribal Chief Chicomacatl, dubbed "The Fat Chief." They combined forces and marched inland to conquer the Aztec Empire in Mexico City in 1521.

Veracruz is known for its pre-Lenten carnival and its traditional music, called *son jarocho*, or the Veracruz sound. It's a loose fusion of indigenous Indian, Hispanic, Caribbean, and African beats. The most famous son jarocho song in the United States is *La Bamba*.

From the City of Veracruz, I took a Marco Polo bus six hours northwest to Tlapacoyan. The bus first headed north along the blond beaches of the Costa Esmeralda on the Gulf of Mexico.

When it turned west, we rode through semitropical forested hills. We passed small villages with schoolkids in gray uniforms and white shirts.

It was market day in Martinez de la Torre and long lines of trucks were stacked high with oranges, tangerines, limes, and bananas.

Roads thinned the farther from the coast we rode. Side roads became dirt roads. Small herds of cattle dotted the hills. Farmers rode burros.

Azaleas and orchids lined the roads. Local Ceiba trees and vanilla plants held mythological powers among the pre-Columbian Indians. The forests hid deep gorges, rivers, and ancient ruins. The foothills led up to Mexico's highest mountains.

When the bus pulled into Tlapacoyan, I could see its strategic geography. For centuries, it was the axis for surrounding villages, also part of an ancient trade corridor from the center of the country to the Gulf Coast.

At its center these days is a bus terminal. It is still an important trade route, and its riches are its people.

CLOUDS TIPPED the foothills around the town. It was drizzling when I stepped off the bus. I gathered my backpack and began my hunt for Butler carnies. In a town where your safety depends on who you are with, it wasn't shrewd to let people know I was alone. Yet I had no choice.

I was prepared to approach every person in town in search of my Butler friends, even if that meant accidentally asking the banditos. I was defenseless.

The first bus-station employee I saw was wearing a St. Louis Cardinals jersey. I guessed he might know English.

I handed him pictures of my lost carny family.

"*Habla Inglés?*" I asked.

No.

Nobody within blocks of the bus station spoke any English. I began showing the pictures to shopkeepers and everyone walking on the sidewalk. I went to a church and stopped people coming out. An older man said he recognized something on my last flier.

"Butler?" he asked.

In an industry town, he didn't know the people, but he knew their employer by its colors. My friends were wearing powder-blue Butler shirts in the photos.

We walked in silence along a short street of faded and chipped cement buildings. He led me to the only new building on the street, painted hot tropical pink.

I'd stumbled upon the headquarters of Victor Apolinar. In my imagination, I half-expected the headquarters to be painted in carnival colors or have a Ferris wheel in the yard.

A man came to the front gate, speaking broken English. He couldn't identify the people in my pictures. I kept asking question after question, but he seemed ready to turn me away.

Struggling to find an identifying clue, I told him Salvador was a Butler foreman who brought his wife up north. That was unusual. The wife was the key. A cell-phone call later and I was reunited with my former carnival boss, Salvador Garcia Alvarez and his brother Rodolfo.

Salvador was so surprised to see me that he theatrically fainted and fell to the floor. He and Rodolfo acted as if I'd found them in a lost city in the Amazon.

Salvador remembered the exchange between us in California and how he'd rolled his eyes when I predicted I would visit.

I'd quit Butler Amusements six months earlier. Salvador went on to travel with Butler to jumps in Oregon and Washington state. I timed the visit perfectly, Salvador returned from the United States the previous night.

More than two-thirds of our traveling carnival unit came from the foothills of the Sierra Madre Oriental. Salvador estimated that fifty-five men and women from Tlapacoyan worked for Butler.

The Tlapacoyan I found was a bustling town. Not only were the sidewalks busy, but the Mexican Day of the Dead was coming the next weekend. The village was decked out in macabre decorations.

A fraternity of carnies was back in town. They were spending their Yankee dollars but were wary of the men lying in wait for them.

Salvador and his wife, Guadalupe, invited me into their home. I'd met Lupe in California. She made food in a grab wagon and helped during setups and sloughs. During her off-hours from the carnival, she cooked for Salvador, family, and friends.

Their children were back home from school to greet their returning parents. Their son Ricardo, 20, was studying to be a civil engineer. Their daughter Rosario, 19, was studying to be a radiologist. Most of Salvador and Lupe's carnival savings went to their education.

The four of them lived on the second floor of Salvador's family home. His father, in his 90s, still delivered milk from the local farms into town.

When Salvador felt tired on an all-night slough in America, he thought of how hard his father worked all his life with a large milk can strapped to his back. Salvador adored his father, a thin, distinguished-looking man who still spoke bits of Nahuatl, the language of the Aztecs. The fish in their courtyard pool were Aztec cichlids, another source of traditional pride.

The family treated me to a ham steak, tortillas, and beans in the downstairs kitchen. We caught up on how the year went at Salvador's Butler unit. Rose Dog worked the entire season. Salvador called him a friend even though Rose Dog resented the Mexican workers. Harvey and his wife, Rhonda, quit shortly after I left.

I asked about Jesus of Sinaloa, who dropped a steel pin on my head during my first Oakland slough. He also shelled out seventy-five dollars for a mother and her children so they could afford carnival tickets.

"You won't believe it," Salvador said. "He won the lottery. Five thousand dollars."

"Karma," I said.

After dinner, I made my way to the Hotel Valencia around the corner, paying for a fifteen-dollar room. Pictures on my room's wall showed local waterfalls, swimming holes, and ancient ruins.

One internationally known waterfall, Tomata 2 on the Jalacingo River, challenges extreme kayakers with a sixty-foot vertical drop. The nearby Filobobos River draws adventurers to class four and five rapids.

At the nearby ruins, the ancient Totonacs played their violent ball games and made human sacrifices.

If not for security concerns, Tlapacoyan would be a magnet for tourists passionate about archaeology, anthropology, and adventure travel. My former coworkers were the products of a place rich in history and natural beauty.

The next day, Salvador and Ricardo took me on an all-carny tour of the town. Salvador identified everybody by name and the ride each worked up north.

We walked through the misty, busy Saturday market, *tianguis*, crowded with food carts, hanging meats, cantinas, and electronic-game booths. Architecture in the town center is Spanish colonial. The Spanish founded a settlement in Tlapacoyan in 1519.

Salvador brought us to his elementary school and to the church where he was baptized and married. He pointed to the fields where he played soccer.

We visited Edgar Flores, whose mother ran a mom-and-pop grocery store. Edgar was a big, muscular man who drove trucks for Butler and ran the Eagle 16, an Eli Wheel.

Everyone we met was fresh from the road and idle. Salvador intended to spend the off-season doing odd jobs around the house. There would be no paid work for these men and women in their winter quarters.

~⌐

JERRY AND JOSEPHINE HALL were relaxing in their living room when we arrived at their home. Josephine was from Tlapacoyan, and Jerry was a gringo from Battlefield, Washington.

I didn't know Jerry in California. He was an electrician and a truck driver for another Butler unit. Thin and middle-aged, he smoked as we talked.

As a young man, Jerry worked as a carny, then joined the Marine Corps. After the Marines, he vowed to be a carny for the rest of his life. He intended to work until he died in carnivals. With Jerry and Josephine, I saw a living dynamic. Love and work blur national borders.

About twenty years ago, the carnival world lit up this sleepy town. Jim Judkins, the onetime circus owner who tapped into the town's labor pool, began organizing an annual December fiesta for the town's carnival workers.

Carnival owners came south to party with their employees. Carnival crews played soccer matches against each other. I remembered the skill of the Mexican players after the slough in Oakland.

Tlapacoyan became part of the Great Mexican Migration north

that is melding the cultures just as the Aztecs, Totonacs, and Spanish merged into something new.

Jerry spent the preceding six off-seasons in Tlapacoyan and considered it his second home. His savings went further.

"I love it here," he said. "It's peaceful."

In a town with roots so ancient, one looks for connections to an earlier time. The Totonacs believed the soul comes from the mother. Much of their art depicts a mother goddess.

The two main Catholic churches in Tlapacoyan are dedicated to Mary, the mother of Jesus. Both feature her prominently above the altar. A stranger might think she was the primary object of worship.

Totonac ceramics differ from Aztec and Mayan art in that thousands of the earliest ceramic Totonac figures are laughing and smiling. Figures guffaw mid-gesture. Others bend backward laughing.

Though surrounded by cultures generating stoic and warlike faces, the Totonac artists created works unmatched around the world for sheer artistic exuberance. They left a happy face for the ages.

Many smiles around town were dead ringers for the Totonac ceramic smiles.

AT THE END of my all-carny tour day, Salvador and Ricardo brought me back to their flat on the second floor of Salvador's childhood home. Lupe made a late lunch of chicken *mole* with sides of carrots, cilantro, onions, squash, tortillas, tortas and tomatoes. *Tomato* and *mole* are Nahuatl words.

Lupe wore a bright red KP Concessions apron with pictures of cotton candy, corn dogs, and soda on the front. I sat at the dinner table and joked about her apron. I mockingly proclaimed I wanted cotton candy, funnel cakes, and corn dogs for dinner.

Hands still in the sink, Lupe laughed. "Then I quit," she said.

When Salvador and I started talking about Bay Point, Lupe joined in the conversation from the kitchen.

The rainstorm on slough night in Bay Point was a highlight for her. Lupe was helping tear down the Hamptons car ride, a kiddy ride with circling attached mini-cars.

The carnival was robbed at gunpoint near her ride. Then high winds whipped the tarp off the Hamptons ride, narrowly missing her.

Despite the robbery and the storm, she and other Tlapacoyan women worked late into the night before returning soaked and muddy to their small bunkhouse rooms. She laughed it off, but I noticed Ricardo listening.

Salvador was like no other carny I met all year in Mexico or America. He was every bit as tough as any Mexican in the crew, but he loved joking around. I never saw him lose his temper.

He also was a running man. He jogged five to seven miles a day when traveling with the carnival. As a younger man, he and his carny uncle played soccer all day and afterward ran another twenty miles across the foothills around the town.

Salvador didn't drink alcohol. He rarely swore. His parents and brother, Rodolfo, were evangelical Christians, but he only reluctantly talked about religion.

He was an autodidact who taught himself fluent English by watching American movies on DVD. He was curious about everything around him.

Going north with her husband made Lupe atypical among village women. She must have looked adventurous to some and crazy to others. Salvador and Lupe shared a tiny bunkhouse all season. It was a close partnership, both in Tlapacoyan and on the road.

Salvador's wife, brother, uncle, and childhood playmates worked on the same Butler unit. For nine months of the year, they lived in a traveling version of their hometown.

WHEN DINNER WOUND DOWN, Salvador said he felt sorry for American families because they don't have what his family has in Tlapacoyan.

"We do not have a big house. We don't have new clothes or a new car. We have happy families. I live in the same house I was born in. I am forty-seven. My children live with us. People tell me American children leave at eighteen."

Salvador was a happy family man. His home was filled with laughter, college dreams, and a mad parrot in a first floor cage who rambles on and bites. He proudly said his happiness was his wealth.

People say the *Ruta de Cortés* passed just south of Tlapacoyan seeking Mexico City's gold. "We Spaniards know a sickness of the heart that only gold can cure," Cortés once wrote. The sickness missed Tlapacoyan. Yet here lies Cortés' gold.

I asked Ricardo if he wanted to go north to work in traveling carnivals. The question made the whole family laugh.

"Never," he said. "I hear the work is too hard."

I envied Salvador's happy home, his Aztec fish, and mad parrot. Soon, I asked if we could go out for a night of real, local son jarocho music. Ricardo and Salvador laughed. At night the streets are not for gringos.

"You go out, someone will say who is he with," Salvador said.

Salvador meant that if I went out alone at night I needed the protection of a local gang. The town was so dangerous, Salvador and his family never went out at night.

THE AMERICAN CARNIVAL experience was different for these Mexican migrants. They crossed language, cultural, and national borders. Mexicans differed in the way they ate, lived, and worked.

Carnival life was fundamentally different for Mexicans. They shopped, cooked, ate, slept, and worked together. From the outside, they appeared united, but they knew the differences.

They were divided by geography. Rural Mexicans tended to work rides and knew little to no English. Big-city carnies from the city of Veracruz and Mexico City spoke English and usually ran the better-paying games.

Family, politics, and status all migrated north with them. Mexicans lived and hung out together. Americans hung out with Americans.

Trips to Walmart, the laundromat, and the *Mercado,* were group excursions. Mexicans pooled their money for food at a Hispanic grocery.

Their kitchens and dining areas were outside near the trailers. Stools, plastic buckets, card tables, propane stoves, and grills lined their bunkhouses and the bunkhouse reefers.

Women cooked for their family or group. Men in the reefers cooked for each other.

At mealtimes, the smell of the beans, rice, and meats overpowered the aromas of the carnival's cotton candy and deep-fried foods. Women cut up the fresh vegetables outside the bunkhouses. Groups of men slurped a fish-based stew mixed with sweet corn.

They prepared for the long season by bringing their TVs, stereos, and posters for their cramped bunkhouse rooms. The better rooms were kept clean and orderly. Women used water hoses to fill soapy buckets to wash the floors.

At the other end of the spectrum were the reefers, which occasionally became rowdy and ripe. Hot, sweaty, working men piled into the reefers at night, squeezing into three levels of bunks.

A local hose fed their showers. When the heater broke, workers were reluctant to shower. It was up to the men to clean their showers, which meant they were left muddy. The Mexican men kidded me about showering in the reefers when the heater broke. Cold water, I'd say, made me *muy macho.*

The reefers often smelled like locker rooms, but they were a great deal for men aiming to save money. Reefers were rent-free, and many times, the dominant smell was food.

Mexican carnies went shoulder-to-shoulder to roll ticket offices and load eighteen-wheelers with heavy gennies, or generator boxes. Fifteen to twenty men picked up 150-foot lead lines, walking lockstep across the lot. Men jumped on truck flatbeds to throw down heavy rubber mats, benches, metal fences, and wood blocks to small crowds.

Americans did similar work but needed to be called together from around the lot. Mexican carnies were already in groups and moved together job to job.

Salvador's management style of the Mexican crew was democratic. Wearing his Atomic Man hard hat, he worked side-by-side at every job. He'd jump in to take on the hardest jobs.

American managers noticed and didn't like it when he worked so hard. They told him to delegate. Salvador didn't listen. He'd say it was easier to get the men motivated when they saw him working as hard or harder than them.

The Mexicans worked fast and joked in Spanish. I once asked Rodolfo what they were joking about.

"You don't want to know," he said. "Every joke is about sex. It's terrible."

I was taller than those rural Mexicans, so when it came time to reach high for a beam or a nut, I was a useful gringo. Too often, I watched them pantomime, "Pick up the other beam. Work over there." My height, not my skill, made me useful.

Many American carnies resented the Mexicans. I heard black and white carnies say Mexicans took jobs away from their brothers and sisters. White carnies lamented the good old days when they were the face of the American carnival.

There is a widespread perception among American carnival workers that Mexican carnies receive preferential treatment because of their power as a group. Yet they sleep in crowded reefers, live abroad for most of the year and return home with just enough money to make it until next season.

MARCO RAN the Yoyo swing ride in Bay Point. One day, a tall, bulked-up African American customer in his thirties became enraged with him. He blamed Marco for not properly strapping in his daughter. She swung unsecured around the giant swing.

"I will fuck you up," he said to Marco.

Running the Lolly Swing ride next to the Yoyo, I heard the customer threats. I considered leaving my ride and going to his rescue. Once again, despite my vow never to fight, I was close to running directly into a confrontation.

Marco was short and strong, but no match for the angry customer. When I asked Marco if he was afraid, he calmly smiled.

"I wanted to say to him, 'You see all these Mexicans around here,'" Marco said. "I think you will not fuck me up in front of them."

Yet Marco could not fight, and neither could his fellow jarochos. People who fight can lose their visas, not just for a season, but for life. The customer calmed down. Marco felt protected because friends and family surrounded him. He was happy when it was all over. He smiled like a mask of the Toconacs.

Before he started working in carnivals, Marco was a part-time auto mechanic whose main job was working at the local tortilla factory stirring the mix. The tortilla factory was the only factory in Tlapacoyan. With no other choices, Marco worked seven-day weeks in suffocating factory heat.

Compared to soul-killing factory, carnival work was easy. He feared being forced back to that factory and working for a fraction of his American wages.

"It was hot, so hot," he said. "America is like paradise."

Salvador's crew in California liked to repeat several catchphrases while they worked. A row of men might haul lead lines across the midway, and someone would shout out, "Every day is like paradise in America."

Marco was a ride jockey supporting his young wife, a newborn son, and a sick mother in Tlapacoyan. It was a mystery to him why he wasn't saving enough.

It is no mystery to me. On our wages, the slightest financial ding wiped out our savings. Marco said he never could buy a home if things didn't change.

"I help my mother with her hospital bills. But food is expensive, even potatoes. I don't know why."

Without a single vice, Salvador earned $345 a week and spent $120 a week. He was a supervisor and did not live in his own house back in Mexico. The commonly held idea that Mexican carnies lived like kings back home from their wages is not true.

~~⌒~~

MEXICAN LABOR KEEPS American carnivals alive, yet it is the most explosive issue in the carnival industry. Carnival owners become enraged at government interference with visas. On the other end, worker advocates rail against work and living conditions.

When I worked at Butler in California, a devastating report came out on the carnival industry: *Taken for a Ride: Migrant Workers in the U.S. Fair and Carnival Industry*, conducted by the American University Washington College of Law Immigrant Justice Clinic and *Centro de los Derechos del Migrante, Inc.*

The study alleged widespread abuses after interviewing workers in Maryland, Virginia, and Mexico.

After working ten traveling carnivals in ten states, I couldn't say the abuses were everywhere, but I could say I saw most of those mentioned in the report.

The study alleged unfair recruitment, wage and hour abuses, health and safety risks, no access to worker compensation, isolated substandard living conditions, and limited access to legal representation. People were promised high-paying construction jobs and then given carnival work.

Taken for a Ride was a blistering indictment of the industry, but no reforms followed.

At the time, importing a single Mexican worker was an investment of more than one thousand dollars for the cost of an agent, transport, and documents. Owners could save the expense by hiring Americans, but they maintained that the investment in Mexican workers was worth every peso.

There's much the American traveling-carnival industry could do to improve conditions, but it refuses to acknowledge the problems. In part, that is because truth is relative.

Every Mexican carnival worker knows the ironic truth. Every day is paradise in America.

~

ON MY FINAL night in Tlapacoyan, Rodolfo brought me to Emanuel the King Church. A born-again revival was at full tilt when we entered.

We sat in the middle of the evangelical congregation. Rodolfo's parents were in a nearby row. A five-piece band, backup singers, and dancers with flags added to the pitch of the sermons.

A huge screen on stage flashed pictures and lyrics. Dressed in a blue suit, white shirt, and red tie, the preacher paced and leaped around the stage. The message was fevered and urgent. Rodolfo shouted translations into my ear.

Tlapacoyan, the preacher said, was a biblical drama come to life. He drew parallels to Exodus, Moses, and the Promised Land. The violence was "like a plague."

"Don't be afraid to go to work," the preacher said. "You have the protection of the Lord, whose blood was shed for you and spills all over the world."

People stood for the songs and the sermons, swinging their arms back and forth. People spoke in tongues, wept, and fainted.

The church was transformative for Rodolfo. He was troubled and prone to the vices of drinking and smoking. His marriage was on the rocks before he was "saved."

Already speaking in tongues next to me, Rodolfo asked if I wanted to approach the stage with him and "accept the Lord." I respectfully declined.

While Rodolfo was at the stage speaking in tongues, two younger women in front of me collapsed crying. I stood above them, swaying awkwardly to the music. When one wanted to get up, I helped her. She hugged me hard. I hugged her back until she stopped weeping.

The spirits in the Ceiba trees and the fertility goddesses of the Toconacs. The Toconac temples in ruins outside of town. The Spanish colonial Catholic churches with the Mother Mary hovering above the altar. In that pitch and fever, prayer and song, people sought meaning in their lives. In trees, in temples, in tongues, in the past and the future, seeking meaning is a universal quest.

Rodolfo and I walked back that night to the Hotel Valencia along drizzly, lamplit streets. He talked about how worried he was about his village. When the men leave to work in carnivals, the bad men who stay behind extort money from the local businesses and carnival families.

Some carnies pay protection money to the criminals to leave their families alone when they are away. They are targets again when they return with Yankee dollars.

"This time of year," he said, "they know you are back from America."

Rodolpho relied on the Lord.

"It is awful," he said. "This was a safe town when we grew up."

I'd visited homes, businesses, and churches. I'd seen where these carnies were born, went to school, and married. I knew them by their carnival rides up north, but their reality took shape as I walked their hometown streets.

At the door of my hotel on the main street, I thanked Rodolfo with my hand over my heart.

The dewy fog made the main street, Calle Ferrer, appear like an image in an *en plein air* painting. The streetlamp lights shimmered in the street puddles. It was a silent as a soundstage. We were the only two people on the street.

Perhaps still overwhelmed by the revivalist fever, Rodolfo took a moment to choose his words.

"You should come back next year because . . . people love you here."

As I closed the door, I realized, this adds another layer to things.

ON SUNDAY MORNING, a light haze hung over the street. An old lady in tattered clothes walked by me with live chickens in a bag. She laid the lethargic chickens down on the sidewalk for sale.

A few people milled around the bus station in the drizzle. It seemed as if the entire time there, I'd walked in a high misty cloud. I boarded an early bus out of town.

Staring out the window, I recalled what I'd witnessed and missed. I missed Mayor Apolinar and never saw any of the violence. I wasn't there long enough.

I witnessed a Mesoamerican people living between worlds. They did not see and feel the same experiences as American carnies. Safety and feeding their families were more urgent for them.

Traveling carnivals depend on those strong people who come back to the United States year after year with the knowledge of how to safely set up a Century Wheel seemingly in a snap.

There's a classic son jarocho song *La Bruja* with a haunting verse:

> *The witch grabs me, she takes me to her home,*
> *she sits me on her lap, she gives me kisses*
> *(she says) "I only wish to eat you."*

Blame it on the superstitious week leading up to Mexico's Day of the Dead. Or blame it on the undeniable power of Rodolfo's revival, but I wondered if American carnivals were the witch. Will these men eat the witch, or will the witch eat them?

The ranks of Mexican carnies were growing fast. They could dominate carnivals like they do agricultural field work and other low wage jobs in the United States.

In the process, some towns in Mexico became wholly reliant on American traveling carnivals to survive. Tlapacoyan is a one-industry town just like U.S. steel towns before they became part of the rust belt. It is easy to see how vulnerable they are to a collapse of a season or two.

I relaxed as the bus hobbled along the bumpy Costa Esmeralda road. I watched the wind blow tufts of white foam off the low surf on the Gulf of Mexico. There was a witch to fear, named Covid-19, but we didn't see her coming.

After returning to Veracruz, I headed south on my own *Ruta Maya* to the Mayan ruins of Chichen Itza in the Yucatan. I wanted to see more of the Mexico these carnies came from.

Traveling by public bus, I saw the Sierra Madre Oriental, the Trans-Mexican Volcanic Belt, Mexico City, the Mexican Plateau, and Chihuahua on my way to Georgia for one last carnival before going to my winter quarters.

I rode to the southern tip of the country and back up through the center of the county. It was a relatively short trip, about a week. I didn't stay long enough anywhere, yet I knew Mexico would fascinate me for the rest of my life.

When it comes to the new face of American carnivals, I'll always think of the Totonac masks with their smiles of mirth and menace.

PART XI
GEORGIA

NOVEMBER

CARNIVAL OF THE TREMBLING EARTH

WAYCROSS

We have met the enemy and they are us.

— *POGO,* A COMIC SET IN OKEFENOKEE SWAMP

I probably still had the dust from Mexico on my shoes when I walked out onto the grassy Okefenokee Agricultural Fairgrounds in Waycross, Georgia.

I saw a dozen local men milling around, unhappy to see a rival for their jobs. In the middle of a group of black men stood a heavy man with a purple Afro-comb in his hair, telling chain gang stories.

"There are millionaires on the chain gangs," he said. "I know. One guy died, and we found his debit card with fifty thousand dollars on it. Don't let anyone hold your money on the chain gang."

There were people on chain gangs with fifty-thousand-dollar debit cards? Others told their own bizarre chain-gang stories. I later learned that Wade State Prison and Wade County Jail are just outside of town.

The man with the Afro-comb later told us that he could get us hired if we paid him ten dollars. He'd bribe the carnival boss. It was a failed scam because I don't think any of us carried ten dollars with us.

We waited all day for Amusements of America to show up. Skinny Southern men smoked and played cards on the band-shell stage all day. Hay bales were stacked in front of the stage for seating. I sat alone on the bandstand stage.

A local man finally walked up to talk to me, but he was no welcoming committee. He said I was wasting my time. The Big A hires the same locals every year, that's why he was sure to get work. A hundred men would be there by the evening. I should hitchhike out of town to another carnival down the road.

Having come all the way from Mexico, I wasn't leaving before Big A rolled on to the fairgrounds. On the other hand, I'd met a real Okefenokee swamp conman. He was authentic, but his pitch was weak.

To get to Waycross, I crossed through Juarez, Mexico to El Paso, Texas. I took a Greyhound bus for a two-day 1,600-mile trip straight across I-10 to Jacksonville, Florida. In Jacksonville, I took a city bus to the outskirts of the city, where I hopped into the flatbed of a pickup truck for the eighty-mile ride to the fair.

Nothing feels so free as hitchhiking on a sunny day in the back of a pickup truck. The truck dropped me off at the front gate.

Waycross is on the edge of the Okefenokee Swamp, the largest blackwater swamp in America. It's a 438,000-acre peat swamp that local Native Americans called the "Land of the Trembling Earth."

The Okefenokee Agricultural Fair was the last major fair of the season, and I needed to round out the year by working in the Deep South. The site was an empty, grassy field when I arrived. The livestock was in the barn, but Big A was still en route from Charlotte, North Carolina.

The five Vivona brothers owned the New Jersey-based Amusements of America. It traveled the Eastern and Southern states, operating more than one hundred rides.

Trucks started rolling in around 7 p.m. The opening was the next evening at 5 p.m., so the crew was going to have to work late into the night.

About thirty local men followed bosses around the grounds. I helped a team setting up kiddy rides on a per-ride basis, but I wasn't yet hired for the week.

I helped set up the Hamptons flat ride. One of the three guys on my setup crew was a local man, recently released from prison for murder. The other two men kept talking about life on their hog farm. The Big A foreman appeared high.

The foreman thought I was a greenhorn, so he asked me to find light-bulb grease. When I said no, he threw a fit. He kept getting confused about the parts. At the end of the night, the foreman walked us back to the boss's RV to get paid.

It was 3 a.m., but the local hires wanted their pay before they went home. The foreman kept knocking on the RV door until a sleepy, angry boss opened it. He said our pay would come the next night. I hoped he didn't see me standing in the back. He might hold a grudge. I wanted to be hired for the entire show.

A cool, mushy fog engulfed the Okefenokee Fairgrounds in the morning. Thick yellow lead lines weaved their way to unfinished rides. A carnival was rising and slowly coming into focus as tired men walked in the deep fog like ghosts in muddy shoes.

The mist curled around the rigging of the Century Wheel. From a distance, a Ferris wheel looks like a cobweb being built by spidermen.

Wheelmen in years past walked the top of the Ferris wheel to test it when it was complete. A carny once told me that he did it jingled "because I balance better when I'm drunk."

Clanks and yells came out of the fog from unknown directions. A potbelly pig and a rooster were heard but not seen. No wonder foggy, swampy areas are so ripe for fables and legends.

As the sun burned off the fog, slowly a rainbow-colored swamp mirage took the shape of a carnival. Carnies set up the last of the rides. Jointees hung plush. Concessionaires heated the grills.Performers practiced their high-wire and magic acts.

I helped set up a kiddy train ride and a swing ride. Each job paid another thirty to fifty dollars. My coworker was an army veteran who served in Iraq, Afghanistan, and Russia. Wayne was earning disability pay from the government.

When electronic music started blasting, Wayne stopped working and started dancing. He stood on his left leg, swinging his right foot like a pocket watch at the end of a chain. The dance was without rhythm or grace, but he wore a shit-eating grin as if he'd invented plutonium.

The Mardi Gras funhouse mesmerized Wayne. The traveling Mardi Gras house has a mirror maze on the first floor and funhouse mirrors on the second floor with an outside swirling exit slide.

"Wouldn't you love to live in a home like that?" he said.

He took pictures of the funhouse on his cell phone. I took pictures of him taking pictures. He wanted to spread the word that he'd found this house of dreams.

The façade was painted in bright, colored confetti with crazed partiers at a New Orleans-style party. It was crowded with buxom overstimulated women and laughing musicians beckoning people inside for wild times.

What greater way to stay reminded of life's fortunes and illusions than waking each day in a house of mirrors, mazes, and slides?

"Wouldn't it be great to have people over?" Wayne said.

Neighborhood people might see the disabled war vet as a newer, more fun Wayne. He wanted to live in a home with a party on the outside and mirrors on the inside. A happy-looking home might internalize the party after whatever interior wars Wayne was still fighting.

WAYNE'S ONE-LEGGED dance wasn't the only conspicuous dance on the midway. The ride jockey across from the Mardi Gras house danced wildly to a techno beat.

A local hire, he was a tall, thin black man who talked with a deep Southern accent. He wanted to be called Dance.

After working the night and morning on setup, bosses assumed I was hired and sent me to work at the Mardi Gras house with Tyrone, a heavyset black man around forty years old.

One drizzly night, Tyrone and I stood on the second floor of the Mardi Gras house looking down at Dance gyrating in the rain with no customers on the midway.

"Pathological," I said.

"Yea, he's good," Tyrone said.

Dance later told me he danced like the Errol Flynns and the BKs (Black Killers), black gangs in Detroit in the seventies. The Errol Flynn dance was named after the swashbuckling movie star. Dance's uncles were in the Errol Flynn gang.

His uncles taught him about life, and they taught him the Errol Flynn dance. I've heard of gangs with hand signals, slang, tattoos, and colors, but this was a gang with a dance.

With uncles in gangs, I wondered if he too was in a gang. Dance would only say he was out on parole and waiting for a court date.

He hustled up a living anyway he could. That time of year was the peak pecan-picking season. Picking pecans is a tradition with long cultural and literary roots in the rural Deep South.

"I sell pecans. I get them in backyards. In the woods," he said. "I work 8 a.m. to 2 p.m. I can make forty or fifty dollars a day if I work."

No doubt he collected his pecans on the golden bicycle he rode to work. It was a new bicycle completely spray-painted gold from the puffy seat to the handlebars, wheel spokes, and rims.

Dance and I worked the slough together. We tore down the kiddy train and a small swing ride. Dance cut his night short with a series of changing stories.

He said he had to leave to tend to his sick grandmother. Earlier, he told me he was going to spend the night "with a white woman." I heard him on the phone telling someone else he was finished with the "white woman" and was going back to his fiancée.

His dancing told a story. It was the Errol Flynn dance of the pecan picker. He scammed. He danced. He got by. Riding his way through life on golden wheels.

Big A brought nearly thirty rides, including a Century Wheel, Ring of Fire, 1001 Nachts, Gravitron, and Cliff Hanger, but the sideshows topped the bill.

There was the Magic of Lance Gifford, the Victoria Circus, and the Globe of Death featuring motorcycles riding inside a steel-mesh sphere. One morning, I saw the twenty-nine-inch "world's smallest woman," Little Liz, walking to the public showers.

The classic "Head of a Beautiful Girl, Body of an Ugly Snake" sideshow was there. For a dollar, marks could see a woman poke her head through a hole connected to a stuffed cloth snake tail. The "body of an ugly snake" prop looked like a worn-out couch.

Before the show opened one morning, I walked by the dunk tank and noticed it had Bobo the Clown written on the side. It was the same type of dunk tank my Chicago coworker Ghost was playing when an angry customer shot him. Maybe it was the same dunk tank. I looked, but no bullet holes or blood stains.

For years, Big A sent rides and workers to Puerto Rico in the off-season. That year, for the first time, it sent a carnival unit to Lima, Peru.

The bosses were desperate for workers, but most workers couldn't afford a passport. Felonies and child-support considerations were weighed. My passport was in my fanny pack. I spread the word that I was interested in Peru, but nobody was interested in taking the new guy. A friendly carny couple came by to give me a word of caution.

"You got to watch out," one carny said. "It's dangerous in Limer."

Thwack!

His girlfriend slapped him over the head, Three Stooges style.

"It's Lima, you fucking idiot," she said. "It's like the capital of something of Peru. A lemur is a monkey. You big monkey."

The Mardi Gras house was one of the attractions being shipped to Lima. The carny living in the ride's tool room thought it was funny that his home was traveling abroad without him.

"Fall asleep in there," he said, "and you might wake up in Peru."

His situation taught me something about carnies and their homes. A local woman agreed to allow him to live with her at her Waycross family home for the winter. He could live rent-free and be her fix-it man until the season started again. He didn't have a home for the winter until he hooked up with her.

That's the relationship some carnival people have with winter quarters. The road is their real home. The off-season means being away from home.

BIG A PAID for every ride I helped tear down on slough. I worked the entire night, tearing down the kiddy train, a swing ride, and the Allan Herschell Carrousel.

I worked alongside Tyrone and another man, both of them sumo wrestler-sized men. They could lift as much as two men. They should have been paid as much as two men.

Tyrone's four-hundred-some pounds came in handy about 4 a.m. when we were hoisting the steel floorboards into the semi-trailer truck. Other carousels have a collapsible pole at the center, but the Herschell required us to pick up the center pole and push it into the truck. We used a forklift for part of the job.

After battling the flu earlier in the night, I experienced a surge of energy late in the morning when everyone else was bushed. Tyrone noticed.

"You are a true carny," he said.

Early the next morning was payday at the office trailer, and some people were getting end-of-year bonuses. Dozens of people lay in the grass or milled about, waiting for the window to open.

A young woman who looked like a teenager talked about having no place to go the next day. Squinting, a cigarette hanging from her lips, she said it was all so absurd.

"I had all year to plan," she said, "Crazy, right?"

The end-of-year pay would not be enough for some people. I knew one carny would report to jail to serve his time for marijuana possession. After a stay with three hots and a cot, he expected to be out by the start of the season.

People leaving for Peru were required to wait another three weeks before they left. That was two weeks too many for some folks.

People collecting their year-end bonus and two weeks' pay walked away with more than a grand. I came away with about three hundred dollars.

"Where are you going now?" Tyrone asked.

"I'm worried," I said.

In the foggy Okefenokee morn, Tyrone won the award for saying the kindest words of my year in traveling carnivals.

"Come back next year. There's a guy in his eighties that works here. You'll never have to find an apartment. You can be with us."

What I heard was, "Never worry about work or home again. Stay with Big A until you die on the midway."

When the last dollar was doled out at the office trailer, it was as if an invisible bomb went off. Trucks, cars, vans, and RVs blew out of the lot so fast they defied the laws of physics.

All that was left behind were muddy footprints, tire tracks, and the swampy air in the land of the trembling earth.

OKEFENOKEE TO WINTER QUARTERS

HITCHHIKING TO SOUTH FLORIDA

I hitched a ride out of Waycross in a van with an abuse victim and her abuser. The abusive boyfriend drove a separate pickup. If you didn't know he was abusive toward women, you could guess it.

A group of carnies and I once watched him drive a forklift past us, and the stories followed him like a backdraft. They each knew examples of his abuse. They puffed cigarettes and shook their heads. Then Tyrone said it

"He'll kill her one day."

She drove the van the eight hours from Georgia to Fort Lauderdale. She was sweet, smart, and tormented. She was going to Peru and hoped to save enough money there so she could buy a truck when she got back and drive far away.

She blamed the carnival life. One of her fantasies was to walk out of the Big A bunkhouses one morning and shout a wake-up call at the whole camp.

"What is wrong with us, anyway? Who in their right mind wants to be a carny?"

She dropped me off on I-95 at an exit for a part of I-75 known as Alligator Alley. As I left the van, I heard her tormentor yelling at her on her cell phone for letting me hitch a ride and for dropping me off where I needed to go.

She was thin and petite, which added to her look of vulnerability. I thanked her for the ride, but I wanted to say, "Sorry."

The next day I was hitchhiking along Alligator Alley when my cell phone rang. The caller ID said, "Tyrone." He was on a Greyhound bus bound for Dallas, on his way to see his first grandson.

He was also going to a hospital to get a festering wound on his leg fixed. He'd injured it working in the carnival three years earlier. He cleaned the wound daily, but it reeked by nighttime.

A veteran of the U.S. Navy, he initially put off visiting a Veterans Affairs hospital because he worried doctors might cut off his leg.

In a mischievous tone, he began the call with a question he thought was haunting me.

"Coming back next year, Mike?"

I imagined him laughing at his own jokes, a giant, jiggling fat man in a tiny bus seat.

"We'll see," I said.

His number is still on my speed dial.

I RAN out of drinking water early the next day and was in bad shape that evening when Osvaldo Guzman stopped to pick me up along Alligator Alley. In a thick Cuban accent, he said he recognized something about me. It might have been dehydration.

Three times Osvaldo attempted to get to the United States from Cuba in makeshift boats. Each overcrowded boat was a hodgepodge of discarded tires and wood. On one trip, he started with seventeen people on a floating deathtrap and set sail for ten days without food or water. Ten people were alive when the U.S. Coast Guard picked them up and escorted them back to Cuba.

Osvaldo made it on the next trip. He secured legal immigration papers, married an American woman, and was the father of a five-year-old son.

At forty years old, he owned his own heating and air conditioning business that he supplemented with an Amway dealership. He gave me an Amway energy drink and vitamins before dropping me off at a roadside rest stop with picnic tables.

As it grew dark, I prepared to sleep on a table. If I slept in the grass, I feared an animal might crawl out of the Everglades and feast on me.

A state trooper pulled up and asked me if I was hitchhiking. Unsure of the hitchhiking laws, the inner hitchhiker lawyer in me pointed out that I didn't have my thumb out. He knew the answer and drove me fifteen miles up the road to a gas station on the Miccosukee Indian Reservation. At least at the gas station, he said, I'd have food and water for the night.

Cars and trucks came and left for hours. Then out of the night fog came a tribal police car making a slow turn into the station. Leaving my backpack and cardboard hitchhiking sign out front, I ducked into the store and began browsing through magazines. I didn't know what the tribal rules were about hitchhiking. I'd lie low until he left. My plan only agitated him more.

Suddenly, he came up from behind and gave me a hard, aggressive tap on my shoulder. When I turned around, the short, tattooed, bulked-up reservation cop stood with his face at my chest. He was aggressively close and looking straight up at me.

"Is that your backpack and sign out front? I threw your sign in the trash. You better start walking off this reservation. This is federally protected land. You walk yourself down I-75 two miles and you will be off reservation land. You want me to arrest you? You want me to send you to Fort Lauderdale?"

He made a not-so-vague reference to prison rape in the Fort Lauderdale lock-up. Again, why do cops pride themselves on prison rape?

"Who dropped you off here?" he asked.

"A state trooper dropped me off here."

"I don't care who dropped you off here!"

He pointed me out the front door and was furious that I didn't move fast enough.

"Well? Get walking!"

After digging into the trash can for my sign, I walked down the exit ramp. It was about 3 a.m. and too dark and dangerous to hitchhike.

I walked into the Everglades. I laid my sleeping bag in a bank of bushes. No need to wake the gators. I fell dead asleep. If a gator tried to eat me, I'd have been on the third death roll before I woke up.

ROLLING up my sleeping bag in the morning, I watched the Florida sun burn off the haze from the Everglades. Five hours later, Nick came rolling up in a white van. He said he knew me the moment he saw me standing beside the road.

"People would see you and say you are a hobo, but I knew. You no hobo. I left home when I was fifteen. I learned how to read faces. I know ninety-nine percent of the time, I see a face, I know him."

Olive-skinned with a broad smile and short black hair, Nick came from Albania. Political opponents there burned his grocery business to the ground and threatened to kill his entire family. He could see I was going through difficult times and wanted to give me a pep talk.

"Albanians are fighters. It is good to fight. It makes you feel young. Young people are fighting all the time. You fight, you feel young. Don't cry. Crying is for losers. Sometimes I feel like crying, but I think crying is for losers. You must fight."

He was fighting for legal residency. About forty years old, he owned a successful business in Naples painting homes, but an immigration judge that week rejected his appeal to stay. The immigration papers were on his lap. He should be depressed, but he was a happy man "with money or no money."

"Happiness is not about being taller or shorter, or skinnier or ugly. Happiness is in the spirit. It is from within. It's from God or somewhere. I don't know ... I am a happy man. You should be happy."

Nick drove me an hour along Alligator Alley to the Gulf of Mexico and the front doorstep of my parents' home. Grace flew in for Thanksgiving. My winter quarters were in Florida.

Winter for traveling carnivals is a time to retool and for workers to recharge. The traditional traveling season is for six months, but some carnivals stretch the season by touring Southern states or traveling to Peru. It's the time of year for joints to stock up on the hottest prizes. Rides get new parts and paint. Tour dates are planned.

What happens in the off-season can make or break the traveling season. A healthy period in winter quarters is as essential to traveling carnivals as sleep is to healthy people. It's a formative time of the travel season's character. The best carnivals don't spend their time in winter quarters sleeping.

February was the end of my winter quarters and exactly a year after I first worked at Classic Amusement in Hayward, California. Murphy was the first person to tell me about the annual International Independent Showmen's Association's "Super Trade Show and Extravaganza," the main trade show for traveling carnivals in Gibtown.

Gibtown was once dubbed the "Weirdest Small Town in America" because it was the winter quarters of sideshow people. The gathering of the carnival tribes happens every year in February. I had so many questions yet to be answered. The yellow brick road led to Gibtown.

PART XII
FLORIDA

FEBRUARY

FREAKS, GEEKS, AND SHOWTOWN PEEPS

GIBTOWN

The bigger the humbug, the more people like it.

— P.T. BARNUM, THE FOUNDER OF "THE GREATEST
SHOW ON EARTH" & "FATHER OF THE FREAK SHOW"

A third-generation carnival man, Ben Nagel was a fan of my blog and offered to drive me around in his truck on an insider's tour of Gibtown.

We drove down Nundy Avenue and across the Alafia River, past the homes of carnival royalty. Nagel pointed at the houses of carnival family dynasties. The Reithoffers live over there. Ward Hall and Chris Christ live over there. It was a Gibtown version of a tour of the Hollywood's stars' homes.

Gibtown is the name carnival people give the combined communities of Riverside and Gibsonton, south of Tampa. It also is known as Showtown USA.

Show people secured zoning in the area so they could train

animals and store equipment in local yards. The local lawns have carnival wagons and Ferris wheels parked in them.

Yet gone are the days when it was a one-industry town with a hundred sideshow freaks making it their winter quarters.

Driving through town, though, it was still fun to imagine when the eight-foot-five-inch "World's Tallest Man," Al Tomaini, and his two-and-a-half-foot tall "half-woman" wife Jeanie ran the Giants Camp Lodge and Fish Camp. They were early residents of the show community running Gibtown after the Great Depression. Al was both fire chief and the chief of police.

Dwarfs received their mail at a post-office counter their size. "Fat ladies" and giants were served beer while sitting at specially made barstools. Conjoined twins ran the local fruit stand.

Gibtown was once dubbed the "Weirdest Small Town in America" because of the concentration of sideshow, circus and carnival people during the off season. During the season, it emptied out like Tlapacoyan does every spring.

Ben and I visited the Museum of American Carnivals. Sideshow banners there included the Devil's Child, Wolf Boy, Ape Boy, Bloody Mama, The Fantasies of Pot, and The Viking Giant.

Across the street from the museum, the International Independent Showmen's Association (IISA) was preparing to be the center of the traveling carnival world for the next four days.

Carnival owners and their top hands were coming from around the world to see the latest in equipment, practices, and technology.

The IISA clubhouse is a carnival shrine. Every wall has original paintings of carnival scenes. Carousel scenery boards hang above the oval bar in the main barroom, giving it a carousel look.

Black-and-white pictures of carnival legends hang on the walls. Scores of international flags hang from the ceiling. Bricks leading up to the front door bear the names and nicknames of great showmen of the past. Captions on wall plaques read, "DL You Drive Em" and "Showman's Showman."

The trade show soon kicked into gear and nights were for food, drink, and dance in the carousel barroom. Whiskey splashed. Beer flowed. Rock 'n' roll cover bands filled the dance floor with partying carnival people.

Thousands of people came, and each of them with thousands of stories. European, Australian and American owners gathered to cut up jackpots. Stories of weather, accidents and fortunes won and lost. Funny, heroic tall tales flowed with the drinks.

Nobody knew for sure what was next for carnivals. Everybody knew the stakes were high. Optimism flowed freely on those nights, yet everyone knew traveling carnivals were struggling.

IN A CORNER of the Showtown restaurant, Elizabeth sat on her dad's lap for breakfast at the Liar's Table.

She was a lively third-grader drawing pictures while surrounded by old carnival men, including her dad, Original Tommy Arnold. In his eighties, Original Tommy reveled in his late-in-life fatherhood.

After I prompted him to tell stories from his past, he told the story of Elvis Presley and how the young singer became the milk-bottle prince of the Memphis midway.

"Elvis won more than we let most people win," he said. "And he kept throwing the prizes to the crowd."

The year was 1957. Elvis scored a hit with *Jailhouse Rock* but hadn't yet been drafted into the Army. Elvis was walking the midway at a Memphis carnival when he stopped to throw baseballs at Original Tommy's milk bottles.

Original Tommy saw to it that Elvis won. When Elvis began throwing prizes to women, there was mayhem on the midway.

"The girls went crazy. He drew a big crowd."

Original Tommy remembered few details other than the line that made his Elvis story a classic carnival tale.

"He spent maybe two hundred dollars on my game. That was a lot of money in those days."

The equivalent in today's money is $1,800, adjusted for inflation.

He might have been the 'King of Rock and Roll' to those girls, but to Original Tommy, Elvis was a mark.

The Liar's Table was the liveliest, loudest breakfast table in Florida that morning with the legends of carnivals cutting up jackpots. Some liars lived in Gibtown, and some were visiting for the trade show from out of town.

Carnival painter Bill Browning created the Showtown restaurant's elaborate story walls. He painted the outside every year when he was active. Browning painted carnival sideshow banners for scores of traveling carnivals, circuses, and the entire IISA headquarters. His art was story art, depicting people in motion on boardwalks and in carnivals.

The need for fresh artwork every year kept sideshow artists busy. In his prime, Browning was easily one of the most famous carnival artists alive. He was retired when I visited, and the walls were fading. The menu special was a throwback, too. Chipped beef over toast with two eggs cost five dollars and ninety-nine cents.

In town from Pennsylvania for the trade show, Flash was at the Liar's Table talking about the good old days.

"If a carny doesn't have a nickname," Flash said, "he isn't interesting."

What's the story, I asked, behind your nickname?

"That's what this business is based on," he said. "Everything the sucker sees out there is flash."

Flash's own carnival story began with a passing remark by a mysterious gypsy woman named Ruby.

"I was walking one day, and an old gypsy woman told me, 'Sell hot dogs and hamburgers. You'll make a lot of money.' And she was right."

Flash went on to buy food concession wagons. I later met his daughter Ruby, named after the gypsy woman.

Flash and his wife brought their children on the road with them. At their peak, they owned eight wagons making popcorn, funnel cakes, and pizza. Flash crisscrossed the country for thirty-three years with grab wagons and poppers.

At the time I met him, he was in his sixties and a bit of a tycoon in

Williamsport, Pennsylvania. He owned the Riverside Campground, a laundromat, a bar, apartments, and a sewage hose and propane business.

"I wouldn't change a fucking day, except, I didn't take care of my health," he said, "and teeth."

The Mayor of the Liar's Table was Freddy Vonderheim, aged seventy-six. He owned both circuses and carnivals, making him a self-described showman transvestite.

Flash and the Mayor were retired from the business, but they could still call out some of the best lines in the business.

The Mayor started a mini-contest with his first rhyme.

> *I'm Donniker Dan the candy man,*
> *with circus strawberry candy,*
> *all you kids who want candy,*
> *please hold up your hand!*

Flash came back with his call-out, ending in a carnival limerick.

> *They were brewing up coffee seconds and thirds,*
> *Those happy-go-lucky carnival birds.*

Elizabeth bounced on her dad's knee as she told the old men she wanted to be an artist like Browning. She loved playing games with the men around the table. She gave big hugs around their necks. I asked her if she liked traveling with carnivals.

"I like it," she said. "I get to go on the rides for free."

During the season, she lived with Original Tommy on the road. In the off-season, she went to a local school.

She loved teasing her old father.

"My dad burns eggs, burns muffins, he burns everything you want to eat except cake and cereal."

Asked about the highlights of his carnival life, Original Tommy pointed to Elizabeth as the highlight of his whole life.

Later in the evening, I was at the main bar at the IISA clubhouse editing video on my laptop of the morning's breakfast. Over came my favorite bartender, Anna May, a lovely woman younger than me and carnival lifer.

She was proud to have raised her kids in carnivals without ever being homeless. They lived in trailers during the season, working games, rides, and ticket booths.

She noticed a picture of Original Tommy and Elizabeth on my computer.

"That's my granddaughter, and Tommy's my son-in-law. Many people in this business are related."

I suspected "Elizabeth the Artist" might someday make lots of people in Showtown USA proud.

Then I unfolded my souvenir to show Anna May. Elizabeth drew it while her dad was telling the Elvis story at breakfast and made me keep it a secret all day.

"Look," I said, "Elizabeth drew me a foot."

Anna May's response surprised me. Maybe because she heard that I was forced to hitchhike to carnivals all year. Maybe because she heard I'd been sleeping under turnpike bridges. Perhaps she heard I also was sleeping outside during the trade show. Whatever the reason, she slid a twenty-dollar bill across the bar to me.

"I heard you could use this," she said.

I slipped the bill into my shirt.

THE CHILD LIVING inside Richard dictated he become a carny someday.

His father died when he was a small boy, plunging his family into bone-grinding poverty. His mother was unable to keep the house warm and put food on the table. He was doing his family a favor by running away to carnivals.

To prove his love of traveling carnivals, he showed me a tattoo across his back of a working Giant Wheel. "CARNIE PRIDE" was in capital letters above the wheel.

He became a carny, he said, because it filled a hole in his childhood.

"It was all about the kids. I tried to give them the experience I didn't have growing up. Then my son was born. He was here in Florida. I was on the road. That sucked ass bad, so I got a sucker job. I hate it."

When I met him, he was a tall, thirty-one-year-old man with a beer gut the size of a toolbox. He and I worked to set up rides around the IISA headquarters for the trade show.

Every night after the trade show, he bellied up to the carousel bar with a cigarette behind his right ear. He ordered Long Island Ice Teas and a pitcher of beer, which he drank straight from the pitcher. All the money he earned went down his throat and up in smoke.

Working on the trade-show rides reminded him of how good he was at the job. The sucker life was getting him down.

I wanted to tell him that his carnival memories were lying to him. Take care of yourself. Stay with your wife and raise your boy. You don't want your boy growing up with that same hole in his heart.

The last time I saw Richard, he was alone near the carousel bar drinking from the pitcher and heavily tipping the pretty, young waitress. She agreed to let him drive her home after work. It was her birthday. He looked up at me from across the bar with eyes the color of bright, bloody red Giant Wheels.

MODERN MIDWAYS OWNER Robert Briggs from Chicago and the McDaniel brothers from New Jersey were in Gibtown for the convention.

When Briggs heard I was writing about his carnival, he looked up my posts. I heard through the grapevine that he wasn't coming after me.

The McDaniel brothers stole my wages, so I expected they might be contrite. But they were defiant. Freddie McDaniel denied that he was blocking my phone calls.

Richie McDaniel startled me from behind one afternoon and shoved me aside, pretending to pick up a free pamphlet at a booth. I tried to say hello.

Richie walked away, saying over his shoulder, "I know who you are."

If that's the best you got Richie, I'll take it. Where's my money?

~~⌒~~

TRAVELING carnivals employ precious people with immortal souls whose work is vital to God's plan. At least, that is the eternal perspective on traveling carnivals.

The Vatican appoints special traveling apostolic ministers to traveling people in circuses, racetracks, rodeos, cruise lines, airports, and traveling carnivals.

The "carny priest," Father Robert (Mac) McCarthy, couldn't travel to the convention. Father Mac spent decades saying Mass on rides and ministering to the working poor. On the IISA community board, he posted a letter saying he loved all carnival people because they "spend (their) lives in bringing joy and happiness to people worldwide."

The acting priest for traveling carnivals at that time was Father John Vakulskas Jr. of Okoboji, Iowa. Father Vakulskas began sprinkling holy water on carnival rides, games, and workers in the 1960s.

Carnival people hold a special status in American life, he said, because they give people a "break from their everyday family life." He made no mention of flat joints, red lighting, or alibi men. There was no hellfire-and-brimstone talk about sinners in need of repenting.

In nearby Sarasota, Florida, Saint Martha Catholic Church is dedicated to serving the circus and carnival communities. On either side of its main altar hang multicolored wagon wheels. Ringling College of Art and Design donated the statue of the crucified Jesus behind the altar. The art school was an offshoot of Ringling Brothers Circus.

At the back of Saint Martha's secondary church space is a circus wagon with an artificial stuffed lion inside.

At the carousel bar one night, I met Father Michael Juran. His career was the most unusual in carnivals. He worked in carnivals, state fairs, and on racetracks as the stuntman known as the Human Battering Ram and the Flying Padre.

When Hollywood came calling, he did stunts in the James Bond film *Man with the Golden Arm* and was Burt Reynolds' stunt double in *Smokey and the Bandit II.*

Father Juran used a bit of the carny vernacular to answer critics of his unconventional ministry.

"We have this Argentinian, (Pope) Francis, who says remember what Jesus did," he said. "He's popping the bubble of the pompous asses."

In his sixties, Father Juran was retired. He'd worked forty years in the priesthood and twenty-seven years as a stuntman. I asked how it felt being a stuntman all those years.

"Thrills, chills, and doctor's bills," he said.

As the Human Battering Ram, he was strapped to the hood of a car as it crashed through a burning wall. At state fairs and racetracks, he'd drive on two wheels. He flew over a bridge in the James Bond film.

Living out of his trailer for Joie Chitwood's Auto Thrill Show, he performed priestly duties in his off-hours. He heard confessions, performed baptisms "without the paperwork," and performed carny weddings.

"Jesus didn't do paperwork," he said.

For those who thought carny weddings on carousels were a myth, he could testify they were real because he performed them. In a carny wedding, couples board a carousel. Words are spoken. Blessings made. The carousel rotates three times around to symbolize the union. At the end of the relationship or the season, the couple boards the carousel again as it turns backward three times, signifying the carnival divorce.

There's no divorce in the Catholic Church, I chided.

"None of it is official," he said.

Father Juran gained the trust of performers and carnival people because he was one of them.

"They'd say, he's one of us, he's a performer too. I'd say God loves you. I'm just like you."

Confessions were heard behind rides or during walks along the midway. People sought him out, or he offered his help.

"They'd say, 'I want to talk about God's forgiveness.'"

Christianity is a religion whose Messiah came from the common folk, not a royal or a person of high status. The divine is found among everyday people, the sinners. It is also a death-defying religion, one whose Messiah defies death and says followers can do the same.

A day later, I saw Father Juran cutting up jackpots with *World of Wonders* co-owner Chris Christ. Refracted sunlight came off the new rides for sale. Christ was squinting and looking away.

I don't know what he knew about Father Juran, but who better than a man working with freaks to understand people are not who they appear to be.

In 2019, allegations of sexual abuse against Father Juran were substantiated by the Diocese of Buffalo, New York, to which he was attached during his traveling ministry. All his stories look different from this distance. What was the truth? The real dark carnivals are inside us.

JIM JUDKINS MAY BE the single most important man in traveling carnivals since the early 2000s.

At the crest of the Great Mexican Migration, Judkins rode a wave of seasonal Mexican labor changing the complexion of the traveling carnival workforce.

Depending on your point of view, Judkins either came to the rescue of carnivals or further addicted them to cheap labor.

As the operator of the biggest labor consulting firm in carnivals, he found, transported, and secured visas for more Mexicans than anyone else in traveling carnivals.

Judkins's JKL Workforce Agency helped thousands of people a year to legally work in the United States. Estimates vary, but Mexicans from all labor agencies at the time made up a third to a half of U.S. carnival workers.

They come across on H-2B visas along with workers from other countries. During my year, I met workers from Asia, the Caribbean, Eastern Europe, and South America.

Judkins advised owners at the trade show on IRS audits, labor practices, worker pay, government bureaucracy, and legislation pending before Congress. Accompanying him were his labor attorney, an undersecretary from the George W. Bush administration, and a Washington lobbyist.

The lobbyist called for owners to write their local representatives in Congress. The attorney told them to keep meticulous tax and accounting records.

Mention was made of their exemption from the Fair Labor Standards Act and how to meet minimum labor standards. Each of the speakers stressed that American immigration policies are prone to delay and legal vagaries.

Nobody mentioned the scathing labor report *Taken for a Ride*, the landmark study released the previous year alleging widespread migrant labor abuses. Nobody in that Gibtown meeting stood up for reforming labor practices and self-policing.

Concessions owner Ronnie Nettenfield stood up to say he was experiencing bureaucratic visa logjams.

"I'm so stressed out about this," he said, "I could shoot myself."

Even a delay of days in getting visas could bring his business to its knees.

"Don't do that," Judkins said. "We'll see what we can do."

Most of Nettenfield's staff was Mexican. His workers came back yearly, calling him "Poppy." He called them "amigos." He thought calling them Mexicans wasn't right. He had a tight bond with his men.

"If I eat a hot dog, they eat a hot dog," he said. "If I eat steak, they eat steak."

After the meeting, I asked Nettenfield if I could work for him during the Florida State Fair. I was local. I wanted to work. Judkins emphasized that locals should be given priority in hiring.

Nettenfield was the owner of popcorn and lemonade stands. He couldn't argue it was a job requiring special skills. Nettenfield turned me down flat.

Reverse discrimination is a common and passionate complaint among white and black carnies. Yet that may not have been what was going on in my case. Nettenfield knew I was writing about carnival people. As D'Olivo said back in California, no owner wants a writer on his crew.

I desperately wanted to write about carnival eats. More people in the world die of obesity than hunger. All I needed was some freakish luck.

BACK IN AUGUST, the *World of Wonders* was playing the Minnesota State Fair near my pool-tables tent. Every work break, I went to see the same freak show. I knew the routines well enough to be an understudy.

Chris Christ sat on a high stool, taking tickets beside the outside bally stage. I walked over to offer my services. If Christ agreed to hire me in Minnesota, I'd be working in a traveling freak show, but I'd miss the State Fair of Texas. I wanted to work in a freak show more than any single state fair.

Christ and was co-owner of the show with his partner, Ward "King of the Sideshows" Hall. Christ was the show's head writer.

"I saw your 'Help Wanted' sign," I said. "I've been on stage. I can help slough. I'd like to work for you."

"We just need women," Christ mumbled.

"I can do that too," I said.

Christ's eyes lit up. It's possible that for just a second, the old showman saw freakish potential in me. The moment passed, and he rejected my offer.

The difference between a carny like me and a real showman was best summed up by Christ on the Carny Lingo website run by podcaster and carnival aficionado Wayne Keyser.

"Ward (Hall) and I are showmen. Don't call us carnies. Carnies are junky ride jockeys that are here today and gone tomorrow. The difference between a carny and a showman is the difference between chicken shit and chicken salad."

Turning back to the pool tables, I felt more like chicken shit than chicken salad. Neither a showman nor a freak.

AT THE GIBTOWN CONVENTION, Ward Hall walked in the front door of the carousel bar with showbiz charisma. Then in his eighties, he was the acknowledged king of the sideshows.

Everyone knew him and wanted his attention. I came a long way to meet him, so I was aggressive in getting an interview. Soon I found myself caught in his publicity whirlwind.

Ward filled me in on a show-business life so eclectic it sounded more like hyperbole. He was an entertainment polymath. He mastered juggling, ventriloquism, and the art of being an outside talker who could mesmerize a crowd.

He wrote four stage musicals and four books. He appeared in seven movies and more than a hundred videos and TV shows.

In New York City, he performed at Madison Square Garden and the Lincoln Center and sang at Carnegie Hall. He was inducted into every American circus and carnival hall of fame.

As I interviewed him, his latest biographer was waiting in the wings.

"I have been in the sideshow business for sixty years," he said. "I've had hundreds of human oddities in my shows. Giants. Midgets. Alligator Skin Man. Bearded ladies. The Monkey Girl. The pinheads. The midgets. The dwarfs. The armless girls. The Living Half Man. All of these people have worked for me in the past."

Sideshows and games once dominated American carnivals. The biggest draws were the fire eaters, sword swallowers, magicians, knife throwers, snake handlers, and human oddities. Big carnivals these days are all about the high-tech rides, making it tough on lower-budget creative types like Hall and Christ.

"A million-dollar midway was once a big deal," Hall said. "Now it's a down payment."

Disfigurement, birth defects, and bizarre behavior often revolt today's audiences. In other times, those were the top draws.

Sideshows were known for trickery with their banners. One sign read, "Six Foot Man Eating Chicken." When the customer entered the tent, they saw a tall man eating fried chicken. Which is one of many other "humbugs" dating back to P.T. Barnum's days in the mid-1800's.

The "See Idiot in Mirror" sign was particularly egregious. After paying fifty cents to get in, the customer saw a mirror labeling the viewer an idiot for paying fifty cents to look in the mirror.

While setting up rides behind the IISA headquarters, I met a showman who once worked a drug abuse show. The banner outside his tent read "The Horrors of Drug Abuse."

Drug abuse drove him insane, the customers were told. He gave the crowd a wild-man routine, screaming and flailing his arms.

Then he reached back, rubbed his buttocks, and stretched his arm to the crowd, showing a handful of chunky peanut butter looking like excrement. To their horror, he grunted and growled as he ate the peanut butter. Sitting at the carousel bar with his beer, he was smiling and proud. There was shock and horror at every show. He thought people liked being horrified. His boss didn't.

The showman was fired because the drug abuse show turned into a geek show. People bite the heads off of chickens and eat poop in geek shows. Interestingly, he was fired because his drug abuse show wasn't as advertised.

MINNESOTA'S long days and August's heat tested Hall and Christ's crew. Its placement at the back of the fair made crowds thin and money tight.

"Minnesota State Fair was typical," Hall said. "Hot. From 10 a.m. to midnight, we worked. Then tear down and driving to the next town. Maybe business is bad and you have to figure out how to keep it on the road despite all kinds of police and fire inspectors, drug tests, insurance . . . Freaks are some of the most resilient people I've ever seen."

Three young women stood on the bally stage in the blazing heat breathing fire all day. The "half man," Short E. Dangerously, balanced on a bowling ball dozens of times a day. Swords were swallowed and knives were thrown again and again. Hall was in awe of his own performers.

The *World of Wonders* planned to stay away from the Minnesota State Fair for another year or two because the sideshows were mostly illusions. Short E. Dangerously was the only real freak at the show. Magic tricks and stunts filled out the rest of the show.

There was a talking beheaded woman. A woman danced with four legs. A fat man laid on a bed of nails. People breathed fire.

"Customers need time," Hall said, "before they come back to see a show about illusions. The world still has many handicapped, deformed, and malformed people who would love to be in the sideshow. But the world is too PC these days."

Society changed. It's less curious and more accepting about human oddities and deformities. Yet it is less tolerant of freak shows, which was once the most tolerant place for freaks.

Medical advancements have reduced the number of people with abnormalities. Many localities ban freak shows. Hall paid freaks to come from Asia and Europe, but they eventually ran off to find their own American Dream

He admired me, he said, for my willingness to quit my pool tables job in Minnesota to perform in his sideshow.

Hall admired me? That sounded like the opening I needed.

"This is how bad I want to work at the *World of Wonders*," I said. "I'll be your ticket taker. I'll work for free. Give me a day to interview everyone. Ward! Free. Free. Free!"

After three state fairs with Adam West, I knew how to turn the tip so even the King of the Sideshows couldn't say no.

THE LAST TEN-IN-ONE FREAK SHOW

TAMPA

*T*he next day I hitchhiked to the Florida State Fair in Tampa, sneaking in the employee entrance and bypassing the formalities of drug testing and background checks.

Wade Shows ran the state fair, so I wore my Wade Shows hat from my time at the Oklahoma State Fair. The guard didn't check for a fair badge.

The *World of Wonders* featured a huge banner line with cartoons of the freaks and illusions to be seen inside. The *World of Wonders* was a ten-in-one show, a sideshow with ten acts under one tent for one admission price. It was once a common freak show format but *World of Wonders* claimed to be the last traveling ten-in-one show.

As I walked up to the sideshow tent, I saw Rash looking into a makeshift mirror on the back of the stage trailer. He was putting on his clown makeup and couldn't be bothered by the new guy.

Nine performers sat around inside the trailer behind the tent, waiting for the shows to begin. Once they started, shows ran continuously all day. People walked in and watched until the shows looped around again every half hour or so. Fifteen to thirty shows were performed daily.

Short E. Dangerously worked 330 days a year, with three weeks off. The juggler and emcee Spiff guessed that he threw twenty thousand knives a year at his assistant, Sunshine. A thin young woman in her twenties, Sunshine also worked the blade box and contorted her body so Spiff didn't stab her with the swords.

Sunshine and Rick, the "six-hundred-pound fat man," were raised in Gibtown. April boasted the best showbiz pedigree. Her father tamed lions and elephants. Her mother worked in an aerial act and helped in her father's show.

Growing up in Gibtown, Rick wondered what it would be like to be one of the carnival people he saw around town. Bored being a cook in a nursing home, he tried to make a living at pro-wrestling, but fat isn't muscle. He opted for the sideshow life as long as it lasts.

That afternoon I saw him eating fried chicken, saying, "I have to keep my act going. Nobody wants a thin fat-man."

Angelica was the "tattooed lady," with tattoos on her face and arms. Americans just aren't that shocked anymore, Hall said, by tattooed ladies and fat people. Some of the people in the audience are more tattooed and fatter.

SWORD SWALLOWER JOHN "RED" Lawrence Stewart was a three-time *Guinness World Record* holder and holder of six more records.

Most of the *World of Wonders* cast slept on the trailer behind the stage, but Red slept in his battered 1990 GMC Rally STX van, parked behind the show. His van was his home on the road, with more than one thousand DVDs and discs for relaxing after work. He managed to fit in a mini-fridge, a microwave, and a trusty coffee maker.

Having held many carnival jobs over the years, Red stopped what he was doing when Hall and Christ came calling for him to star again in the last ten-in-one show in America.

Red performed shirtless in a Scottish kilt and sporran purse. His bare chest, legs, and arms were heavily tattooed. He pulled his hair back in a ponytail.

His sword-swallower act was world class, but don't stereotype

Red. He prided himself on his expertise in Fourth and Fifth Dynasty Egyptian mummies, an interest he acquired from his archaeologist grandfather.

He studied Tibetan Buddhism at the University of Colorado, Boulder. Meditation was his escape on the road.

"It helps some," he said, "so I can put my mind elsewhere."

Red worked sideshows off and on for decades, developing his own way of looking at freaks.

"The so-called freaks were just like normal people to me whether they were different in shape or mind," Red said. "I considered everyone on the planet a freak in their own right."

HALF MAN SHORT E. Dangerously also was a knife thrower, a fire breather, and a glass walker who walked on his hands.

Born with a condition called sacral agenesis, he was about three feet tall, but the talkers outside said he was twenty-two inches tall.

His lower-spine deformation left his legs underdeveloped and unresponsive. In Shorty's day, a full amputation of the legs was the most common procedure. The condition occurs in one in twenty-five thousand live births.

Freak shows were once a lucrative career option for people with his condition. Pictures of famous past half men adorn the IISA clubhouse wall.

Shorty was a DJ at a strip joint before becoming a sideshow performer. After joining sideshows, he began touring Australia, Brazil, Germany, New Zealand, and Venezuela.

I was interviewing him backstage when he heard his cue. He hopped down from his chair and walked on his hands to the back curtain. He looked back at the room full of performers before going on stage.

"Time to make donuts," he said. "I know, sometimes, I can't believe all this myself."

All of the performers considered themselves fortunate to be

sideshow entertainers, if not all freaks. It's not a stretch to wonder if some able-bodied performers envied Shorty's genuine freak status, given the money, travel, and fandom.

Shorty's childhood was happy. He felt healthy. He loved music, women, and traveling the world. Fans in faraway countries wrote to him on the internet. He felt loved.

He wasn't bullied growing up in Columbus, Ohio or during summers in upper Michigan with his family.

"I took my condition just fine, and so did the people around me. If they didn't, then they didn't need to be a part of my life. Plain and simple. There were a few assholes along the way, but it was dealt with accordingly."

His life before becoming a sideshow star also wasn't that bad. He was popular with the dancers at the strip joint where he worked as a disc jockey.

"I was a favorite of most of the dancers . . . There were plenty of wild nights."

He was inspired by the sideshow tradition.

"I do feel like I am part of something. It's becoming a dying art, and I only wish I discovered it sooner. I consider myself an entertainer first and foremost, but I'm also a showman. I just happen to be a freak . . . Being on stage is an incredible rush."

As for the future, Shorty fostered no dreams of settling down.

"I will never get off the road. I would like to have my own show in the next two to five years or so. So yeah, more countries and more roads."

What if he could do it all over again?

"If I had to pick, I would be a rock star. Metal. We were a cover band in high school. Lots of Metallica covers. I was the frontman."

CHRIST AND HALL lived many different lives during their long careers. I asked if they wish they'd lived any other kind of life outside of sideshows.

"If I could live it all over," Hall said, "I'd be an evangelical healing preacher or a trial lawyer."

Christ was once a sword swallower, knife thrower, fire eater, and magician. He and Hall dabbled in wrestling, boxing, and ventriloquism.

"I like being a creative person," Christ said. "I wouldn't want to spend my life in a factory with widgets."

As I walked off the Florida State Fair lot, one last nagging thought came to me. Ten carnivals in ten states and my last one in a freak show, but they never let me step on stage because they didn't see the inner freak in me.

PART XIII
THE YEAR OF BEING WITH IT

EXTRAORDINARY DREAMS OF
ORDINARY PEOPLE

My future was decided for me at 12 years old. I went to a carnival and I saw a man, Mr. Electro . . . he reached down with a flaming sword, full of electricity, and he pointed it at me and said, "Live forever."

— RAY BRADBURY, AUTHOR OF *SOMETHING WICKED
THIS WAY COMES*, ON A DAY SPENT AT A TRAVELING
CARNIVAL THAT CHANGED HIS LIFE.

*I*n Grace's carnival dream, I'm in my red carnival shirt on one bended knee. My arms are stretched open wide. She is running to me and jumps into my arms.

It was a replay of our reunion at the front gate of the Minnesota State Fair.

"That wasn't a dream," I said. "It was a memory."

It was the summer after I left traveling carnivals. She didn't like being dismissed easily. Her carefree mood flashed serious.

"No," she said. "It was a dream!"

She was right. Her side of the year wasn't filled with Ferris wheels and carnival tricks. She imagined it all from afar. From her front-yard treetop. From her bed with carousel horses painted in a circle above the headboard. Her dream wasn't a memory. Her dream was a message saying, "Don't ever leave me again, dad."

When I returned from carnivals, Grace developed a book idea and self-published *Power of Purple: Jackie's Purple Ninja Story*. The super-hero was a grade-school girl, much like herself. And the heroine's dad was absent.

Grace kept me in touch all year with the family side of carnival life. Keeping one's family together is a carnival worker's toughest job.

Families own and run carnivals. Families run rides, set up the game joints, and serve the great gobs of fried food and candied treats. Families live in Tlapacoyan and Gibtown, where their traveling-carnival men and women leave their hearts.

Because the McDaniel family red-lighted me, I spent my time in winter quarters to file a complaint with the State of New Jersey. I made dozens of calls to bureaucrats, none of whom had ever been asked to help in a carnival wage theft case.

Carnies don't have time to follow up like I did, yet it was the most common complaint among carnival workers. At least twice, the state sent agents to McDaniel headquarters but failed to make contact. The most they could do was put a note on the McDaniel credit report.

About eighteen months after I left New York, I received a check from the McDaniel brothers in the mail for $288. It was symbolic, but it also was a small fortune to me at the time.

Leaving carnivals wasn't smooth. When the year ended, I shared something more than experiences with many carnival people. I had no income and no permanent home.

Scott at the State Fair of Texas worried that his carnival life wouldn't let him go. He was headed toward a have-not life in a gotta-have-it world.

"I haven't had a real job since I was sixteen. Now I have a prison record and just carnies for references. People don't like carny refer-ences. They think we're all drug addicts and idiots, which is pretty true. I'm thirty years old now. How can I save one thousand dollars for a deposit on an apartment?"

Former carnival workers were living in each of the three shelters where I stayed, including Anchorage Gospel Mission, Memphis Union Mission, and St. Paul's Union Gospel Mission.

I saved money during the year by living on a food budget of one dollar a day. It went slightly higher if I was at an all-you-can-eat pancake diner writing all night. Most days I ate straight from a cold can of pinto beans and nothing more. I paid for McDonald's dollar-menu items to get Wi-Fi services.

Along the way, I likely became the #1 hitchhiker in America with more than 13,700 miles hitched along America's showcase roads.

I wrote on cardboard hitchhiking signs the names of interstates 5, 10, 25, 30, 35, 40, 70, 75, 80, 90, 95, and the fabled Route 66.

This cardboard carny hitched across thirty-six states and Canada. I sailed up and around mountain ranges named Appalachian, Rocky, Saint Elias, Sierra Nevada, Smoky, and Sierra Madre Oriental.

In Alaska, I sat in the flatbed of a speeding pickup truck watching forest fires and meteor showers melting together. I never wished to be anywhere else in the world. Alone for days under the Texas panhandle sun beside I-40 and sleeping along Alligator Alley made me feel like the freest man in America. Strangers told me their most intimate stories while we crossed the Mississippi, Rio Grande, and Yukon rivers.

When people ask who picks up hitchhikers these days, I mention an Arctic Circle teacher, an Arkansas preacher, a Chinese cook, a balloon clown, a magician, a denturist, an environmentalist, an FBI bureau chief, two Navy intelligence officers, a nuclear engineer, a pizza delivery driver, authors, cops, drifters, hillbillies, hippies, mechanics, miners, refugees, religious zealots, rodeo riders, truckers, and a former wolf who became a man. I'll never be able to repay my debt to them or to the adventurous outpost nurse and artist in the Yukon.

On top of the hitchhiking, I rode 5,740 miles by bus and another 2,130 miles by train. I traveled 21,570 miles in search of traveling carnivals and the world they traverse. This was North America on the cusp of unprecedented climate, technological, and economic change.

A love of change is part of us now. My biggest change was an internal shift. I was an immersion journalist until I quit at Saint Timothy's in San Mateo, California. My farewell made me realize that I may not be a real carny, but I'm part of the story this season.

Carnivals and carnies remained my focus, but the gut-wrenching farewells kept repeating at carnivals coast to coast.

A family friend later volunteered her theory.

"You were listening to them," she said. "They weren't used to people listening to them like that."

Yet sad farewells are for people leaving a great place. The unspoken truth about carnival life is that so many people love it. Leaving it is sad. The carnival is their home. At the end of the season, some people don't know where to go.

People live their entire lives in the all-consuming carnival world. I was invited to do the same near the Okefenokee Swamp. The saying goes, "With it. For it. Live it. Love it."

Every day in carnivals, I sang along with the music of the midway. I made up stories for riders and customers. I helped people have fun. Every night I slept so deeply, I must have sunk to middle earth. Every morning seemed like the start of something new. Each day was material for thought.

Part of the joy I felt was the novelty, which was another reason I was no carny. Being a carny is normal to a carny. Mornings were drudgery if they partied the night before. They thought about money, family, health, mortality, and their struggles for meaning. I thought about them.

Carnival people are the untold stories in America. They put millions of people on rides a year. The carnival industry rakes in hundreds of millions of dollars every year. The carnival worker deserves to be seen.

The mystery at the bottom of carnivals is the carnival class. It includes musicians, painters, carvers, tattoo artists, and sci-fi writers in the next bunkhouse room. Carnies are children, parents, and grandparents.

Carnies get together cutting up jackpots even when they don't believe the tall tales. They sing and rap in harmony in vans all the way back to the bunkhouses.

Carnies are the working poor, victims of the smallest moments, from sneezes to achy teeth. A life's savings can be wiped out by a dropped smartphone. They are life's underdogs at the mercy of pinprick luck.

Carnival workers feel personally responsible for lifting people's spirits. Almost every ride jockey told me, "It's all about the kids."

Nights and days swung from the sacred to the profane. The preachers and priests brought their Bibles. The Tug Thug brought his women. Sleeping under starry skies in the Chugach Mountains in Alaska contrasted with the rainy nights in a cow-shit cesspool outside Chicago.

The carnival world is like the music of the midway. You focus on the music you want to hear. It was my privilege working with carnival people who came from across the country and around the world.

I worked with carnies from South Africa, Asia, the Caribbean, Europe, and South America. Big-city carnies mixed with Native Alaskans from tiny fishing villages. Carnies from the Deep South moved easily with crews in New York.

My background didn't hold me back because identities shift in carnivals. I was known as Crocodile, Cowboy, El Grande, High Street, Mike Love, Slim, and The Priest. When I deep-sixed my real name, I felt like a fiction in a traveling fiction land.

Maybe not, though, as who really knows anyone? Particularly someone with a name like Angel, Atomic Man, Batman, Biggin, Boogie, Breeze, Castro, Chango, Chunk of Cheese, Cockroach, Confederate Max, Cosmo, Country Love, Curley, Darko, Dizzy, Dum Dum, Fireball Pete, Flash, Gator, Ghost, Gotti, Jimmy Tattoos, John the Horse Walker, Kid Gypsy, La La, Louisiana Brian, Luke the Puke, Lurch, Marine Eric, Metal Head, Monster, Muscles, Nick the Prick, One Shot Carl, Original Tommy, Randy the Hat, Roger the Artist,

Robert the Killer, Robert the Toup, Pork Chop, Rose Dog, Short E Dangerously, Sis, Slippery Pete, Smalls, Sparky, Spiff, and Uncle Fester.

The experiences of the Mexican carnies were a revelation to me in how they worked and suffered the pains of separation from their home and families.

They knew how to wrestle iron giants to the ground fast and fit jumbo jigsaws into trucks like masters. I joined their work crews, showered in their reefers, went to their hometown. They worked the same carnivals as the Americans and yet were living between two worlds.

Being the best carny or showman was tied to a sense of self-worth. Ride jockeys drew the longest lines. Jointees outsmarted every mark. Grab wagons workers made the best corn dog batter. State Fair cooks could stop your deep fried heart.

People were open about seeking meaning in their lives. Some people sought it through religion. I spent time going to churches, prayer meetings, and evangelical services. From a born-again carnival in Alaska to carnies speaking in tongues in Mexico, people in carnivals searched for transcendence.

Yet most carnival people skipped Sunday services. They talked about their struggles to make sense of the world during setup, slough, and on long rainy days. Living a life with meaning was often on their minds, and they were winging it as they go.

What I saw depended on where I stood. And I stood operating carousels, a Lolly swing, Flying Dumbos, an Eli Wheel, a Cliff Hanger, a Mardi Gras house, pool games, shark games, basketball games, and the Tubs of Fun.

I worked the R-keys, lady fingers, impact wrenches, zip ties, bolts, cotter pins, ratchet straps, and metal pins. Duct tape held together rides, joints, and carnival lives.

The carnival adage goes, "Haul it, move it, bolt it, block it, level it." I lifted generator boxes, lead lines, ticket booths, ATM boxes, and carnival vans stuck in the mud. I lifted every last bit of pig iron on the midway. Then I hung the flash and went for the cash.

There were all-night sloughs in lightning storms. Bruises, cuts, and aching muscles. The finger-smashing truths of carnival life are that muscle and guile pay the bills.

Where you find the greatest happiness, you find the most pain. Pain loves carnivals, too. Separation from loved ones. Beds with bugs. Bunched up shirts for pillows. Cold water hose showers. Work without a clock. Pay like disappearing ink. Rotten teeth, black lungs, swollen livers, and mental illness went untreated.

Migration separates. Weather mugs. Poverty warps. My bike, tent, and clothes were stolen. When Patrick White died, we were thunderstruck and saw ourselves ending like him.

Poverty came with its own entourage, including drug and alcohol abuse. I didn't party with the crews, but the fallout was plain to see. At least one of the people I worked with that year have since died of drug abuse. I knew their babies and their loved ones.

Women in carnivals experienced different challenges than men. I met many happy women. Happy with their families and their relationships. Happy with life on the road, like Connie in New Jersey and Anna May in Gibtown.

Other women had it tougher. Raising children on the road is challenging on a razor-thin budget. Women left their kids behind with extended families. In New Jersey, Dana was beaten savagely. Heidi tried but failed to kick her drug habit in Texas. Wanita was verbally abused in Fairbanks bars. I drove from Okefenokee to Fort Lauderdale with a battered woman.

Foster mothers I met consistently said they left their first husbands because of their drug and alcohol abuse. A woman without a man often suffered abuse from both women and men, being labeled a possum-belly queen, aka an easy woman. Women worried about an unattached woman being around their men, making single women feel like they are more on their own.

As a younger man in my twenties, I met a lovely sixteen-year-old runaway girl working in a carnival. It was sexy and exciting to see her living adventures on the open road. I still don't know what I really saw because I later met dozens of people who ran away to carnivals as teens. Many were fleeing juvenile detention, foster homes, or a hell-on-wheels father.

Reckless personal questions hurt people, and I may have asked too many people about how they ran away.

I watched tears roll down the cheeks of men and women, their childhoods still so close to the surface. Ward Hall ran away for the second and final time when he was fifteen years old. Huey at Butler ran away at age sixteen but planned it first at age eleven. Some carnies ran away before they could fluently read. One foreman asked me to read for him.

When I first arrived in carnivals, the level of poverty was shocking. Beds in the Mexican reefers were stacked three bunks high. Cow pies surrounded our trailers like landmines. People slept inside rides. There was a disregard for labor laws. Bait-and-switch tricks were played on Mexicans.

American carnival workers think Mexican carnies are depressing their salaries. Owners think low wages are necessary for the survival of traveling carnivals. Mexicans were fighting an uphill battle for a subsistence life on both sides of the border.

Traveling carnivals need reformists working for better conditions. Mexican unions, American activists, and academics have shown an interest in exposing abuses. Universal healthcare would introduce social workers and medical professionals to carnivals. It all seems unlikely in the near future, but I've seen people win at the impossible tubs.

THE TECH REVOLUTION is more likely to be the biggest reforming influence on traveling carnivals.

Tech will blow away many tedious, back-breaking manual labor jobs. New carnival workers will be forced to learn tech skills, making them more valuable. The survival of carnivals won't be up to carnival workers or owners. Bigger forces are already at work.

Tech will change carnivals more than outdoor lighting and gas-powered vehicles at the turn of the twentieth century.

Massive population displacement is on the horizon with global warming. Traveling carnivals will have an edge in migrating societies.

Before the current climate change crisis, the American Dust Bowl in the 1930s was the biggest human-made ecological disaster. Millions of people were displaced and plunged into near-starvation poverty. Carnivals adjusted with games for pennies, nickels, and dimes. Instead of worthless plush, people during the Dust Bowl era won bushel baskets of food.

When much of Miami is under water, carnivals will go where the city moves. A good global-warming game prize might be an oar.

If a kid in the San Francisco Bay Area grows up to invent the ultimate happiness pill, traveling carnivals will figure out a way to mix it into corn-dog batter.

Traveling carnivals will change more in the next twenty years than they have in their first one hundred years.

On the rides and gaming side, there'll be gesture control, facial recognition, voice recognition, high-image graphics, high-def displays, virtual reality, augmented reality, wearable gaming, cloud gaming, mobile gaming, and on-demand streaming games. Interactive rollercoasters are already being developed.

On the operational side, watch for self-driving trucks, self-sloughing rides, and 3D printers capable of printing rides and themed buildings at key jumps. Computerized LED lighting will turn Ferris wheels into billboards. Virtual payment terminals will deepen a gambler's pockets. Drones will light up the night skies.

Augmented humans, half-human and half-android, might be the new freaks in *The New World of Wonders*. Android carnies will treat natural-born humans like marks. Instead of the fake hypnotism of Mike's Rainbow, androids actually could hypnotize us. Human desires will be broken down into hackable logarithms.

All this is not imminent, but it is all foreseeable as we round the corner of a new technological age and a global-warming crisis.

In 2014, I found about 350 traveling carnivals listing themselves online. At the start of 2020, during the outbreak of Covid-19, the Carnival Midways online site listed a few more than 200 active carnivals in the U.S. It's a safe guess that next year there'll be fewer.

The traveling-carnival industry is still relatively young. I am nearly half the age of the industry. Traveling carnivals were born in times much like our own. It was a time of economic depression, pandemic and a technological revolution.

The Panic of 1893 was part of a depression that lasted most of a decade and was on a par with the Great Depression. The "Asiatic flu" killed an estimated 1 million people in the 1890s, infecting up to 60 percent of the earth's population. Trains, cars, automation and electrical power were poised to revolutionize the planet.

These days, Covid-19 may infect up to 70 percent of the world. Generations of carnival families are devastated as state fairs and festivals are canceling or reducing crowd sizes. The coming macroeconomic impact will be historic. At the same time, technology and the internet are revolutionizing our world.

The big picture is remarkably similar to that of the 1890s. I can't predict how or when, but I will predict a spectacular comeback for traveling carnivals like those before.

The lessons I learned on the road apply to life outside carnivals. Play is worthy of stingy time. Imaginations must be fattened. A great carnival can change our DNA.

Since I left carnival life, pop songs remind me of midways. Commercials become ballys. I walk by lakes looking for monster goldfish won in a carnival. At sunset, I watch for the sun poking through the rib iron of a carousel.

I still feel the tug of the carnival seasons. In spring, I sense people antsy to get back on the road. In the fall, I see the flying flowers, monarch butterflies, on their way from Canada to their Mexican winter home.

I can hear carnival voices. No funny, no money. No flash, no cash. Happy children are the hope of the future.

There is no better way to spend your life than pursuing the art of making people happy. The people of the carnivals are worthy of attention. Their stories matter because they are part of us. We are connected more than we know. We are all living in stories, and theirs move.

The Latin term for humans is homo sapiens, for "wise men." Wise doesn't quite fit. It has been suggested that a better Latin label for us might be *pan narrans*, the storytelling apes.

This storytelling ape set out to capture the stories of the cotton-candied, winner-winner chicken-dinner thrill merchants of American traveling carnivals. I told myself stories, too, and the ones I chose made it a phantasmagorical year.

Up out of this beautiful, bruising world come carnival people weaving their way between inner cities and small towns. Wheels and imaginations rise up wherever they go. They are on a ride of life, and wonder is only the beginning.

BE SHOCKED & AMAZED

VIDEOS AND BLOGS MADE WHILE IN CARNIVALS AND HITCHHIKING

A major part of experiencing American OZ are the videos and pictures featuring the characters and majestic landscapes of the United States, Canada and Mexico.

There are music videos on Youtube and multimedia shows with photos from the year. The blogs drew 100,000s of visitors.

You can check out them out at the sites below or at my website at MichaelSeanComerford.com. At American OZ's blog site's original title *Eyes Like Carnivals* are the stories written during the year in all-night diners, truck stops, and carnival bunkhouses.

Again, you can review the book, it's simple, fun and free, free, free! Your friends will marvel at your taste. You can review at Goodreads or your favorite book buying site.

RECOMMENDED BOOKS & LINKS
PUBLICATIONS WITH AMERICAN OZ THEMES

American Dirt - Jeanine Cummins

Joyland - Stephen King

An American Summer - Alex Kotlowitz

Dancing in the Streets - Barbara Ehrenreich

Rolling Nowhere - Ted Conover

The New New Journalism - Robert Boynton

Roadside Americans - John Reid

TJ The Jag, The One and Only (Facebook)

Power of Purple: Jackie's Purple Ninja Story - Grace A. Comerford

Dare to Dream Green (Website) - Grace Comerford

Reader reviews are easy and free, free, free! Help the people and stories of American Oz gain the voice they deserve. Please leave a review at Goodreads or your favorite book buying site.

Made in the USA
Monee, IL
24 August 2020

39626217R00196